THE
MYTHOLOGY
of
DOGS

Canine Legend and Lore through the Ages

THE
MYTHOLOGY
of
DOGS

Gerald Hausman

AND

Loretta Hausman

ST. MARTIN'S PRESS

New York

To the dogs who civilized us when
people said we'd gone to the dogs.

Production Editor: David Stanford Burr
Design: Judith Stagnitto Abbate

Library of Congress Cataloging-in-Publication Data

Hausman, Gerald.
 The mythology of dogs : canine legend and lore
through the ages / Gerald Hausman and Loretta
Hausman.—1st ed.
                p.   cm.
        ISBN 0-312-15177-2
        1. Dog breeds.   2. Dogs—Anecdotes.
3. Dogs—Folklore.   4. Dogs—Mythology.
    I. Hausman, Loretta.   II. Title.
    SF426.2.H39   1997
    636.7'1—dc20   96-30642
                                          CIP

First Edition: February 1997

10 9 8 7 6 5 4 3 2 1

Acknowledgments

THE AUTHORS WISH TO ACKNOWLEDGE the following individuals and institutions:

Bob Weil, Senior Editor, St. Martin's Press; Rebecca Koh, Associate Editor, St. Martin's Press; Ricia Mainhardt Literary Agency, Brooklyn, New York; Researcher, Alice Winston Carney, Sacramento, California; Mel Young, The Pampered Pup, Matlacha, Florida; Barbara Kolk and Staff, American Kennel Club Library, New York City; Pine Island Public Library and Staff, Bokeelia, Florida; Mariah Hausman, Miami, Florida; John Bredin, ArtWave, St. James City, Florida; Photographer, Barbara Davis, N. Fort Myers, Florida; Mike Marseglia and Dan McGowan, Old McGowan's Farm, Bokeelia, Florida; Francis Fretwell, Moore, South Carolina; Marian and Bubba, Brooklyn, New York; Hannah Hausman, University of Miami, Coral Gables, Florida; Phil and Joan Rosenberg, Island Computer, St. James City, Florida.

Contents

THE
MYTHOLOGY
of
DOGS

Introduction

I AM GLAD TO be able to write this introduction to *The Mythology of Dogs* by Gerald and Loretta Hausman because this book is a valuable addition to the literature on dogs. Also I am always grateful to have the opportunity to say something about dogs because I owe them so much. At the personal level, some of my very best friends and companions have been dogs. Professionally, as a veterinarian and animal behaviorist, I have learned much from them about the art and science of healing, and about inter-species communication, animal awareness, feelings, and the power of empathy.

The dog was the first creature on Earth to become a member of human society. To be accepted into the community and to earn a place in our families and hearts had more to do with the nature of the dog than with our ability to dominate and domesticate this particular species.

Indeed the nature of the dog is such that it would not be an overstatement to say that the dog helped civilize the human species. Evidence of the civilizing influences of the dog on human nature and culture has been carefully compiled by the Hausmans. Their book, in the best tradition of historical, mythological, and anthropological investigation, provides an entertaining and penetrating overview of the various dog breeds, ancient and modern.

The more ancient the breed, like the saluki and Irish wolfhound, the more folktales and mythologies await discovery. In this treasury of dog myths, those who enjoy the company of particular breeds will certainly discover something new about their dogs that the Hausmans have excavated in their extensive literature research. Other readers, probably like myself, who have no particular attachment to any specific breed will also not want to put this book down. The reason for this, which is also the unique strength of this book, is that each breed of dog gives us a particular insight, a unique facet of a multifaceted "canine complex."

When we put all the different breeds and their associated legendary, physical, psychological, mythical, and other unique attributes together, coupling these with the various human purposes, needs, and aspirations these devoted canines have satisfied for millennia, then what do we have? A clearer view perhaps of the dog of dogs, *Canis familiaris*, the original, primal form whose ethos is as evident, pure, and unchanged, in every dog from Chihuahua to Great Dane, as it was in the beginning. Today's "mutt," the mixed breed that I call the natural dog, is essentially a democratic amalgam of diverse breeds so reassembled as to represent the resurrection of the primal dog. The swift, lean, and super-bright look-alike pariahs, or pi-dogs of Africa and Asia, inform us of this ancient prototype before it was disassembled into a diversity of breeds.

The Mythology of Dogs takes us to the dawn of human and canine history as civilized, domesticated beings. It pushes even further back in time to when humans were gatherer-hunters and dogs were our allies in a mutually enhancing relationship, long before the first livestock were tamed, herded, and protected by our dogs.

There is no evidence in this book to support the erroneous belief that the origin of the domestic dog is lupine; that all dogs come from wolves. Dogs are surely not Judas wolves, descendants of a domesticated lineage of wolves bred to hunt wild wolves and to protect livestock from their hungry kin.

This myth of dogs' origin is without substance, I believe. The dog of dogs, a close cousin of the wolf, existed as a separate, God-made species long before humans established a domestic relationship with the dog. Certainly, as this book reveals, dogs were sometimes cross-bred with wolves. But when we put all the different breeds together, each reflecting like the many surfaces of a finely cut precious stone, the diamond-soul of the dog, we get a clearer image of the primordial form: the natural dog. Each surface reflects something of ourselves, too, in the faces of Pekes, poodles, bloodhounds, and beagles, because we humans played God with canine genes and psyches. Though to some degree re-created in our own image of perfected utility, standardized type, and idealized form and personality—sometimes to the detriment of the dog's well-being—each breed still remains true to its original nature and Creator. And as different breeds from age to age see cycles of popularity and ancient myths and legends spring to life, so our lives continue to be enriched by their unquestioned presence. We may thank our ancestors for having helped create some remarkable varieties of dogs, and congratulate ourselves for helping conserve the very best of those ancient breeds of earlier civilizations. But above all we should thank God for dogs and wonder how we could ever have a life without them.

—MICHAEL W. FOX, Vice President
The Humane Society of the United States
Washington, DC
August 1996

Authors' Introduction

I T C A M E A S a surprise to learn, while working on this book, that over a period of thirty years of marriage, we have owned together almost thirty dogs. Add to this equation the Canidae with which each of us grew up, and the total comes to twenty different breeds between us. So, we have always been large with dogs and dogs have always been largely on our minds and in our hearts, and, as well, a large part of our monthly budget.

However, these considerations have nothing to do with why we began this book, which grew out of our great curiosity about the nature of dogs and perhaps the most fundamental question of all: What makes a dog a dog? The best answers to this question seem to come from human prehistory and those oral narratives that place man's best friend side by side with God. So, we began our search into the mythology of Canidae with the premise that Dog did not "begin" merely six thousand or so years ago in historical time, but much before that in mythological time.

Dog, as a primordial being, began, as Ferdinand Mery said in *The Life, History and Magic of the Dog* because of the frailty of humankind: "In the beginning, God created Man, but seeing him so feeble, He gave him a dog." In the Canidae narratives of native peoples, there is none of that human ethnocentrism with which author J. Allen Boone writes. "I had long been under the impression that while I lived on the upper levels of existence, all animals . . . had to do their living on much lower and relatively unimportant mental and physical levels; and that between them and myself there could be certain rather limited service ties, but not much else."

In the myths of our ancient past—that is to say, the prehistory of our race—Dog wasn't relegated to servitude, but delegated by God to lend a helping hand to humankind. As one storyteller reported, the natural superiority of Dog is implicit in the earth-religions of indigenous people throughout the world.

> Dog myths say . . . that Dog can hunt and Man can't. They say that Dog has the use of fire and that Man has never seen fire. They

explain that Dog has Woman, Man hasn't met her yet. They reveal that Dog has a close relationship with God, while Man is just beginning to know him.

Many people from whom we asked for specific breed information responded by asking us to clarify—"What is a myth?" Their contention was that dog myths were like old wives' tales, rumors of truth fraught with misinformation. Myths, our breeder friends told us, needed to be corrected, not perpetuated.

We won't deny that a lot of dog myths surviving over the last millennium have been boiled down over time to an adage or an aphorism, which is neither clear nor meaningful in our present context. So, in order to address this difficulty, we stuck with stories that explicated, or dramatized, specific breeds. In each selection in this book, there is a definite kind of dog that we were able to physically identify with our tales. On the other hand, if there happened to be an important breed we hoped to feature, but couldn't find a single myth to go with it, we had to drop that dog from our roster. Naturally, the most numerous myths came, part and parcel, with the same ancient breeds: the mastiff, the hound, the toy. The more recent the breed or the more unspecified the breed, the harder it was to find a myth to go along with it. All in all, the task was very, very difficult, as there are few books specifically on dog mythology and only one that we know of, Maria Leach's *God Had a Dog*, which covers myths culture by culture. Her book, however, is a rather complex anthropological work, and not easily accessible for the reader.

In ADDITION TO the general myths applicable to our sixty-seven major breeds, we've included another forty associated tales, bringing the total number of dog myths to ninety stories altogether. The myths come from virtually every world culture that exists on our globe. Each dog is introduced by documented historical facts which are followed by mythological histories from oral and written tradition. Sometimes the two cross lines and appear to be the same. Who can know, for sure, which is which? Did Mary Queen of Scots, before her fateful beheading, truly have a Maltese under her skirts? Or was this an embellishment on an earlier myth that someone heard?

It is certainly true that myth begets myth, while history tries to narrow the field and make the improbable seem outside the possibility of truth. A good working definition of myth—and one that we have used in compiling our tales—is that it is the closest thing we have to a sacred oral history. However, the great body of largely unwritten material we have drawn from is not, as many people think, confined only to our ancient past. It contains, as well as the old echoes, both the present and the future. All three offer viable histories of a symbolic kind.

How the Afghan got his wet nose by plugging up the holes in the Ark is no older, in this timeless sense, than how the Newfoundland aboard the Titanic tried to save his master by swimming and barking in circles after the great ship went down.

The thirteenth-century Welsh Gelert story, one of the most famous dog stories ever told, traveled from Gelert, Wales, to twentieth-century Las Vegas, Nevada, and barely skipped a beat—essentially it's the same story.

The original version features a medieval Welsh wolfhound, who bravely saves his master's child by killing a marauding wolf. The contemporary episode, set in Las Vegas, the Fate capital of America, substitutes a Doberman pinscher, who corners a burglar in a closet and bites off three of his fingers. Both tales are built on maximum irony and their own punch-ending surprise, but there's no denying their relationship to one another.

The old and new myths herein have survived us because we've survived them. Moreover, our mythological subject, the mystery Canidae, our friend, the Dog, refuses to be easily catalogued. The terms of his written history would seem to be that, since he is not able to tell it by himself, he will confound those who try. So, if this book has, in some manner, gone to the dogs, it's most probably because a Great Dane and a dachshund—two of the oldest breeds—wouldn't leave the room where the book was being researched and written.

Along with our own helpful canines, countless people—from kindly country vets who shared a tale or two to the dedicated Internetters, who captured some heart-warming and some bone-chilling stories—gave us lively, publishable material.

Breed clubs turned over their newsletters to us; a few helped by offering stories by phone and by fax. The American Kennel Club in New York graciously offered us rare archival books and their expert reference staff. Then there were well-wishers, too many to name, who mailed us their memorable stories. The best, of course, came unexpectedly in the midst of doing something else—the ones that came in out of the cold, unannounced. That's what happens when you have lots of dogs; other dogs want to know about you, they want to smell you from head to foot. After years of this, one has an archive of walk-in dog stories that beg to be told.

So, here are the myths, the histories, and, at the end of each, a "Lore of the Dog" section, which describes the physical and mental characteristics of the breed. Where one begins and another ends is as questionable as the first spark that lit the firmament. However, if you believe the wise old aphoristic tales, Dog was there and saw it first. God said so.

AFGHAN

Noah's Dog

JOHN BREDIN

THE AFGHAN HOUND'S early history is, like his cousin, the grey-hound, one of ancient honor. The dog is depicted on tombs, printed on papyrus, pictographed on walls, and chipped into rocks going back to 2200 B.C. Some dog experts such as Michael W. Fox suggest that the Afghan is the dog Noah took aboard the Ark. There are myths to substantiate this, but naturally there is no historical proof. However, the Afghan hound is known to have coursed game in the Nile Valley during the reign of the ancient Egyptian kings.

One thing that has made the Afghan so popular over the centuries is the versatility of the breed. Afghans will ably hunt deer, rabbit, wolf, gazelle, jackal, and even marmot; and their use as frontier sentry and mountain sheep-herder may be added to the roster of roles the dog has accumulated in his four thousand year history. This adaptability accounts for the Afghan's adoption by British army officers in the latter half of the nineteenth century. World War I, due to borders being closed, virtually stopped the spread of the breed, but it picked up again in 1925 in England, and then again in the United States, so that by the mid-thirties there was an Afghan Hound Club in America.

Although the Afghan's presence in the Bible may be more myth than fact, one can still follow a "biblical map" upon the plain that is now part of Nigeria. Here, in the old African kingdom of Bornu, the ancient hound's relatives were said to set forth and multiply. The word "Bornu," in fact, means "the country of Noah." The geography itself is a vast tableland near the edge of Lake Chad, where African myths say Noah's family touched down after the Great Flood.

Author Edward C. Ash suggests that our recorded four thousand years is a mere fraction of dog time on Earth and this being so, the Afghan is as old as the glittering rocks on the plains of Bornu. One story says that Noah took two Afghans on the Ark, and these were among the last creatures to board the vessel. The Ark was so full by then that the poor Afghans had to stand at the door with their noses exposed to the wind and the rain. Another myth explains that during the tempestuous forty days and forty nights, the Ark sprung some leaks. Noah was able to plug most of them, but there were a couple that he couldn't stop. So, he appealed to his faithful Afghans and they stopped the leaks by putting their long noses in the holes.

Both of these tales explain, in mythological terms, why dogs have wet noses, but what they do not explain, and probably never will, is why dogs— above and beyond the obvious rationale of food dependency—have thrown their lot in with the human race. Perhaps, as some say, it is "the nobility of sacrifice" that one recognizes in the face of a dog, and in none is this more clear than the wise-eyed Afghan.

The Lore of the Dog

This regal member of the greyhound family is a courser, sight hound (primarily using sight as well as scent and hearing), and kingly mannered hunter whose feathery trousers and coat (except along the spine where it is considerably shorter) shields him from thorny shrubs and bushes when on the chase. Physically, he resembles an overcoated greyhound. His aristocratic head, complete with visor, is all feathers and silk. Most commonly the Afghan is either black with spots of chestnut, fawn, or tricolor.

Male Afghans are 27 to 29 inches in height and weight is 50 to 64 pounds. Large footed and pivotal hipped—the hip bones are actually set higher and wider apart than most dogs—the Afghan can traverse the roughest terrain, moving nimbly across scorching sand, rock-strewn plain, and hills of fallen timber.

This dog has great endurance for the chase, powerful thrust in the capture; Afghans have actually run down leopards. His speed, while a little less than the greyhound, is nonetheless inspiring. Once having achieved his perfect pace on a leash, the Afghan can place his back feet in the track of his front feet.

The aloof Afghan has been called haughty and distant, but he is primarily only standoffish to strangers, whereas with immediate family members he is noticeably affectionate and even playful. The reason for Afghan singularity may be credited to the special skills he employed in the hunt. Outdistancing horsemen, the Afghan was left very much on his own. This developed an independent spirit, which might be mistaken for what some trainers have called "slow learning." However, the Afghan's nature is as free as his gait.

AIREDALE AND WELSH TERRIER

The Dog of the River Aire

JOHN BREDIN

T HE AIREDALE WAS developed around 1850 by crossing the English black and tan terrier, now extinct, with the otter hound. The name comes from the river Aire, a watery otterscape near Leeds in England. If size and keen scent are the gift of his otter hound origin, then the Airedale must have gotten some of his talent elsewhere because he's been used to hunt a variety of small and mid-sized creatures—namely water rats, weasels, foxes, and badgers. This largest of "earth dogs," or terriers, has been used on larger game too, often bounding deer and charging boar.

In the 1920s in America, the Airedale was so well thought of that there was even an expression to typify his lively character in a person. A man-about-town was highly praised as "a regular Airedale of a fellow." During the two World Wars, the Airedale served as a messenger in the gloom of the trenches, a job he did with great effectiveness. The breed was officially recognized in 1879 under the name Airedale, and although the dog was quite popular in America from 1915–1945, his popularity began to diminish after the fifties. Today the Airedale is recognized for his keen intelligence, his unpredictable wit, and his quirky terrier's disposition.

SOME SAY THAT the Welsh terrier, another descendant of the English black and tan terrier, is, aesthetically speaking, a small version of the Airedale. This remarkably eager hunter-and-digger was employed on the old English hunts to rout out foxes, badgers, and rodents. Working in concert with the faster-paced hounds, who ran ahead of him, the Welsh terrier followed behind, waiting to go-to-ground. The way it went was thus: First, came two or three brace of foxhounds, so called, then the terrier squad, which included the Welsh terrier and perhaps a Dandie Dinmont or two. When these breeds were yodeling in the distant dells, the hoi polloi of dogdom were unleashed— "mongrels, whelps, and curs of low degree," as Sir Walter Scott called them.

The terrier gang, of which the Welshie was a part, went to earth as quickly as they could, going underground in pursuit of whatever quarry was inclined to take that avenue of escape. When they broke free of the ground, it was because the fox, for example, took to the open field, whereupon the sleek greyhounds ran him down. It seems cruel, and perhaps even unthinkable today, that so many Canidae were sent off after one brief puff of fox, but such was the climate and temper of the time.

JOHN STEINBECK, A dog lover if ever there was one, wrote that the moral qualities which we as humans most admire in dogs are usually those we would wish to have for ourselves. This is logical, and yet, as a man who was painfully aware of his frailties, Steinbeck recognized a variety of human tendencies, both good and bad, in the dogs that he knew and loved; and he wrote about many of them.

One particular Airedale that Steinbeck observed was a character who lived at a gambling house called the Silver Mirror. Here was a hustler of the Canidae clan who had developed an appreciation for blackjack. Whenever someone won—whether at craps or blackjack—there was Omar the Airedale, looking half-starved and utterly deprived of human kindness. Of course, Steinbeck confirms, "Omar invariably got a steak." Predictably, Omar died some years later of "obese old age."

This tale neither supports nor denies the theory that dogs have the ability to reason, and can put their mind to good use whenever they want a free meal. It does suggest, however, that dogs are not more, and certainly not less, than human. Steinbeck said that all he wanted to do was "put them in their proper perspective, and thus to make dogs look as much like people as people look like dogs."

He once asked, "If all dogs were the noble beasts we pretend, how would we know a real hero when we see one?" Perhaps he was aiming, early on, at an antihero dog, a dog lower than a cur, but not less than a man. In any case, the next Airedale he wrote about was one of his own. Although he insists that he is not picking on the breed, Steinbeck does admit to being guilty of "irreverence."

In this unfortunate episode, the dog exhibits cowardly, back-biting tendencies, which many Airedale owners, he suggests, will deny.

It seems a mongrel dog of no certain lineage—shepherd-setter-coyote—trounced Steinbeck's Airedale every time he went past the dog's domain. The beatings got to be a daily thing: "Every week my dog fought this grisly creature and every week, he got licked." And so it went, week after week, until one day Steinbeck's dog got lucky, and taking the bully by surprise, gave him the thumping of his life. Finally, when the grisly dog "hung his head in the loser's corner," the author's unsportsmanlike Airedale decided to fight dirty. Aghast, Steinbeck watched his dog—after justly winning the day—ruthlessly lay into the loser's private parts. When the Airedale was finally pried away from his victim, the latter, according to Steinbeck, "was finished as a father." Morosely, he winds up the story by commenting that "there can be dogs without honor, even as with us." It's a small thing to concede, given today's unholy standards, but when he wrote this in the Disney-era sixties, it was newsworthy—or at the least controversial—to say that a dog was less than a dog.

AUTHOR AND EDITOR Ted Patrick, a friend of John Steinbeck, liked to polish Airedale pedestals, which may have been the foil that got Steinbeck started on his antihero anecdotes. Patrick speaks of an Airedale that barks at a bunch of Boy Scouts who tramp past the house where he lives. There is no great ferocity in the bark, Patrick explains, just a desultory, unaggressive reminder of the universal watchman at work. However, one of the Scouts throws a big rock at the barking dog. The rock hits home and knocks the dog out cold.

Two weeks later, the same Scout troop passes the recovered Airedale's porch and suddenly the dog streaks into the boys' midst, selects the rock-thrower among the mass of uniforms, and avenges himself with a good bite.

One might ask: How did the dog know which Boy Scout had thrown the rock? Did he dream his revenge? Was he planning his grand attack during the two weeks that the boys were absent? Did he run toward a smell, or a face? Or neither? And what does the story tell us, if anything, about this curious breed?

Airedales, like all breeds, come with plenty of mythical baggage. There are some stories that tell of the Airedale that sits in a corner and does nothing but growl. There are other likely tales that praise the dog's wit and his vast grasp of human vocabulary. In other words, a particular animal is woven into the general pattern of dog traits by the application of a convincing story. Thus the myth precedes and often precludes the truth, and all because a convincing writer told us so.

Can we learn anything from these commonplace myths of "good dog, bad dog?" Ted Patrick claims that reasonable assessments are unlikely—not until the quixotic creatures called dogs learn to talk, and can best the worst of us at our own game of writing beautiful lies.

Mythically speaking, dogs may have forgotten more about us than we shall ever learn from them. So said Pliny, Pythagoras, Cicero, Herodotus, and Steinbeck—or one of them, anyway. Ask any Airedale.

The Lore of the Dog

The Airedale is a big rangy dog with small dark eyes and a long flat skull. The nose is long with beardlike fur around the bottom, giving the appearance of a mustache and goatee.

The ears are small and V-shaped, and folded to the side. The tail, set high but not curved, is of medium length. Overall, the dog is strongly built and quite symmetrical.

The fur is stiff, dense and wiry, not curly. The colors are brown with black or grizzled markings. Height is 22 to 25 inches and weight is around 50 pounds.

The Airedale has keen eyesight and hearing. A courageous dog, once bred for hunting bears and wolves, he makes an excellent family, guide, and guard dog. His nature is easygoing and his temperament is all fun-loving terrier. An attentive master is considered best for this dog, who will often fantasize enemies, hunts, and adventures while prowling across the living room carpet.

Airedale owner Ted Patrick recalls one such dog that showed his devotion so completely that each morning he presented Ted's mother with a new item of his affection. "I remember one morning it was a freshly killed rabbit; another, a bottle of somebody else's milk; another, a fresh loaf of bread that had been delivered to another porch; another, a rag doll; another, a nightgown removed from a clothesline and ripped in the process."

THE PERKY WELSH terrier, the compact relative of the Airedale, is no less devoted or impassioned. Strong and wiry, this "little Airedale" has a head like a hammer, a black nose, and powerful jaws. The eyes are deep set and quite expressive; the ears V-shaped, set high with the flap facing forward rather than falling to one side. This dog's neck is long, the body is muscular, and the tail is arched and docked. Leggy and cat-footed, the Welsh terrier will hunt anything that will go aground.

The coat is wiry and dense and the colors are black and tan, grey, black grizzle, and tan. The height is 15½ inches and the weight about 20 pounds. These are good apartment dogs, but they must have sensible early training to acclimate them to later life. They are naturally wary of strangers and make excellent watchdogs. Like the Airedale, the Welsh terrier is very intelligent.

SOME AIREDALE OWNERS feel that their breed should be at the top of the IQ list. Author Booth Tarkington was one such proclaimer, as it was his nephew's Airedale that discovered the international art of cab-flagging.

It happened this way. The dog's owner, Booth Jamison, was attending Princeton University, a school that did not allow dogs in the dormitory. So, when the Airedale came to campus for a visit, Jamison sent him home via cab. Some days later the dog showed up on campus with another Airedale friend when Jamison wasn't there. Disappointed—but undaunted—the canny Airedale hopped in the same cab he'd taken before; and thus got a comfy ride home.

After this, whenever the dogs felt like it, they headed to Princeton, and, whenever Jamison was out, they'd hail their favorite cabby, who collected his fare back at the boarding house where the dogs resided.

AKITA

The Emperor's Hunter

BARBARA DAVIS

EXCAVATIONS INTO THE shell mounds of the Ainu on the northernmost tip of Honshu in Japan reveal burial sites of dogs and men from prehistoric time. Although dogs were sometimes used as payment for taxes in the fourteenth century, the Akita Ainu's earliest records date back to the seventeenth-century nobility of feudal Japan. The word "Ainu" in Japanese means "sons of dogs." The respect accorded to these animals comes from a legend which states that Ainus are people descended from the union of a dog and a woman.

The emperor, Yuryaku (A.D. 457–479), upon seeing a house that resembled his palace, ordered it to be burned to the ground. But when the owner presented him with a fine white dog, the emperor changed his mind and rescinded the order. This dog was an ancestor of the Akita who later on became a member of the court. Ownership of the Akita was eventually denied to all commoners.

In speaking to—or even about—an imperial Akita, the courtly Japanese employed a unique vocabulary specially created for the breed. Each individual dog had a caretaker whose dress was matched by the rank of the owner. In fact, the leash used was indicative of the Akita's (and his owner's) status. The emperor's own Akita was reported to travel about on a sedan chair and to wear a gold collar.

———

THE PRIMARY USE of Akitas, prior to their royal adoption, was for hunting. Their fine nose, alert ear, and sturdy, well-furred body made them the best possible snow hunters. These were dogs that could run tirelessly after game—deer, bear, and boar—in the snow, and while they were able to hold a bear at bay, they were so versatile that they were also used to retrieve waterfowl.

In addition, the breed was invaluable to fishermen, driving fish into nets during a fish run. The onshore fishermen gave a command to the dogs, waiting in boats just off the shore, who plunged into the water and formed a cordon that closed in on the fish. The Akitas were rewarded with fish heads only if the dogs actually retrieved a fish.

Along with hunting and fishing, the Akita became a formidable fighting dog. Although still given royal treatment, the animal was bred to fight and, in time, the breed suffered such attrition as a result of this sport that it nearly vanished altogether. The fighting was repeated as often as twelve times in a given month. It wasn't until the late nineteenth century, when Japan began to be influenced by European culture, that this practice was put to an end and the Akita—almost extinct—was brought back in good numbers. By 1927 the Akitainu Hozankai Society was established as a breed club. In 1931 the government of Japan declared the Akita a national monument and a national treasure.

HELEN KELLER, THE internationally renowned champion of the deaf and blind, is credited with bringing the Akita to the United States. In 1937 she received an Akita puppy from the Japanese government and brought it home to America. The American occupational forces, after World War II, admired the Akita's adaptability, loyalty, and nobility. They, too, brought the dogs home and in 1956, the Akita Club of America was founded. However, it took another twenty years before the breed was found acceptable by the American Kennel Club.

ONE OF THE earliest Akita myths is an Ainu folktale about a man who visits the land of the dead. There, he finds, as in many American Indian myths, a village, much like his own, inhabited by people that he once knew. However, unlike similar Native American tales, the people of the dead do not seem to see or hear the Ainu, and he passes unnoticed except for one thing. His presence is picked up by dogs who bark at him. This myth has worldwide echoes and it supports the widely held folk belief that dogs possess feral vision, a sightedness that pierces through the veil of death. Dogs, it is generally believed, can see ghosts.

Another Akita myth is the so-called "tattler's tale." Once, long ago, all dogs could speak. However, one time, Dog saw his master having an affair and he reported it to his master's wife. Thereafter, the story goes, Dog lost his ability to talk. Thus deprived of human speech, and, in a sense, silenced, he now is only able to bark.

Among the North American Indians, the Dog receives a death penalty for this same crime. The Native American Caddo myth tells how dog and master turn into stone at the end. In most aboriginal myths of this sort, the dog is demoted.

In keeping with the ancient stories, the Akita did not bark during the hunt and his silence was considered his finest virtue as a hunter's dog. An old Japanese myth illustrates this perfectly. It seems that a hunter and his dog were in the forest together when the dog, seeing a bear, brought his master into a fatal confrontation with the beast. Afterwards, coming home alone, the dog lied to his master's wife. He said that it was the man's dying wish that he should marry her. The bereaved wife didn't believe the dog's lie, and as the dog went on and on about it, she threw a handful of dust into his mouth, and that finally silenced him. The tale reminds us of the Ainu belief of a primal dog/woman union. It also suggests that dust is both our origin and our end. "To bite the dust" is to be duly—and doubly—silenced.

The Lore of the Dog

The Akita is a heavy boned, muscular dog, whose image in Japan is one of health and well-being. In fact, a child's birth is often heralded by the presentation of an Akita statue.

Sturdy as a block of wood or a piece of jade, Akitas have small erect ears and tails that roll up, once, or even twice, over the rump. They have an undercoat of thick, soft fur and an outer one that is straight and slightly off the body.

The shoulders are strong, the chest wide, the hind quarters in proportion to the front legs. Overall, the dog's appearance is statuesque. All colors are possible with the Akita, and there may or may not be a mask. The huskylike face is alert most of the time, giving the dog a strike-on-command presentation. Long, deep looks from this alert and attentive dog will produce a worry line or furrow just above the eyes. Akitas stand 23 to 28 inches and weigh 77 to 88 pounds.

Akitas are friendly and courageous dogs. They are eminently trainable and, in fact, they even languish somewhat when not at work. As they were once used as fighting dogs, their inclination around other animals, but especially other dogs, can be threatening, unless, of course, other training has intervened.

Family is important to this breed, but they often become agitated (and/ or unpredictable) in the presence of children who are not known to them. Strangers are also suspect until proven friendly or trustworthy. This is not to denigrate the dog's extraordinary family loyalty. In the words of Dr. Michael W. Fox: "There is a statue of an Akita in Tokyo in memory of the dog who waited at the station for his master to come—years after his master's death. This spot is a popular rendezvous for dating couples: omen of fidelity?"

Highly sensitive, Akitas do not need loud commands to heed a warning or to understand the emotional impact of a human situation. The dog is valued for intelligence, decorum, and a watchfulness that has permitted many Japanese mothers to leave their children, often for hours at a time, in the care of the family Akita.

American Staffordshire Terrier and American Pit Bull Terrier

"The Sturdy Staffordshire"

BARBARA DAVIS

RUGGED AS THE region of rills and the hard-hearted miners in England who gave him his name, the Staffordshire terrier is not a tunneler or a digger, but a fighter of distinction. The dog was originally bred for the fighting pits of the nineteenth century and his prowess in the ring, the pit, and the backwoods of America have brought him enduring fame. This dog is the product of cross-breeding the bulldog and a terrier, most likely the fox terrier—the former giving him the gravity of a square fighting dog; the latter offering him tenacity and agility. This direct descendant of the bullterrier came to the United States in 1870 where he became known as the Yankee terrier or the American pit bull terrier.

Crossing the Atlantic gave the Staffordshire terrier an advantage in size and conformation, as these were both stressed in the dog's American breeding. Now outweighing his English cousin by some 10 pounds, the American dog is still a feisty fighter, a fine watchdog, and a scanner of scoundrels. They say, in fact, that this dog can determine evil intent from slack manner in anyone. Just as he once had to size up an opponent in the cruel pit, he can cast a quick eye on a man and come up with an appropriate strategy of demeanor.

THE ORIGINAL "LITTLE Rascals" comedy team had a white-bodied, black-eyed pal named Petey, who helped keep his children out of trouble—that is, when he wasn't evading the dog catcher's net himself. Petey was almost as famous as Tige, the mascot of Buster Brown, who, as a logo, lived inside a shoe. Then there was the RCA pit bull named Nipper, whose successors now seem to be a pair of mom and pup Jack Russells who like to watch their big-screen TV.

In Tim McLaurin's novel *Keeper of the Moon: A Southern Boyhood* the author, who grew up in the hills of North Carolina, recounts the tale of a legendary pit bull and his mythical master. The story, according to McLaurin, is true, the only invention being the language used to describe the two characters. The dog, Roy Lee, is "tougher than two alligators" and eats "nails and gunpowder" for breakfast. His owner, a human counterpart to the dog, is Tote Faircloth, a Fayetteville welder, whose fame for hard drinking and rattlesnake toting perhaps earned him his name.

Roy Lee, McLaurin says, "had only one gear—forward." He's the fightingest thing in those back hollows and hills of North Carolina, but he allows children to ride upon his back. His passion for fighting is born of an intense dislike for all other dogs. He does not pick fights willy-nilly, though; there's a professionalism in the way he walks and swaggers, like a gunfighter who has his ethical tendencies, his rationale for fighting, his style.

Tote is reluctant to have Roy Lee fight on one particular day because the younger opponent is barely past puppyhood. Furthermore, the young dog's owner is joined by his son, who has played with the dog and dotes on him. Tote, however, finally gives in and the consequences, excerpted below, tell us much about the way these dogs were, and are, bred, and what a fight really means to them. In the final analysis, fighting becomes an art of self-expression, more than a blind killing reflex. Mainly, though, this is a story of men against men, man against his own perverse nature. The pit bull is a kind of pawn in the war of human values:

The black dog was by build and nature a "leg dog," using his shorter stature to bulldoze under Roy Lee to get at his legs or belly. Roy Lee was a "throat dog," instinctively going for his opponent's windpipe. The dogs feinted and parried, the younger dog using superior speed and strength, Roy Lee relying on his experience, leaning on his opponent, tucking his front legs far back to keep them out of his jaws. When both dogs got strong holds and kept them for a couple of minutes, they were broken apart. Roy Lee breathed hard, but was unhurt, just a small gash opened on his lower jaw. The black dog bled from his mouth and ear.

"Let's don't fight him no more," the kid said to his daddy, eyes wide at the sight of his bleeding pet. The man ignored him. A woman came up behind the boy and laid her hands on his shoulders.

Roy Lee hit the black dog again, slammed him to his back and got a good hold on his throat. The black dog gasped for breath and struggled to free himself. Roy Lee fought only with his mouth, lying limp while the other dog wasted energy trying to get loose. He choked and sucked at the air, unable even to growl. The boy whimpered and asked again for his father to stop them. Finally, the black dog broke Roy Lee's hold, but was behind on breath and short on energy. Roy Lee hit him again, this time bit into his soft belly. The black dog turned and snapped Roy Lee's leg, but he jerked it from his jaws and out of reach before he bit down. Roy Lee chewed at his belly, shook his head violently back and forth. Suddenly, the black dog yelped a shrill cry of pain and frustration.

"Stop them, Daddy," the boy cried, tears suddenly in his eyes. "He's getting hurt."

"Stop them, Larry," the man's wife said, a big-hipped woman in jeans. "You're scaring him."

"Y'all shut the hell up," the man said, his eyes still intent on his dog. "Damn dog was born to fight." An embarrassed murmur rolled through the crowd.

When the black dog squealed, Roy Lee fought harder, bit deeper into his belly and shook, then released his hold and sprang for his throat again. The black dog met him with open jaws, but Roy Lee feinted, let the dog's inexperience carry him by, then nailed him from the rear. He soon had his opponent on his back again in a throat hold. The black dog gasped.

"We ought to stop this," Tote said to the man. "Your dog's game. He's just young."

"He's gotta fight to learn," the man snapped.

Roy Lee's tail twitched back and forth as he choked the younger dog. The black dog got weaker, unable to break the hold, his breath now coming in short gasps. He tried to squeal again, the sound high pitched like a dying rabbit.

The boy sobbed. His mother pushed him toward the rear of the crowd and took a step toward her husband. "You don't stop them, I will, Larry," she shouted shrilly. "The dog's gonna die!"

The man whirled about and lashed out with one arm, slapped the woman hard across the face, caused her to pitch backwards to the ground. She put her hand to her mouth, her eyes stunned as she stared at her husband.

Tote stepped forward. He shouted, "Roy Lee!" and touched his dog's back. "Off now, off, Roy Lee," he said. "Ease off now."

Roy Lee broke his hold immediately, and Tote pulled him backwards by the tail. The black dog tried to get up once and attack, but his legs buckled. He rolled to the side and panted for air.

"Fight's over," Tote said to the other man, buckling the collar around Roy Lee.

"Let the damn dogs fight," the man said loudly. "My dog ain't finished."

"Mine's finished," Tote answered.

"You scared?" the man said. "I thought you was supposed to be so tough." His fist closed slowly at his side. "You look chicken to me."

A hush fell over the crowd, the only sound the boy crying. Tote stared deep into the man's eyes. "I ain't scared, son," Tote said. "But I ain't letting my dog kill yours."

The man pointed his finger at Tote. "I still say you're chickenshit."

I saw that same look enter Tote's eyes, the sheen I noticed when he was lying in the hospital bed, as if he was tallying up life spent fighting and boozing, with only a fading reputation to show for it, a cancer in his chest that would eventually kill him. Any one of a dozen would have stepped in for Tote if it came to blows, but I feel Tote could probably still have taken the guy, fighting like Roy Lee had, on experience and guts and the grace God seems to give some people. I suspect as Tote stared across the ring, as the man's insult still rang in his ears, he saw the resemblance of another would-be warrior, one who'd still be living today if he'd had the sense to keep driving.

"I ain't scared of you," Tote finally said. "Not of a man who would slap his own wife."

The man's gaze faltered, his eyes flicked to the ground, then to his wife and son. Tote turned and led Roy Lee to the truck, the old dog limping slightly. Tote placed his feet carefully, like walking a beam. The two shuffled away from us, brushing together occasionally as if they leaned inward to one another for support.

This might seem to some like a picture from the past, an event inscribed on the rural South of long ago. But the truth, according to McLaurin, is that dog fighting happens today and the story is true to the ethos of dog and man. The men pay obeisance to their clan, their ability to survive within it; and their dogs reflect these old values. In truth, it is the men who fight, not the dogs, and victory or loss accorded to each as it must and as it will. "It happens," Tim McLaurin told us, "it happens."

The Lore of the Dog

The American Staffordshire terrier and the American pit bull terrier are medium-sized, muscular dogs. Known as a fighting machines, their physique was designed for the locking-on of jaws, the dancing and feinting in the ring, and, generally, the aggressive mannerisms of a professional boxer-wrestler-judo master. The skull is broad, the muzzle short, giving the pit bull a top-heavy look. The ears, half-pricked and rather small (often docked), lend the face an alert readiness. The eyes are black and round and of medium size; they appear, at times, to gaze deeply into people, as if sizing them up. Whether this is a leftover reaction to the pit bull's fighting ways and fighting days, we cannot be sure; but it is a characteristic.

The body is solid with straight front legs and well-muscled thighs. The feet are strong and padded and made for holding a position on the earth. Pit bulls have short tails which are carried horizontally; their coats are thick, short, and shiny, and they come in all colors. Their height is 17 to 18 inches and their weight runs 38 to 44 pounds. According to most authorities, the American pit bull is heavier than his English cousin with a larger head. However, the two dogs, though separate in name, are quite often identical; in fact, they are often dual-registered.

In spite of the dog's reputation as a rapacious fighter, the properly trained pit bull can become an excellent house pet, guardian, and children's friend. In fact, the animal is especially gentle with children. The code of honor as seen in Tim McLaurin's tale is credible in the ring, but not necessarily out of it. The dog is not as quick-trigger as the stories make him out to be; he is affable and companionable most of the time. However, he'll fight when his territory is threatened or when provoked by other dogs, or by people, which sometimes happens because of the dog's supposed ferocity, a reputation perpetuated in recent years.

That well-known instinct, the will to win, is deeply bred and will not go away; but the image of a killer, waiting to tear apart his victim, is not even present in many of the myths of old. More famous than the dog's ferocity is his ability to accept punishment with equanimity. There are lots of stories that tell of a dog who can literally be wrapped around a crushing tire as the car is moving, and yet the dog will still come up smiling. The pit bullterrier has a great code of honor, a brave heart, a winning manner. He knows he is better than most of the folks who own him. One word best defines the sturdy Staffordshire: Indestructible.

BASENJI

The African Barkless

A s a game beater for African tribal masters, the basenji's barkless history is one of the oldest in dog lore. Egyptian carvings from five thousand years ago indicate that these dogs were brought as gifts to the pharaohs from Central Africa. Disappearing from known existence at the fall of ruling Egypt, the dog was "rediscovered" by an English explorer in the late nineteenth century in what was formerly the Belgian Congo, now Zaire. Nicknamed "the-jumping-up-and-down-dog" for his habit of leaping high to see over the elephant grass, the basenji is generally known for his alert nature. He has also been called the Congo Dog.

Although paleontologists have no record of the basenji's link to a primal canine, author and dog expert Michael W. Fox has suggested that the basenji may be an intermediary between modern domestic and wild dogs, a dingo-like canid; this precludes the wolf being the primal ancestor of the domestic dog. In 1895 an English explorer discovered the basenji at work and he told how the native people of the Congo used him for all aspects of hunting including pointing, retrieving, and driving. In addition, the basenji was used as a ratter, to hunt down twenty-pound "reed rats." The dog's silence may have been bred for this purpose, as reed rats are very cautious creatures. The basenji was first brought to the United States in 1937, and though formerly uncommon, the breed has grown greatly in popularity.

THE FIRST ANCESTOR of the basenji was adopted by the Nyanga people in the Belgian Congo. He became not only a great hunter but also the culture hero of their mythology. It is said of the basenji that, being a godlike animal, he proved too fast for normal men to keep up with him. So, the Nyanga people decided that this dog should have a bell. This way, whenever he drove his quarry beyond the ken of human trackers, they could hear where he was and be able to catch up to him. Arguably, then, the first dog collar was a piece of sacred wood covered with antelope skin, inside of which was a small, resonant piece of bone.

Bells and gourds were also used as heralding devices, and these could be heard from some distance; but these could have created the effect of a "beater" to scare up game as well. Indeed, the dog bell may have brought barklessness into the throat of the basenji. No one knows for sure why the dog refrains from barking (since it does have a normal canine larynx), unless, according to the early myths, the collar did the barking for him. Ironically, it was the basenji's first appearance at a dog show in Great Britain that broke his ancient vow of silence, causing him to let out a plaintive yodel.

THE BASENJI WAS the great bringer of fire. One day a man named Nkhango went searching for honey and discovered a dwelling deep in the forest. This was the house of a god, and before it sat a dog named Rukuba.

Nkhango asked the dog what it was that he sat before, and Rukuba explained that he was seated before the thing called Fire.

"I should like to have some of that," Nkhango said.

"Well," Rukuba said, "if I should steal some of it for you, what, in return, would I receive for myself?"

"I will take care of you forever," Nkhango replied. So Rukuba stole Fire, and gave it to Nkhango before his lord returned to the house. All was well thereafter with Nkhango, whose gift to his village was well received.

But it did not work so well for Rukuba, who was kicked out of his lordly home. Eventually, he turned up on Nkhango's doorstep, saying, "You said you would take care of me." Nkhango was glad the dog had come and he kept his promise; so did the generations that followed, all the way to the present time.

The Lore of the Dog

With perky ears and curled tail, the basenji is a small, compact, lightly built hunting dog, who has been compared to a tiny deer in his agility. He stands about the same size as a fox terrier with a deeply furrowed forehead and a neck that is arched and proud.

The fur is smooth, glossy, and odorless, and, unlikely as it seems, this dog cleans himself just like a cat. Coloration is copper, black, black and tan, with white markings. This dog stands at around 17 inches high and weighs 20 to 22 pounds.

Devoted, playful, and normally quiet, the basenji is unique among dogs for it does not bark, but it does yodel, chortle, murmur, and snarl.

Basenjis are at home in country or city surroundings, and are therefore ideal house pets. They are known to be aloof with those whom they do not know, yet their family will find them intelligent, cheerful, and affectionate. Some owners complain about basenjis not working out well with children. Others state that they are affable with them. They can be quite aggressive, perhaps owing to their "wild lineage."

BASSET HOUND

The High-bred, Low Down Hound

BARBARA DAVIS

Descended from the old St. Hubert hounds of France, bassets are supreme badger hunters. Sportsmen in the United States have used them for hunting fox, raccoon, opossum and squirrel, and the dogs have a special affinity for flushing rabbit and pheasant. This dog was not known anywhere except in France until 1863 when it was presented at the first dog show held in Paris. Twelve years later its popularity in England, furthered by admiring royalty, was secured.

There are a great many variations of the basset breed, but perhaps the one best known in America is Le Coulteulx (derived from the French breeder of that name). This breed is of decidedly French lineage—the word "basset" deriving from the French "*bas,*" or low. It is a dog with a bloodhound head, a foxhound coat, and the running gear of a heavy-boned dachshund. He has been called the "Cyrano of Dogs" for his great and sensitive nose, his tragi-comic, droopy sadness of face.

During the Tenth Dynasty in ancient Egypt on a pillar at the tomb of Antefaa II there appeared four markedly different archetypal dogs: a Nubian greyhound, an Australian dingo, an Asian mastiff, and, finally, a curious small dog, which later appears in the Twelfth Dynasty of Seostris (2100 to 1850 B.C.) and is quite similar to today's basset hound.

Shakespeare recognized the dog's literary appeal in *Midsummer Night's Dream,* describing his piecemeal form as "crook-knee'd," "dew-lapped," "matched in mouth like bells." His ears, Shakespeare said, swept away the morning dew. This is no metaphor, so he must've meant it literally.

The basset is a dog of flagons and apples, bottles and flasks, and his ears are as pendulous as his pedigree. Bassets were, traditionally, a sixteenth-century French nobleman's companion to the autumn hunt. While the dog burrowed deep into the ground after a badger (they also tracked roe deer, wolf, and boar in northern Europe), the titled sportsman fed upon succulent game fowls and hams.

One can envision the portly hunter sitting upon a pavilion or cart, complete with fire grate—if the weather was cold—sipping and supping while the real hunter, his prize basset, was tunneling to tomorrow.

THE FINE BREEDING of the hound, in general, is not accidental in literature or in myth. Early references remind that hounds are, as Tennyson said of cleanliness, "next to godliness." In Punjab, India, wild dogs that roamed the hills were considered Hounds of Heaven and were left undisturbed. Perhaps the music of the hound, his eloquent and piquant baying, which in hunter's terms is called "giving voice," is yet another indication of his proximity to godliness.

ELVIS PRESLEY GAVE the basset his due when he sang Big Mama Thornton's classic blues lyric "Hound Dog" to a basset on the *Ed Sullivan Show* in the early 1950s. However, Thornton probably envisioned a more southern canine for her song, perhaps a blood or coonhound.

Bassets do have bluesy voices and they speak whiskey-rough, like Delta singers. Still, they know their French pedigree serves them well and they make frequent demands upon it. Pouting, for instance, when courtesy or kindness is slow being met.

Despite the great blues and sorrow stored in their eyes, bassets have a good sense of humor—but only when disengaged from the serious business of hunting. Then, and only then, do they seem to like, and sometimes serve up, a good practical joke. Whether this means tripping on their own ears to get a laugh, dancing on clackety-claws across a tiled floor, or chasing cows, which they neither despise nor admire, is anybody's guess. The high-low Basset is a bred-to-the-bone character, an eccentric who requires a straight man, or woman, to perfect his act. If this is your dog, get ready for tragicomedy.

The Lore of the Dog

It is said, "No good hound is a bad color." Bassets come in coats of many colors, but they are most commonly white, with chestnut or sandy markings—the typical foxhound hue. Their fur is short and their skin loose.

Bassets are short-legged and heavy boned, with low-slung yet sturdy running gear, permitting easy access to ground scents. They have pendulous ears and large feet. The average height is 14 inches; weight is between 40 and 50 pounds.

Words that come to mind with regard to the basset are bashful, thoughtful, mournful, disdainful, cautious, modest, melancholy. However, they can easily be playful, petulant, poky, perverse, outrageous, and outspoken.

They train easily for the hunt, but not necessarily for obedience trials. They have a strong self-will and a presence of mind that can only be described as irksomely human: They want to do what they want to do when they want to do it. If scolded wrongly—or even rightly—they sulk, but not just as other dogs do. Bassets have been known to hold a permanent grudge.

On the other hand, they will also hold a permanent liking for someone, even when that person has only met them once. In other words, they have a memory like the proverbial elephant. Both hearing and scenting on the basset are unusually finely tuned.

Bassets enjoy free-ranging activities. Those that find themselves tied up or chained too often may become perverse. Certain members of this breed have traveled far and wide across the countryside, visiting friends and neighbors; perhaps this is the result of a nonhunting, leisure-minded, rambling basset.

As house pets, bassets are loyal, affectionate, and good with children. They have been cited as "incapable of biting." While not known for being great watchdogs, since their manner is a bit too laid-back, they do, however, have an amazing voice box, and the carrying sound of a basset is miles wide and acres long. Their bark can be as dramatically present as their bite is nonexistent. The downside of bassets is that they are—and look—stubborn. Good luck asking a basset to play follow the leader.

BEAGLE

The Beagler's Merry Beagle

BARBARA DAVIS

Long before the 1950s in America, when the beagle was the most popular dog around, this sportsman's friend was a favorite of the people of Great Britain. Queen Elizabeth I was known to have a few "singing beagles" and her English yeoman raced after them on foot. Yet the beagle predates the Elizabethan period by at least five hundred years. The ancestors of today's breed were kept in England for the hunting of small game. The larger hounds of the 1600s were called buck hounds because they chased down deer. The smaller variety, known as beagles, ran after rabbits (the fox was not yet in fashion).

Interestingly, it was a popular engraving of the time called "The Merry Beaglers" that ensured the notoriety of this dog in England. Parson Honeywood of Essex kept so fine a pack of tuneful little hounds that the art world honored them, and the rest is history. Sportsmen who did not see the engraving did not know the hound; but these were few indeed.

In America, prior to 1870, the hounds of the southern states, known too as beagles, were primarily white and bore more resemblance to the basset hound than to Honeywood's strain. It was not until the 1860s when General Richard Rowett brought the first high-class variety of beagle to

America that a variety of finer beagle strains began to appear in the United States. Less expensive than fox hunting, *beagling* was a form of diversion that Americans could afford. There was the bounding hare and the bugling beagle. There was the open countryside of an autumn afternoon, and there was a pack of pursuant beagles in full, fall cry. However, the lovable little beagle, with his swinging ears and wide-set eyes, began capturing more hearts than hare. Out of the rabbit patch, then, and onto the warm hearthside. By the faddist 1950s, the beagle fit in as the number one home-dog, nudging the sad-eyed cocker spaniel into second place.

THE BEAGLE'S REPUTE as the finest of rabbit dogs taps the keg of myth. In Tall Talk, or, the "calling of the dog" (which is quite close to "putting on the dog"), Mississippi tale-tellers spoke windily of their hunting expertise. These stories were wild and winsome and greatly exaggerated— "windy, stretchy and bendy," they said in the tall-tale trade. When a story-teller told the most outrageous myth or tallest tale, he'd be congratulated with "You called the dog!"

One famous "calling of the dog" concerns a myth that runs through the oral folk literature of the South. It's the story of "the Split Dog."

In Mississippi, there's a yarn about a beagle whose love of the hunt is so great that one day, chasing a rabbit, he runs into a farmer's scythe and gets halved in the process. The owner of the little beagle takes him home, swathes him in bandages, and puts him in a box under the warm stove, where he forgets about him. Three weeks later the dog emerges as good as new, except for the fact that he's put together wrong—hind end to front end. Never mind, the story goes, he could run forever that way. Winded on one pair of legs, he switches off and runs on the other pair. He runs frontwards, backwards, either way. He wags both ends at the same time, and either end can catch a rabbit!

The same tale is told in North Carolina by a black storyteller who's got the dog put together "two feet up and two feet down" so that, when he got tired, he'd roll over and resume running. A European version splits the hunter and the hunted in the following way. The dog, while on the run, is divided by multiplication—that is, by giving birth. At the same time, the rabbit has a litter. So there's six of each, including the parents, and the chase goes on, as does the storyteller, probably for eternity.

The Lore of the Dog

The beagle is the typical hound tricolor: white, black, and tan. Measuring 13 to 16 inches and weighing 18 to 30 pounds, this small harrierlike hound has two types of fur—silky and slightly coarse. The ears are long and hang against the sides of his face. The tail stands up, as if it were a flag of gladness; beagle tails wag excessively.

This is a compact, nicely built dog whose musculature is designed for long tracking through heavy brush and rolling field.

Winsome, intent, friendly, clean, adoring of children—the beagle is all of these and more. The dog that flashes through the briar patch will faithfully lick a toddler's hand and not act rebuffed when that same infant sits down on him.

These are cottontail hunters of the first order, but they are equally dedicated home-enhancers, merry little companions for any family member. Their musical singing voice is as much a part of their personality as their wagging tail. They have a generally unbarking attitude in the home, but they are quite frolicsome.

They do not like to be left alone and some people say they are difficult to housebreak. Beagles, it should be noted, need to run, preferably with other dogs.

BICHON FRISE

The Bearded Dog of Malta

MARIAH FOX

THE BICHON FRISE is one of our oldest breeds, and though historians disagree about its origin, they do concur on one fact: that the small, usually white-coated bichon has an ancestor who was present before the time of Christ.

Some believe the little dog known as bichon frise (literal translation: "stirred-up beard") is a relative of the Maltese, a surf and marsh, south-central European dog from the old trade-island of Malta and descended from the Spitz-type.

Others claim the spaniel, the miniature poodle, and the Cayenne dog were combined to produce the bichon, whose original name was Barbichon, and whose primary home was Italy.

The Maltese and the bichon do share common ground, if not common fur. Both are of Mediterranean origin dating as far back as 600–300 B.C., and each have some kinship with the Barbet, a small dog of water and swamp with soft, wooly, frizzled fur.

How large might the *famille de bichon* extend? In 1836 a Dr. Reichenbach listed the following associated breeds: "the Bolognese Toys, the Silky Poodles, the Bouffet, the Burgos, the Brevabilis, the Flammens, the Pyrome, the Bichon, the Maltese and the Lion Dog." A more updated review in Paris, "Votre Ami le Bichon," put the family of bichons into four categories: the Maltese, the Bolognese, the Tenerife, the Havanese.

FROM THE START, the bichon was adopted and cherished by the wealthy class of tradesmen and later on by the fashionable European Court. The Italian Renaissance (1300s–1600s) brought these small, courtly dogs into prominence in Italy and the rest of Europe. They flourished under the soft hand and ruffled silk of such kings as Francis I of France and Henry III of England. The Havanese it is said, journeyed from Bologna to South America where it was bred with the South American poodle. From there it went on to Havana to become the Havana Silk Dog. All in all, these dogs traveled the royal circuit.

However, by the turn of the century the little dog experienced a fall from grace. As a royal dog depicted on refined European tapestries and seated on picturesque thrones in Madagascar, he descended to the status of a tramp's pet—the reverse of the rags to riches scenario.

It's not entirely clear why the bichon lost favor, but by the early 1600s, the small friend of monarchs had become a dog of the streets, a smudgy little sheep dog. Soon the diminutive aristocrat danced to a different tune—literally. He was now a trick dog. As the myths explain, he turned into "the dog of the organ grinder of Barbary." However, the bichon commanded—always has, always will—affection from whomever he associated. If he no longer placed his breath upon signet rings, he did make children laugh and cheer.

Following World War I, however, the bichon gradually began a second ascent into the laps of luxury, where he has faithfully remained ever since. The official standard of the breed was adopted in France in 1933.

The following bichon myth comes from Greece, but it is common in many world cultures where it explains the special virtues of dogs and cats, snakes, boys, mothers, thieves, and fishermen.

> Once there was a young man who lived alone with his mother. "Go out and sell something," she said to her son, "and we'll have something to eat." So he took a load of oleander and sold it for a couple of coppers. On the way home, he saw some boys torturing a snake.
>
> "Let it go," he offered, "and I'll give you these coppers."
>
> The boys agreed and the snake went free. When he got to the door of his home, he saw that the snake had followed him.
>
> "So," his mother said scornfully, "I tell you to get some money so we can have something to eat, and you bring home a worthless snake."

"We'll see if it's worthless," the son said.

A few days later, he went to sell some more oleander, and he got two more coppers. On the way home, he saw two men, who were about to kill a dog.

"Don't kill it," he begged, "and I will give you my coppers."

So he gave them the coppers and they let the dog go free. Then the dog followed him home just as the snake did. Now his mother was very angry and she scolded him as before, but he would only say, "It doesn't hurt to be kind."

Now, once more the young man cut oleander to sell; and once more he sold it. But on the way home with the coppers in his hand, he saw some children torturing a cat.

"Here," he said, gesturing to them. "If you will let the cat go, I will give you these coppers."

The children freed the cat immediately, and, like the snake and the dog, it followed him home. When his mother saw this, however, she went into a rage.

"I send you to get money and you bring home cats, snakes, and dogs!"

So he said to her, "Maybe they will be of use to us." But his mother continued with her angry abuse. After she went away, the snake came up to him and said, "I know of a way to get some food for all of us."

Then the snake took him to his father's house and there he said: "Father, this is the young man who saved my life; surely you can give him something for this kindness." Whereupon the father of the snake went away and swiftly returned with a signet ring.

"Press the stone of this ring," he said to the young man, "and all your needs will be met."

The young man went home and sat beside the dog, the cat and the snake. He looked at the signet ring. It looked ordinary to him, but still he pressed the stone, and, at the same time, he wished there were food in the house. Immediately his mother came to him. "My darling son," she exclaimed. "There is bread in the cupboard and wine on the table."

"That is not all," the young man said, smiling. Then, pressing the ring, he wished for a castle overlooking the sea. At once he found himself standing before a great castle whose turrets disappeared into the clouds. Below the sea rustled like silk. Beside him were his mother, the snake, the dog, and the cat. He was content with his wish. "Let us go in, Mother," he said. "I am sure there is a great dining table all laid out for our arrival."

And there was, and everything went well for the young man and his mother. And also for the snake, the dog, and the cat. But one day a sly servant saw how much riches were provided by the signet ring. So he stole it in the night and got into a boat and set sail for a distant island.

Now it was the dog's turn to help. He said, "Don't fret, I know just how to take care of this situation. The scent of a thief—even on water—is not hidden from my nose. I will swim with the cat on my back and together we will find the untrustworthy servant and bring back the ring."

The young man was glad to hear this and he sent the dog and the cat on their way.

Now the dog was a fine swimmer and he carried the cat on his back, and though the water was wide, he smelled the trace of the thief, and tracked him to the island where he was trying to hide.

That night, as the thief lay in the rich bed he had provided for himself in the great house he had wished for, the dog crept in with the cat on his back. "I will boost you up to the bed where you will stick your tail into his nose," the dog said.

The cat did this thing and straightaway the thief sneezed, and out of his mouth came the signet ring, which the cat caught. Then the dog took the cat on his back and ran to the sea where he swam for home.

When they were near the shore and could see their master's castle, the dog said to the cat: "Why don't you let me have a look at the ring, for I have always wanted to see it close up."

The cat didn't think it was such a good idea, but against his judgment, he handed it over. Clumsily, the dog dropped the ring into the sea. But as the ring spiraled toward the bottom, a fish saw it and swallowed it whole. Moments later, a fisherman on shore caught that same fish and began preparations for his dinner.

"All is not lost," said the cat as the dog reached the beach. "We must entertain that fisherman, and he will return to us what is ours."

The dog liked the cat's thinking. A short while later, they each showed up at the fisherman's fire, and entertained him with dancing and singing. The cat sang beautifully and the dog danced wonderfully and together, they charmed the fisherman into giving them a small gift.

"You two have made my evening complete," he said of their little circus on the sand. "So now let me share my gift from the sea," and the fisherman tossed them the entrails of the fish he had cooked.

The cat bowed. The dog somersaulted. Then the two of them ran off, holding the two ends of the fish's stomach in their mouths. As soon as they got out of sight, the cat used her sharp teeth and claws to open the entrails—and there, snug inside, was the signet ring.

And that is how a young man and his mother, a snake and his father, a cat and a dog, a thief and a fish and a fisherman each got something that he wanted—if only for a time.

The Lore of the Dog

The bichon is a puff of white fur, but not a cream puff, by any means. This is to say that he is not a toy, but a small sturdy dog. The face, soulfully human, has dark haloed eyes which look directly forward.

The moderate muzzle is short, not pointed. The ears are drop and covered with long flowing hair. The plumed tail matches the dog's jaunty temperament, and together with his dark-eyed inquisitive face, he seems to be asking a question. The arched neck goes smoothly into the shoulders and the chest is well developed. The coat, soft and curly, is hypoallergenic, exactly like that of the poodle. It is virtually nonshedding. Although the coat is naturally curly, when brushed it feels like velvet plush.

The practical advantage to this dog's fur is that it sheds water well and is excellent insulation against inclement weather. Matting is problematic, and the bichon requires diligent grooming.

The height is 9 to 12 inches, the weight is 10 to 18 pounds depending on height.

The bichon frise is strong-willed, but this will to win and to charm is matched with great dignity and intelligence. He is, therefore, a fine companion dog, one who is comfortable with other animals and with children.

His outgoing manner is accompanied with a fun, loving personality and the attributes of a little clown. He loves to play, but he is not hyperactive.

Though not designed to be a guard dog, his alert manner will always announce strangers.

BLACK-AND-TAN COONHOUND

The Dog that Barks Trees

MARIAH FOX

THE COONHOUND, ONE of the great tracking dogs of America, is as ubiquitous in some parts of the Deep South as kudzu vines and cotton bolls. The breed comes from the American foxhound, the Virginia foxhound, and the bloodhound, whose early ancestor was the famous Talbot hound owned by the eleventh-century Norman nobles.

Today's black-and-tan still hunts raccoon, opossum, deer, bear, bobcat, and even wild pig; and he still doesn't like to get off the porch swing when someone comes to sit down on it. Traditionally, the American coonhound was bred to resist the cold hunter's wind, rain, and poor weather in general; however, here's a dog who, when not working, is a sprawler, a dawdler, and a do-nothing lounge lizard.

Although the coonhound wasn't officially recognized by the American Kennel Club until 1945, the dog is an American—make that a "murrican"—original. Black-and-tans go well with sourmash, copper kettles, and moony nights under the dogwood leaves. They're part of the southern and Appalachian vernacular, and a certain mountain mystique and pine-flat, corn-pone reasoning has been built up around them over the years. Well suited to folkways and myths, the black-and-tan blends into the leafy language that has sprung up around him. Georgia storyteller O. Victor Miller speaks of a coon hunt in the piney woods of his homestate:

> Doll and Jethro kept trailing their coon, and they finally treed it two hours after the hunt was over. The dogs were on a pine they'd gnawed the bark off and exposed the cameo meat. We shined the pinetop and saw the coon's eyes twinkle green then flash red. I just stood there a little winded in the sweet night air, with the buzz of the cicadas and treefrogs, the *my-rump* of the bullfrogs, and the sweet-sad whistle of the whippoorwills beneath the moon-dimmed stars.
>
> When a coon dog sniffs, there's a total involvement of the blood and sinew as though the scent flows like electrical current through him and sets him aquiver from whiskers to tail. On a trail or at a tree, he becomes as pure a creature as there is, driven and timorous, made whole by his union from centuries of breeding. But the chase revives the hunt in a man's blood too, mixed with a kind of diluted longing and fear that defines his kinship with the dog and the racoon too.

Now, this same sound that led the early hunters to their quarry is echoed today in the voice of the black-and-tan coonhound. Such phrases as "barking up," "barking treed," and "giving mouth," which describe that moment when the coonhound's prey is brought to limb, are a kind of poetry unto themselves. Moreover, the timbre of the dog's voice is "Opry music" to some and it tells whether the coonhound is on the run, or if, instead, a cold scent has been struck.

Running coonhounds begin by baying open-mouthed and long-voiced. When they are up close to the tree, however, the song is short and sharp, and there's an urgency in it. Once the quarry's treed, the hound puts up a slower bay; the notes are prolonged with interstitial silences carefully set between them. The hound is listening between bays for the crunch of a hunter's boot.

Tradition says that only one dog in the pack should "give mouth" at the end of a successful treeing. The other dogs whine and prance, and perhaps whirl around a bit when overcome with angst, but their training tells them to wait until their master comes.

Myths of the belling hunt abound in the backwoods gambit tales of possums, coons and, sometimes, bears. Some of the best of these myths feature the classic, lop-eared porch lounger—the big voice of the midnight choir, the black-and-tan coonhound.

One backwoods bit of blarney explains why the dog has such long ears.

Flipping and flopping, the ears send the scent back up to the hound's nose. In fact, all hounds clear their nasal receptors by raising up their nose. This is followed by a second of silence, almost akin to a prayer, during which the dog's nose is "cleared" for further tracking.

Pack hunters, coonhounds move in unison but bay and breathe in turn, as the need arises, which is why the off-and-on music is so drunkenly beautiful, if you chance to hear it on a crisp night when the moon's dripping honey on a drift of fallen oak leaves.

COONHOUNDS ARE CONSIDERED awfully smart by their trainers, but they're more stubborn than army mules. Many an erstwhile tale sings the dog's praises while hammering at his uncanny recalcitrance. Maybe it's willpower that keeps the dog on track during the hunt; maybe it's lunacy.

A midwestern folktale speaks of the coonhound that was so smart that all the hunter had to do was show the dog a board (the same size as the skin he wanted to tack onto it) and the obsessive hound would run into the woods and fetch a raccoon exactly that same size.

One day the hunter's wife put her ironing board on the back porch. The dog ran off looking for a raccoon the same size, and didn't come back for nearly two years.

The Mississippi version of this myth has a honeysuckle sweetness to it: The dog's owner searches high and low for that stubborn hound, and finally finds him exhausted in the woods, lying on his side and puffing like a freight train. The hunter feels so sorry for him that he carries him home in his arms and puts him down in front of the crackling hearth and feeds him cornbread and fire-warm honey until the dog can't eat anymore.

Truth is, coonhounds love to be fondled, fussed over. They want a certain amount of pampering and being told they're the cat's meow.

ARTEMIS, GREEK GODDESS of the hunt, was protected by a pack of hounds—a lop-eared, loose-faced, particolored, spotted band of hunting dogs. These same animals figure, later on, in Anglo-Saxon and Celtic mythology. They are none other than the redoubtable Hounds of Heaven that chase men down the darkened days and drunken nights.

It's all part of the great cyclic myth of the famous European autumnal hunt—the dogs, the hunter, the moon, and the quarry all blending into one perfect moment of hunterly bliss. Grafted onto this romance is the hound of hounds, a dog so supreme that, according to dog expert Patricia Dale-Green, the animal took on a "dark or light aspect," a semblance of good or evil.

This means that good hounds, or heavenly ones, might provide their owner with riches and/or the power to heal. Bad hounds, as most of us know, are the representatives of the Devil, the surly denizens of Hell. More is known about them in our lugubrious literature than the Hounds of Heaven. Hell Hounds are both dangerous and cunning, and capable of pulling a good man into the pit of degradation, desire, or perverse longing for the pleasures of the flesh.

The hound is also mythologically related to Apollo and other Greek gods. Dionysius was said to keep a pack of hounds in his temple in Sparta which savaged anyone who obstructed his musicians. As Dale-Green says, in *The Lore of the Dog* ". . . sacred hounds took part in temple rites" at the temple of the Sicilian war-god Adranus.

In the sacrifice of the hunt, then, as the October blood is spilled like wine, we come to understand that the voice of the hound is as old as human consciousness. A dog that can bark a tree bare in the light of the moon can make a man into a shining saint or a sullen sinner. When we hear the song of such a dog we know why the hound commands so much of the couch for himself—he's saving up for that sublime moment when, that Celtic tongue will turn silver again.

The Lore of the Dog

Coonhounds have pendulous ears and a pendulum tail and a body that wags when they walk. The tail is almost always wagging, too, unless the dog is asleep, but sometimes it wags even then. They are 25 to 27 inches tall, weighing 50 to 75 pounds.

The coat is short and thick, black and tan, and the classic coonhound has tan markings on chest, legs, muzzle, and throat. The rest of the body is silky black. Overall, this dog looks like his bloodhound cousin, except he has more visible bone and fewer wrinkles.

The black-and-tan coonhound, as a working animal, is a serious-minded individual. Do not try and deflect him from his purpose, the sacrosanct hunt. You will not be successful.

Coonhounds are intelligent (within their sphere of interest), vigilant (within their sphere of smell), and otherwise obedient and family-oriented. Their loyalty is legion, the subject of sentimental poems of praise and stentorian eulogies.

However, when they are not working, these dogs are the definition of torpor. On a hot summer's day, they like to melt into the floor. Once again, a word to the wise: Don't try and move a black-and-tan thus reclined—sleep is as important to him as his passion for the hunt.

At work black-and-tan coonhounds are picky walkers, delicate on their feet, and they often walk as if on thin ice. Their best known feature, their nose, is used to extraordinary purpose. They move behind it, following an infallible olfactory sense that enables them to track with faultless accuracy.

BLOODHOUND

Saint Hubert's Hound

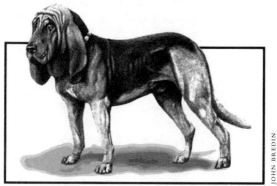

JOHN BREDIN

THE BLOODHOUND, IN name, comes not from "blood-thirsty," but breeding or "blooded stock." The thoroughbred bloodhound is a direct descendant of the old Saint Hubert hound. Saint Hubert (A.D. 656–727), the patron saint of dogs and the hunt, was a famous hunter whose hounds were used to hunt stag. His conversion to Christianity happened after a vision, in which he saw Christ on the cross gleaming between the antlers of a stag. Legend has it that following this experience he gave up hunting and dedicated his life to more spiritual pursuits.

Although some legends say that bloodhounds came to Europe with pilgrims from the holy land, history favors their being bred by monks in the Abbey of St. Hubert, at Mouzon, in the Ardennes region of France. From that time forward, during each succeeding year, the monks sent six young dogs to the king of France. The king, in turn, passed the dogs on to the nobility, and the breed spread, so that in less than a quarter century, bloodhounds were in the Pyrenees and in Great Britain.

At the feast of St. Hubert in the Ardennes, huntsmen on the third of November celebrated the Mass of the Dogs. The chief huntsman appeared at the parish church with a pack of venerable bloodhounds, the oldest member of which received a blessing of holy water. This medieval mass of the dogs was celebrated until the end of World War II when, for reasons unknown, it was abandoned.

———

In AMERICA DURING the mid–nineteenth century, the bloodhound was an invaluable member of many law enforcement agencies. Criminal identification by bloodhound was actually considered an acceptable piece of evidence in a court of law. American bloodhounds were so good at tracking that some were said to pick up a scent that was nine days old. Unlike their human counterparts, these impassioned hounds didn't seem to mind if their quarry was dead or alive, or if their trail was old or new. What mattered was their nose to the news.

BLOODHOUND MYTHS RUN throughout the ballad literature of the British Isles. In the Welsh, "Romance of Pwyll, Prince of Dyfed," a huntsman on a pale horse pursues a stag driven by a pack of white dogs with red ears. These are the Hounds of Hell whose image is also identified with the flight of the wild goose. According to Celtic myth, the northward migration of wild geese would summon souls of the damned to an icy Hell. Imagine these geese passing unseen on a frosty evening and giving voice like a pack of yelping hounds. The hounds, in many of the old ballads, are called Yell Hounds. Their yelp and pursuit is entwined with the autumn hunt, the passage of geese, and the desperation of lost souls. The dark huntsman goes by various names, depending upon the origin of the folktale. In Northumberland, he is the great King Arthur, but he is best known in English folklore as Gabriel. Why Gabriel? Perhaps because he is a summoner of souls in the Bible, essentially a judge. As the angel of death, he is the final judgment. There is an English church carving, presumably a lintel, in whose oaken spell we may see Gabriel, the huntsman, with his brace of hounds. The old icon explains why, even today, we've put bloodhounds in the company of the courtroom our modern place of judgment. Modern American tabloid (comic strip) literature from the 1930s shows these judicial dogs wearing long black robes, just as English tales of old had them gathering souls across the gloomy skies of early winter.

In THE FOLKLORE of healing arts, the significance of the hounds is that they are the foretellers of death. As Gabriel, Prince of Thunder and Lightning, gallops over chimneys and homes, his fire-breathing, blood-spotted hounds bellow at the soul-summoning air. Hearing their cries in the British Isles once meant that someone in the household was about to die.

Hence, the mood-enhancer in the movies—head-arched hounds baying at the moon just before a villain dispatches his latest victim.

A Celtic myth tells of the Little People, whose underground cavern-world is connected to ours by a torchlit tunnel. The king of the Little People is a red-faced, fiery-bearded man who travels about on a goat. In one of the tales, the Little King attends the wedding of Herla, the British monarch, and gives him an invitation to "come underground." Herla accepts and is given the gift of a tiny bloodhound who, the Little King warns, must stay in Herla's hand while he is mounted upon his horse.

Moreover, no one in Herla's party is permitted to dismount until the hound jumps to the ground. In the myth, Herla has been away from his own kingdom only a few days, but on returning to his country, he meets an old man, who speaks of a lost queen and a missing king. Unnerved by this news, many of Herla's men leap to the ground and swiftly turn to dust. The rest of the party, so they say, are condemned to ride the hills forever.

So concludes the myth of the "Celtic Wild Hunt." When the story came to the New World (with Dutch and English overtones) it was fashioned by Washington Irving into "The Legend of Rip Van Winkle."

THE MYTH OF a hellish bloodhound was, of course, employed by Sir Arthur Conan Doyle in his famous Sherlock Holmes mystery, "The Hound of the Baskervilles." The tale was suggested, Doyle confessed, by the premature death of Fletcher Robinson and "a spectral dog near his house in Dartmoor."

There's little doubt that the old Yell Hound, or Yeth Hound, myth was used by Doyle. "A hound it was, an enormous coal-black hound, but not such a hound as mortal eyes have ever seen. Fire burst from its open mouth, its eyes glowed with a smoldering fire, its muzzle and hackles and dewlap were outlined in flickering flame." Holmes discovers—after killing it—that the dog's glowing apparition was merely the result of a "cunning preparation of phosphorous." However, in flying through the air at his pursuers, the amazing hound became one of Gabriel's ghostly companions. Thus are myths made and remade over the millennial fires of the imagination.

The Lore of the Dog

The face of the bloodhound is more powerful than sorrowful, more dignified than despairing. The dog usually appears judicial, the weight of heavy considerations causing a kind of gravitational pull downward. The extra skin around the head causes him to look wrinkly and old, even when young.

Average height is between 25 and 27 inches; weight varies from 88 to 105 pounds. The coat of a bloodhound is short-furred, the skin thick and loose; colors are black and tan, red and tan, or tawny.

If you're looking for a guard dog, perhaps you ought to look elsewhere, for these gentle creatures are of a one-minded disposition; they like to track. That is their whole life and it leaves little room for anything else. They can, however, be friendly, affectionate, considerate house pets; but they are unusually sensitive to criticism. Like other breeds of hound, these are generally obstinate.

Their public persona is that of a pipe-smoking, nose-snuffing, sometimes southern-drawling cartoon character, who was made famous in various kinds of notable cartoons. There is Huckleberry Hound, the neighborhood good guy. Pluto, the sniff-to-the-end-of-everything, irretrievable goof. Inspector Hound, the impeccable sleuth. Trusty, the fatherly philosopher (in *Lady and the Tramp*). And don't forget McGruff, the Crime Dog from the public service announcements on TV. "Help take a bite outta crime."

All of these characterizations come from the exaggerated seriousness of the bloodhound and his solemn outlook on life. His view seems to be that things can only run from good to bad to worse. He is there not to make them better, but to unravel the mystery of universal misfortune.

BORZOI

The Swift Dog of the Russian Steppes

BARBARA DAVIS

BORZOI IS NOT only synonymous with speed, it literally means "speed" in the Russian language. The breed itself began in the wolf-thronged steppe lands of the upper Volga in the sixteenth century, around the time of Ivan the Terrible. Bred from Asian greyhounds and other indigenous dogs, these coursers were used for sport, and, in the minds of the nobility, for the necessary predation of wolves.

Russian wolf hunting grew into such a passionate national pastime that entire estates during the reign of the czars were given over to the art and wisdom of borzoi training. The hunting party itself may have included as many as one hundred borzois, one hundred foxhounds, and as many as one hundred trainers, in addition to the large number of hunters. All were transported by train—sometimes forty cars in all—to the hunting sites along the forested, rivered, snow-bound prairie country of czarist Russia.

The earliest seventeenth-century borzois, introduced by the Grand Duke of Novgorod, came replete with Tartar and Mongol traditions. But these animals were not built for the cruel winters, so the duke bred them with the heavier coated collielike native breed and the Lapp sled dog. The result was a dog designed for speed, resistance to cold, endurance, sight-hound excellence, and wolf hunting prowess. Today's borzoi is little changed from this original animal whose tail-whipping grandeur is ill-suited to apartment life.

Borzois were slaughtered during the Russian Revolution because, in the minds of the proletariat, they symbolized the decadence of the dying nobility. In America, they made their debut as an import from England during the late nineteenth century, but it was the ones that came directly from Russia, in the 1890s and early 1900s, that were used in the American West to kill coyotes and wolves. Today, borzois are still bred in the former Soviet Union and used for show and for hunting, but only a limited number of them are imported to America. (The problem is that the dogs usually lack the paperwork that would confirm them for U.S. standards.)

THE BORZOI WAS originally trained, according to ancient Mongol traditions, to chase up to a wolf and bump shoulders with him as he tried to flee. Seeking to knock the wolf off balance, and thus bring it down, the borzoi worked in tandem with two others of his breed. The standard measure was three borzois against one wolf, so that when the quarry collapsed, the team moved on to the next one. This left the downed wolf to the hunter's lance, or, as the case was often cited, to the hunter's muzzle, for then the wolf was taken alive.

One Russian tale tells of a pack of wolves that managed to outdistance the mounted lanceman and the borzoi's trainer. Far out upon a sea of snow, and with a Siberian night closing in, the borzoi team of two tried to keep pace with the pack of wolves.

The loping gallop of a long-winded wolf is without peer on the prairie lands. In deep snow, particularly, there's no way for dogs to catch them. Trained to harry, not to hurt or kill the quarry, the borzoi always waits for arrival of the huntsman.

In the tale, the wolves sensed their advantage and turned the hunt around. They became the hunters and the borzois turned into the quarry.

Here, myth enhances the borzoi's reputation for keen intelligence under great duress. The lead dog was a fast runner named White Falcon, who saw at once that he couldn't outrun his canny adversaries, so he decided to use another tactic, one more commonly employed by the wolves themselves—trickery.

White Falcon, running alongside his teammate, traversed an ever widening circle. In the failing light, the wolves pressed on as White Falcon turned a curved line in the snow into a hidden gyre. His circle, wide and thus unnoticeable, was turning ever backward in the direction of the huntsman.

The wolves, secure that the dogs were out of their element in the darkening sea of sparkling snow, stepped up the pace, making the borzois, they thought, run even harder. The borzois, for their part, were weakening, and only White Falcon knew that his turning gyre, his dangerous orb, was not looping farther out, but was tightening in, returning to its point of origin.

Almost in sight now was the huntsman and his trainer, and the third member of the borzoi team, a pregnant female who'd been leashed for obvious reasons. She was well-tethered by the trainer, but by the time the chase was in view, the wolves had caught White Falcon and his companion, and she leaped free and raced to their aid.

White Falcon's plan had worked, but the price—utter fatigue—was too great, and when the wolves closed on them, they were in desperate shape. Thus did two worn-out borzois and a plucky female, heavy with pups, face a wizened wolf pack in the fading light of day.

The pregnant dog, White Falcon's mate, was the first to go down in the wake of whirling animals; by the time the huntsman reached her, White Falcon and his companion were by her side, both males wounded but standing.

The female borzoi was alive when the huntsman got to her. Curled in the blood-spattered snow, she was giving birth. Two of her newborn puppies died, stillborn, but the third came back in the heavy shirt of the huntsman, and as the story goes, this immortal pup yet thrives.

It is, they say, the royal line of the borzoi.

The Lore of the Dog

The borzoi is Roman-nosed, saber-tailed, and every inch the Russian aristocrat. Add to this long willow legs and the curving, courser lines of a body built for speed. Some say the wasped, elongated body surpasses even the greyhound in speed. Dog author Ralph G. Kirk describes the borzoi this way:

> The nose pointing into the wind like an arrow, the soft ears folded
> back so tightly that the tips of them actually lapped. No stomach—
> the line from chest to loins curved up in marvelous beauty so close
> to the spine that it seemed to threaten the severance of the hind
> quarters altogether.

The Russian winter coat of fur—white, tan, black, and gold (and varying shades and mixtures of these)—is long, wavy, curled at the neck, feathery on chest and legs, and, overall, heavy enough to withstand the coldest weather. (They are, therefore, heavy shedders.) The chest has great vertical depth, "there being almost no spring of ribs to spread her chest against the wind," says Kirk. The feet have well-arched knuckles, giving cat-quiet step and graceful articulation to the artful borzoi. Shoulder height is 26 to 31 inches; weight ranges from 55 to 105 pounds.

Shy, docile, obstinate, affectionate, loyal, and intelligent, the borzoi is a fine companion, but, because of his courser's blood, this dog needs a lot of exercise in order to be happy. Borzois demand attention on a regular basis, or they may become distant.

Some say the borzoi is too large to be controlled by small children, though this is a relative matter, dependent upon the individual household.

BOSTON TERRIER

The Boston Bull

JOHN BREDIN

IN THE OLDEN days, all terriers were small earth dogs that ran after rodents and other burrowing animals. At least that is how they were designated, just as, for instance, all large dogs were mastiffs and all hunting dogs were setters and spaniels. Terriers were an indefinable lot of little hole-seekers. Dog authority and author, Roger Caras, from whom we learned the above designation, has loving words for the terrible terrier clan: "Terriers are generally but not always smallish dogs with a fire inside that simply cannot be quenched. They are scrappy, playful, sometimes hyperactive, generally exceedingly loyal characters. They are the clowns of the dog world and are expected, even in the show ring, to be hard on each other."

The Boston terrier is one of our native breeds in America, an animal whose popularity was once on a par with apple pie. The cross, the American Kennel Club (AKC) tells us, is between an English bulldog and a white English terrier; and the result is one hell of a smallish, bullish swaggerer.

Records of the breed date back to the late nineteenth century. The first fanciers of the dog were in Boston, naturally, and they presented them as Round Heads or bullterriers, which caused some disgruntled owners—those who owned bulldogs and bullterriers—to strongly object to this classification. At the same time, the AKC, being uncertain of the new breed's future progress, held off from giving their prestigious admission. The dog was admitted

officially in 1893 when, after twenty years, the Boston Terrier was still breeding "true to type" and was confirmed as a Yankee original.

Those who see the Boston terrier as cute and cuddly should guess again,
for this dog was bred for the Boston fighting pits; and the time when he
actually fought there is not so long ago in Canidae history. From the Boston
terrier's acceptance by the AKC, his popularity has risen and fallen with the
times. Today his standing as the representative of old Boston Commons is as
unquestioned as his city bred companionability. This little Bostonian, who
was once dubbed Round Head, was sometimes called the Black Satin Gentleman in England, for he was jacketed in black and stood very dapper in
spotless white shirt front.

There is a myth of psychic power that seems to have grown up around
the Boston terrier. Joseph W. Wylder, for example, in *Psychic Pets* has written
of a remarkable terrier named Missie, ". . . one of the widest known and best
documented psychic pets of recent times." The London *Daily Mail* acclaimed
Missie as one of our generation's foremost prophets. What did the dog do to
earn this praise? She developed a system whereby she could give numerical
information to people that was infallibly correct. Missie is said to have been
able to tell how many coins someone carried in a purse, and she would give
this information by an appropriate number of barks. Her real genius, though,
was for prediction, which she did by answering questions of a numerical sort
by barking her answer. Many disbelievers tried to eschew her pronounce-
ments, but no one could prove her to be inaccurate. She even knew the time
of her own death, and she announced it before she died.

A recent confirmation of the Boston terrier's psychic sense is shown in
the comedy film *The Gun in Betty Lou's Handbag* written by Grace Cary
Bickley. One of the main characters is a Boston terrier with a gift for understanding human speech and human action. The dog appears omniscient and
creates dramatic tension by knowing more than its owners do. Often owners
of these dogs will tell you that they have a special grasp of numbers, times,
and schedules. While, all dogs can be said to have this gift, this breed may
have more of it than any other.

THE FIGHTING TERRIER myth also comes with the territory and
people like to tell how a Boston terrier can hold off a mastiff. Unfortunately,
this may not be a matter of inconsequential boasting. For these feisty fellows
would rather fight than fold. One with whom we are acquainted happens to
be fourteen years old and still going strong. Not long ago, he was attacked
by a young and robust Rottweiler. Being all but blind in both eyes and a
little shaky from age, the Boston terrier had a tough time defeating his ag-

gressor, who charged out of the darkness to tear him apart—and did. The Rottweiler actually tore the old patriarch's hind leg off. Yet the Boston terrier would not quit, would not give up, would not let go his hold on the Rottweiler. The scene itself seemed to have come directly out of *Monty Python and the Holy Grail* ("But a flesh wound!")—the episode where the one-legged wounded knight fights on, even though he keeps losing limbs in the encounter. That is what happened here, as well. The happy ending to the tale is that this particular Boston terrier is out and about, once again, doing his mile and a half of exercise every night. These are undaunted and unquenchable warriors who, blind or not, see just as well without their eyes.

The Lore of the Dog

Called the Yankee terrier, the Boston Gentleman, the Boston bull, or the toy bulldog, this breed, though relatively new, is founded on an unshakable premise. Bulldogs and bullterriers are dynamite together. It is probable that the French bulldog had something to do with the Boston terrier's bat-ears and perhaps some other less noticeable qualities as well. Overall, the Boston bull is a mighty midget with the nicest face, the most compassionate and impressive eyes, set well apart in an elegant, Herculean head.

The chest is broad, the ribs deep, the legs straight and strong and well-spaced—but not bowlegged like the bulldog's. The tail is either straight or curled; the coat short, shiny, smooth. The colors of the Boston bull are brindle with white markings, black with white markings, or brindle with black markings. According to standard, the dog has a white muzzle with a white blaze over the head, collar, breast, and forelegs. There is also white on the hind feet. Height is not specified and the weight should not be more than 25 pounds.

The Boston terrier is very adaptable to a family with or without children, but remember that a child must be taught to be considerate because these dogs are sometimes touchy. They really need to be kept indoors, as they are sensitive to cold and heat, but they also need regular play and exercise. They shed moderately and should be brushed at least once a week.

This dog is a good companion for the elderly since he aims to please and is a little charmer. A small, neat, affectionate apartment dweller, it seems the old ancestral fighting instincts have been replaced with the dog's natural intelligence, sensitivity, and alert protectiveness.

BOXER

The Smiling Pugilist

MARIAH FOX

THE GREAT DANE, the bulldog, and the terrier can each be found in the sixteenth-century background of the boxer, but while some argue over this very credible pedigree, others complain that "the dog wasn't even invented" at that time.

The definitive lineage of the boxer would seem to come from the German *bullenbeiszer* and *barenbeiszer* (the bull-baiter and bear-baiter) dogs. Certain experts, though, shake their heads and comment drily that the boxer has an extinct ancestor, the *brabanter* or *boxl,* from which they say it rightly got its name.

What to believe? The myth and the math rarely correspond exactly and only sometimes are commensurate with public opinion, which moves about quixotically, and quirkily, from one generation to the next. What we have, obviously, is a stub-tailed wonder, a dog of many dimensions who's known to be a fighter with a sentimental heart.

Historians point out that the boxer got to be a prominent fellow in the nineteenth century, just as the anti–dog fighting laws closed down the grisly sport of Dog versus Dog. The unique facial structure of the boxer, which is comparable to a bulldog, has something to do with his short-lived fame as a fighter. He's got an undershot jaw and an upturned nose, and he can lock-on and not let go. The low-slung jaw, when sunk into an opponent, doesn't interfere with the turned up nose. His fighting prowess is part of his checkered, his chopped, and his channeled physiognomical history. In fact, some say the boxer got his name from the habit of standing on hind legs and boxing with his front feet.

Boxers ran messages on the battlefields of both World Wars, and the dog was one of the first breeds in Germany to be selected for police training. The upswing in boxer popularity in America occurred during the 1930s when one imported champion won all the blue ribbons. Since then the boxer's been an American standard, though not so popular now as in the fifties when, along with the beagle, everybody seemed to own one.

The boxer's fondness for work is also part of the animal's mythos. There are lots of stories of boxers doing free fieldwork for the local police station, or just liaison work around town. They're busy dogs whose business is the world, the neighborhood, the family. They like to move about in the day or the night, doing something, anything, even just hot-footing along the sidewalk somewhere.

The story is told of the boxer living in a suburban neighborhood, who found it was necessary to make a series of rounds every day, casually but interestedly, examining every house on the block. The completion of his daily inspection ended at a home where the dog always got a small reward for his work, a cookie. Day in and day out, the solitary boxer worked his way to this last house, his final rendezvous point, where, all things being equal, he stopped, ate his cookie, and returned home.

The boxer did his work, amazingly enough, without the knowledge of his owners. Little did they know that their trusted household guardian was out and about, watching everyone else's estate. This boxer tale illustrates a common boxer trait: the dog's sociability is mingled with a deep sense of community responsibility. Some say this derives from the breed's early policework; others say it's just a boxer's love for organized human habitation. In any case, there's hardly a boxer alive that doesn't like to soft-foot about with an eye to his surroundings, and the doings thereon and therein.

Emily Brontë, the English novelist, once owned a boxer in whom she placed great adoration and trust. Reportedly, Keeper, as he was called, strode at her heels on long walks around the moors. In fact, his presence—and not Heathcliff's—was the shadow that accompanied her through the foggy, foggy dews of her highland home.

The bond between them was so deep that the final act of Emily Brontë's life was done for her beloved Keeper. Though mortally ill, she got up from her bed, went outside, and fed Keeper a last supper. After which she died.

For three years, prior to his own death, Keeper mourned his beloved Emily, grieving without relief until he too passed on. Charlotte Brontë's biographer, Elizabeth Gaskell, said of Keeper: "Let us somehow hope, in half-red Indian creed, that he [Keeper] follows Emily now, and, when he rests, sleeps on some soft white bed of dreams, unpunished when he awakens to the life of the land of shadows."

Gaskell is referring to the fact that Keeper enjoyed sleeping on beds, and the only time Emily ever really disciplined him was when he once slept on the best bed in the house. Afterwards, as Keeper bore her no malice for his indiscretion and her wrath, she knew that dogs, unlike humans, love only for love itself.

THERE IS AN old Swedish myth that tells of three beautiful princesses, who have been abducted and held prisoner by giants. The king promised anyone who could rescue them the reward of a daughter's hand in marriage and half of his kingdom. Many wealthy warriors tried to find the three women, but to no avail. Then, along came a lad, who, much like the ne'er-do-well youth of "Puss and Boots," had three remarkable dogs.

One was called Holdfast, presumably a bulldog. Another was Tear, a Doberman pinscher, and the third was Quickear, most likely a terrier. Put the three dogs together and you have one very normal boxer, for, as we know, the boxer is made up of these three distinct breeds.

Anyway, the tale concludes, as one would expect, with the dogs performing acts worthy of their names. The giants are subdued, the youth receives his just reward, and all ends as it should, with flower petals and wine.

Thus are the vicissitudes of myth combined with the attributes of excellent breeding to produce an inimitable dog, the boxer. Part bulldog with a bit of Doberman, and a pinch of terrier—the whole animal a myth boiled down to blood and bone. Yes, here is a dog of singular, yet unknown, upbringing, who has it his way, whatever way that is.

The Lore of the Dog

The chiseled, wrinkle-free head and squarely built body accord him, as some say, beautiful ugliness, ignoble nobility, the prize-fighter's mug. His black mask and muzzle give him a jaunty self-assurance. There's nothing in excess on the well-trained boxer frame. It is as if he'd taken off every unacceptable pound to make weight in the ring.

The boxer's feet are compressed, catlike. The shoulders are muscled, as is the rest of the body. The coat is short and shiny, ranging from fawn and brindle, with shades that go from light yellow to dark red. White markings are on the muzzle, chest, neck, and feet. Traditionally, boxers have docked ears and tails. Of average size—22 to 25 inches and 50 to 70 pounds—the boxer is a middleweight.

Although they look threatening and are good watchdogs, boxers are quite sociable and friendly, and completely devoted to the family. Fundamentally playful with family and friends, boxers are quick to break away from their classic fighter's pose to have a little fun. They have a sparkling light in their eyes, and are softies at heart. The slightly arched skull, powerful muzzle, and undershot jaw make him look like a no-fooling-around tough guy, which he is, but not all the time, and definitely not with his family.

Tail-wagging is legion with the breed and it seems to involve the dog's entire pelvis. Boxers are often car-and-bike chasers. They like to bounce and are often "in your face," to the degree that some clubs recommend not owning one "if you don't want them to lick you."

Owning two of the same gender is also not recommended, as they will fight. In the absence of a secure fenced area, boxers should be walked at least a mile a day.

BULLDOG
(ENGLISH AND FRENCH)

Bulldog Rules

JOHN BREDIN

P ROBABLY DESCENDED FROM the Asiatic mastiff, the bulldog was
bred in Great Britain during the 1200s. Before that time, the Romans had a
similar breed of dog so ferocious that an ordinance forbade the passage of the
animal on the street, even upon a chain. The English game of bullbaiting
began with "Butcher's Dogs" (Rottweiler, Dogue de Bordeaux), which were
relegated to the sport, quite by accident. Exactly when this was in fashion
isn't quite known, but during the thirteenth century, Earl Warren observed
a bunch of these dogs chasing a harried bull through the cobbled streets of
Stamford.

Mr. Warren enjoyed the sight so well that, six weeks before Christmas
of each year, he arranged for the event to be repeated. Thus originated the
cruel but greatly adored English blood sport of bullbaiting which was patron-
ized by royalty and commoner alike. The Bulldog was originally bred only
for ferocity and courage in the pit. In 1835 an outcry of public opinion arose
against the sport, though dog fighting did remain in force for many years
afterward. The bulldog's famous lock-jawed tenacity enabled him to clamp
onto his opponent—bull, bear, or dog—and to hold on until the following

year, or until the opponent dropped. The bull, as was usually the case, had one of two options: to run or to fight.

In running, the bull was usually clubbed by men and beset with dogs. In fighting, the bull had a good chance to gore his canine opponent, but the bulldog's chances of sinking fang and holding fast were surprisingly greater than the upswung leverage of horn.

It's a wonder, in most respects, that the dog's psyche survived the brutal fate of hunter, attacker, and killer because the little bulldog took on foes that he had no wish to antagonize. Today, he's still more ferocious of face than anything else, and, for the most part, bulldogs are given to watchdoging: staring half-lidded out of a dog house with folded paws and a mug that could chase away the sunshine.

THE FRENCH BULLDOG came about because, following the abolition of bullbaiting in England, in 1835 (and later, dog fighting), the British refused to abandon their beloved bad-mug pal. The people of the English midlands, where the dog was so very popular, took him with them when they emigrated to France to exploit the trade of lace-making which was more in vogue in France than in England. So, off went lace makers and their dogs, the two becoming, in time, a Francophiled version of their ancestors.

Today, the French bulldog is the mugsy twin of his English cousin, but, since he never knew the trials of the bull pen or the dog pit, he has a rather sweeter disposition (which also comes from his later cross with terrier dogs) than the English bulldog.

THE BULLDOG HAS always been an animated cartoonist's dream. For the past fifty years, we've come to know that good old, flat-faced, unshaven, cigar-chomping bulldog. There's something so human about the characterization, as if we'd made up a dog to go with a guy down at the end of the bar.

The classic bulldog myth always begins with a bully and a back-street. . . . Could this be a bull and a butcher's yard? One such yarn we picked up in Maryland. In the town of Westminster, shortly after the Second World War, we are told, it happened that a very aggressive bulldog lived completely unsupervised and left to his own recognizance. He made himself known by stalking the streets during those hours when passersby were most frequent. This was in the morning when people were going to work and in the evening when they were coming home.

In the morning the dog was seen standing like a bronze statue, not guarding, just grinning. He was not a chaser, but wherever he positioned himself, he expected a taste of something meaty. Such was his reputation; such was the embroidery of myth that clung to his countenance.

People got in the habit of keeping their children inside when the bulldog was outside; and it became de rigueur to run to one's car, leaping into the front seat and slamming the door to avoid the impact of crushing jaws.

No one, it seemed, ever challenged the dog—least of all any other household dogs, who, like the townfolk of Westminster, wouldn't go out when the bulldog was on the prowl.

He ran the town. He cowed each and every person. He had a grandiose pugnacious reputation—but no one ever saw him in action; they just imagined that they did. Stories led to more stories, and these became legends, and, finally, myths. Thus was the dog blown up larger than life.

Then one day a new guy came to town and changed the way people looked at bulldogs ever after. The way it happened was that, instead of bolting to get into his car, this man walked. He took his time, too.

Outraged at the insouciance of the newcomer, the bulldog strutted up to him and dared him to take another step. The immovable animal's slack-jawed face was grim and cruelly marked, and he growled deeply and menacingly.

But the new guy remained unmoved.

In a high, nasal, singsong voice, he whispered a silly little nonsensical song. The bulldog's jaw dropped.

Here, boldly drawn, was the curious mythical role once chosen by Odysseus, the time he was met by a pack of killer dogs. Did he run from them? Did he quake with fear? He did neither. He sat down and then he let the staff fall from his hand. The dogs' growls wavered when they saw Odysseus's empty, open-handed entreaty. Stunned, they studied him for the slightest sign of malice. But he bore none. Seated, he was level with their eyes. Weaponless, he sought not to do battle.

Bad dogs, it has sometimes been remarked, behave a little differently when their opposition refuses to quail and yet, deigns not to fight, as well.

So it was long, long ago with Odysseus.

And so it was once more in Westminster, Maryland.

The dogs that would've torn Odysseus limb from limb sat down and licked their paws and whined, and wondered if anything was wrong.

The bulldog of Westminster sat down and did the same.

And the cool-eyed stranger sang the mighty dog's praises and told him that he was a bold and beautiful bulldog of the terrible sort, and that he was formidable and awful, and that the whole world was quivering at the mere thought of him.

"But," sang the stranger, "aren't you just a little bit lonely? Don't you know that being so awful, you have no friends? Don't you ever want to be scratched on the head or patted on the tummy? Don't you ever want to be liked instead of looked at and loathed?"

Well, as everyone knows, kind words are honey and mean words are vinegar. Whether it was the newcomer's soft voice, as some insist, or whether it was his surprising way of sitting down on the sidewalk, the outcome was the same. In no time, man and dog became good friends, and it wasn't long after that bulldog had other friends, too. In fact, after a while he had a whole town of friends.

He still stalked around gruffly, as if he owned the neighborhood, but now he did—he really did.

The Lore of the Dog

It's difficult to speak of the bulldog without resorting to compound metaphors. Beginning with the pugilistic mug: so decidedly human and magnified that the head seems to subordinate the rest of the dog. Yet the other parts are equally noteworthy.

The bulldog is pear-shaped with the large end of the fruit low inside the widespread forelegs, which sometimes appear like marble columns going straight into the ground. The hindquarters (the small end of the pear, if you will) recede into narrowness, causing the dog to look, as people say, "like a battleship." The head is wide, the forehead flat, the muzzle short, broad, and turned-up. Jowls, thick and pendulous, are noted for drool.

Bulldogs have rose ears, thin and folded back. The feet are round and compact and heavy knuckled. Coat is short, smooth, and comes in red and all other brindles: white; red; beige; pied with, sometimes, a black mask or muzzle. Twelve to 16 inches high, the bulldog may weigh as much as 55 pounds.

The bulldog has become a symbol of the British and this is often designated by his full title, the English bulldog. The distinguishing qualities of the dog include courage, tenacity, and equanimity. Like the people to whom he is endeared, the bulldog does not back off.

However, this unsurpassed watchdog is a loyal, gentle, and reliable family friend. Bulldogs can be quartered in small homes or apartments and they do not need the heavy exercise of some larger breeds.

They are hardy and have few maladies except that the flat face, bred for clamping of jaws, is not comfortably designed for normal breathing. So some bulldogs develop breathing difficulties and many have a characteristic snort.

Breeding over the last one hundred years has made this "beautifully ugly" dog an aristocrat rather than the aggressive predecessor that fought blood-circus foes such as bulls, bears, and other dogs. This is a serious dog, however; some say he has a sense of humor, because he often seems to be laughing.

THE FRENCH BULLDOG is similar to the English bulldog. However, he is smaller, lighter boned, and it would seem that his removal from the arena of fighting placed him into a slightly different mold. Straight-legged, bat-eared, and unfrowning, this Gallic dog is quite simply less dour than his cousin. There is a French refinement in his body and face, as well as his personality.

The coat is short and fine, lustrous and soft. Mostly brindle, but sometimes fawn or pied, the French bulldog is 12 inches high and weighs 13 to 26 pounds.

This dog is noted for courage and is a fine watchdog and a good mouser and ratter. French bulldogs are patient and companionable family dogs.

BULLTERRIER

The Pit Dog

JOHN BREDIN

THE BULLTERRIER, WITH the glossy white coat, was probably developed by mixing the white terrier, the Staffordshire terrier, and adding a dash of dalmatian and pointer. This probably happened around 1860 when Birmingham's James Hinks was the leading English bullterrier breeder. The dog (the Staffordshire) came to America in the 1870s where it became known as the pit dog, the pit bull terrier, and the Yankee terrier.

Rudyard Kipling, as many are aware, was an exemplar of dogs, and he writes of a bullterrier that he once chaperoned while stationed in India. This dog, Kipling explains, was a burden, an inheritance, a hostage, a nuisance—but, in the end, an education.

Kipling didn't want the dog because he already had one—another terrier, in fact. So the addition was entirely unwanted.

He makes clear, however, there was little to be done about it, and thus came bumbling into his life the most fawn-spotted, heavy-boned, whipping-tailed bullterrier there ever was. Little did Kipling know that he was about to get a short course in the psychic behavior of bullterriers.

The way he got the dog is yet another story. Briefly, it goes as follows: Kipling had saved the life of a soldier, a man whose thanks consisted of turning his dog over to the writer. "Sir," said the saved fellow, "I give you a dog because of what you got me out of."

Stories of weaker origin have begun with more preamble than this, and
Kipling takes heed of the wording—"a dog." But not just any dog. . . .

Accepting his dog dues under duress, Kipling takes into his care yet
another pillow-pummeling canine companion. But he quickly sees that this
new terrier is no pillow-fighter. This one's the real thing, a watchman's
watchdog, a beast so frightening that no one, not even the armed regiment
across the way, dares to come near.

In one incident that lives up to his name, the Bull, as he is known,
pulverizes a pack of yellow pariah dogs that have threatened Kipling's rat
terrier.

The squat, rolly, smile-on-lips, slant-eyed bull closes in on the feral pack
and dispatches them with clean, well-aimed swings of his great oblong head.
With a few well-timed flicks of that anvil-shaped skull, he scatters them. Then
he pads softly back to Kipling, smiling like a crocodile. Delivered, untouched
by tooth or claw, is Kipling's little rat terrier. Hmmm, Kipling muses, maybe
the dog's worth keeping, after all.

But just as Kipling decides that he wants the dog, the dog decides he
wants his old master back. He takes to haunting the streets, wagging his tail
when he sees anyone in khakis. Kipling makes up his mind to return Bull,
but the soldier whose life he saved won't hear of it. A deal's a deal, he says.
Kipling begs the man to reconsider, but he turns to granite with resolve.

Once a week, though, the old soldier drops by for a visit. On these days
Bull waits attentively, listening for the squeak of the door, or even for footsteps on the road.

Kipling's no fool when it comes to dogs and he sees that Bull's the
proverbial one-man animal. There's no recourse, he feels, but to force the
dog back on the honorable soldier. Just when he decides to do this, however,
Bull's former owner is sent far away into the high country of India.

Bull's not supposed to know this, but he does. First, he mopes, then he
pines. Then, running a high fever, he plops himself down and starts to die.
The symptoms look vaguely like malaria. Kipling watches the hearty terrier
waste away and begin to fade like a shadow.

The remedy, of course, is for the author to go on a trek, a personal
quest to find Bull's soldier. In the meantime, since the dog seems to be ex-
piring from malarial infection, Kipling doses him with quinine, and barely
saves his life.

But how to keep Bull alive while the two of them make the long journey
into the mountains?

Kipling uses the writer's trade—words. First, he tries simple, unabbrev-
iated English words. The dog, he finds, knows them. And he knows them

exactly. Kipling tells Bull that they are going on a long trip (tail wagging), to the village of Kasauli, the place his soldier is staying (furious tail wagging).

This is repeated like a dose of medicine fifty to one hundred times each day at the rate of ten tail wags per line. Whenever Kipling notices Bull is looking a bit sickly and he starts hanging his anvil-shaped head, the author repeats the magic message and speaks of the trip into the snow country. The dog's eyes burn and his tail cuts across the still air like a scythe.

As soon as he can get away, Kipling takes Bull to find the old soldier. The nearer they get, the broader the dog's smile, until, at last, when they draw in sight of the mountain regiment, Bull's eyes squint with pleasure and he leaps into the air.

He knows this is the place—but how?

And in the midst of many, he finds his man.

Kipling writes:

> He departed without a word, and, so far as I could see, without moving his legs. He flew through the air bodily, and I heard the whack of him as he flung himself at Stanley, knocking the little man clean over. They rolled on the ground together, shouting, and yelping, and hugging. I could not see which was dog and which was man, till Stanley got up and whimpered.

A little later, Kipling observes the reunion meal that consists of sardines, jam, cold mutton, pickles, and beer. Between mouthfuls, Stanley tells Kipling that he almost died of malaria—this, at the same time Bull was dying down in the desert.

And so Stanley, the old soldier, and his square dog are reunited in the mountains of India, and as the cold twilight comes creeping across the snowy hills and the lights of Simla begin to sparkle, Kipling buttons his own little rat terrier into his coat, and they become two of the four happiest people on the top of the world.

The Lore of the Dog

The bullterrier has an oval egg-shaped head, powerful jaws, piercing narrow, triangular eyes, the steely body of a soft-pawed tank. The short tail, thick at the base and tapered at the end, is carried horizontally. The hindquarters are straight and heavily muscled. Usually white with a colored marking over eye or ear, the bullterrier may also be brindle with white markings. He stands 21 to 22 inches in height and weighs 52 to 62 pounds.

Bred for ferocity, this dog can't be separated from his martial arts upbringing, his fighting machine lineage. Named the White Cavalier, he was trained to fight surpassingly well, but not to seek or provoke a fight. According to experts, the bullterrier is entirely given to performances of bravery on behalf of his master or mistress. There is no question, however, that the dog has an old soldier's sense of humor, dry as a desert martini. Today's bullterrier, while still an inveterate ratter, does few of the blood-thirsty things that he did over a century ago; as a badger-router he was superb and as a dog fighter supreme. Now bullterriers are family dogs and extraordinarily obedient, loyal, and steadfast guardians.

CAVALIER KING CHARLES SPANIEL

King Charles's Charlie

BARBARA DAVIS

HISTORICALLY, THE NAME "spaniel" was loosely used and any breed that did what a spaniel did—whatever that was—and even if it bore no resemblance to the correct spaniel breed, was so named.

Yet the little King Charles spaniel (Charles II of England, 1660–1685, was never without one.) stands outside classification by having a selfless temperament, an ego-less disposition, a fervent desire to aid the afflictions of humankind, and a cuteness all his own.

Sometimes called the carpet spaniel or Charlie, the dog was perhaps once used in the field, but later became known as the perfect fashion pet for ladies. That is to say, a dog of royalty. Fashion—not a quirk of the dog's own nature—made him into a comforter of women. A creature known then, and today as well, as a lapdog.

Lapdogs of the seventeenth century—the so-called Spaniell Gentle—were warmers, coziers and comforters, yet they had another practical purpose: drawing fleas and other tiny vermin away from their owners. They were said to hide under petticoats, to lie silky-eared and soulful upon the laps of the aristocracy.

Indeed, a prescription once recommended that the queen of England keep a "Comforte Dog" (King Charles spaniel) on her lap to treat a cold. In the days of drafty castles and chilly carriages, and through the uncertainty of the plague years, the cavalier was the lap-watcher of monarch and lady. Pythagoras once explained that small dogs of the spaniel variety were able to store the breath of a dying person and carry it with them, thus keeping the spirit alive. They also offered "lick-therapy," the tongue being a medicine; the French believed that a dog's wet tongue could cure ulcers.

The Greeks felt that the dog could protect them not only from terrestrial foes, but from evil spirits as well. If a person felt the onset of said spirits, he carried a dog with him at all times. The belief that a dog's presence would keep evil at bay is with us today, as dogs are frequently used in care centers of all kinds, especially with the elderly and children.

Small dogs, because of their portability, were granted much more than medicinal powers. They became spiritual advisers, silent sojourners residing in the crook of an arm, the curve of a lap, and, alongside their beloved's head, on the subtle dent of a pillow.

Thus to have a dog beside you if you were feeling unwell was to possess a talisman against harm, a physician/shaman/priest/best friend, who would never leave your side, no matter what condition—financial or physical—you found yourself in.

AUTHOR SHARON HOPE writes, "So fond was King Charles II of his little dogs, he wrote a decree that the King Charles spaniel should be accepted in any public place, even in the houses of Parliament where animals were usually not allowed."

Painters adored the toy spaniels and they were featured in the works of Titian, Van Dyck, Gainsborough, Rubens, and Rembrandt. Characteristically, the artists depicted a spaniel with a flat head, long muzzle, high-set ears, and almond eyes. In the nineteenth century, however, the dog's breeding was markedly more organized and scientific, producing a Charlie whose face was flatter and whose head was rounder.

Proof that life imitates art, and not the other way round, today's cavalier King Charles spaniel resembles the Old Masters' renditions. How this came about was that Roswell Eldridge, an American dog fancier from the 1920s, went to England to find a Charlie that resembled the old paintings.

He could find no such dog, however. So he offered a prize at London's Cruft's Dog Show for a male and female King Charles with the features found in the paintings that he loved. Breeders took him up on his challenge and in 1945 the new "old" breed of Charlie came to be the cavalier King Charles spaniel. (The name refers, in part, to the Cavalier period of King Charles.) However, inasmuch as breeders were unwilling to abandon the flat-faced spaniel, this dog is known today as the King Charles spaniel or the English Toy Spaniel.

If you're confused by the alterations in Charlie's recent and not-so-recent past, consider that either dog is at home on your lap, and that both have the fondest of soul-settling eyes. Otherwise, why would they ride today on the laps of movie divas, captains of industry, and princesses of fashion? When Charlie snuggles, so does the heart. It's an old medicine for melancholy, but it still seems to work quite well.

LA FONTAINE, THE French fabulist, tells the tale of "The Little Dog," a small spaniel. There was once a beautiful woman, he explains, whose name is Argia. One day a handsome young man named Atis, falls in love with her and vows that he'll do anything to win her hand. As luck would have it, a fairy appears before Atis, and promises to help him win the lovely Argia.

Now the fairy transforms herself into a spaniel and Atis into a vagabond minstrel, a ne'er-do-well lad, traveling about the land with bagpipe and dog. He is so miserable looking in his ragged tatters and with his face sooted by so many drafty campfire nights, that no one would guess he was once a handsome youth.

Upon arriving at Argia's door, Atis and spaniel perform their most winning songs and tricks. In delight, Argia exclaims that she must have the spaniel—at any price.

Atis refuses her but uses the dog as barter for his own strategy of love. "Look how valuable my dog is," he says. Squeezing the spaniel's paw, Atis shows Argia a bit of magic.

Out of the fairy dog's paw there tumbles a fortune of riches: pearls, diamonds, and gold. Immediately Atis gathers them up.

"You cannot have the dog without me," swears Atis, and finally, the bedazzled Argia, against her better judgment, gives in. She now accepts dog and master together. That night, having won the hand of his love, Atis turns back into himself. The joyful Argia embraces her little spaniel, who remains a dog forever—and not just any dog, as well we know.

THERE ARE A number of morals in this little tale. First, and most obvious, is that, in the case of the spaniel, all good things come in small packages. Second, there is more than a little mystery in the spaniel's history, for the curative powers of this small dog have been known for a long time. The squeezing of the paw is a bit like the rubbing of a genie's lamp, but the riches are spiritual, not material. In fact, the mention of the pearl is also symbolic of the biblical pearl of virtue, or the wisdom of King Solomon. Of course, the association of toy spaniels with affluence is historic rather than philosophic. Transmogrification and fairy lore are entwined in the little dog's past. By and large, good things do come in small packages and love, if true, has a gentle spaniel's eyes that can transform anything into riches.

The Lore of the Dog

The first thing you notice about this dog is the pool-like, empathic eyes that seem to draw you in for keeps. Owners describe them as looking like a cocker spaniel puppy all of their lives.

They are silky-coated and silken-eared and the face, unlike the flattish look of the toy spaniel, is well-rounded, the muzzle longer and tapered, but not pointed. The ears fan slightly forward to frame the face.

The body is short, the chest deep and the back level. The tail, carried level with the back, is sometimes docked. Feathering occurs on ears, legs, and tail; foot-feathering is a characteristic of the breed. Overall, the fur is very soft to the touch. Colors are black with areas of bright tan; solid red; white with chestnut markings; or tricolored (black, white, and chestnut).

The height is 12 to 13 inches and weight is 13 to 19 pounds.

Sweet-tempered, outgoing, gentle, outdoor-and-indoor-loving, the perfect bedside or traveling companion—the cavalier King Charles is all of these and more.

The dog's aura of historic magic and loyal demeanor make him a wonderful confidant for children and the elderly. However, Charlies regard all people—including strangers—as potential friends, and while they'll bark when someone new approaches, this is more of a greeting than a warning.

In spite of their reputation as indoor pets and lapdogs, they love a good romp outside. Charlies have a good sense of smell and sight, and can be used for short hunting expeditions.

They do not like to be left alone, and if not given exposure to unfamiliar sounds at an early age, the cavalier King Charles may turn timid. Altogether this is a fine family dog.

CHIHUAHUA

The God Dog

JOHN BREDIN

T HE ANCIENT NAHUATL nations of Mexico, represented by the
Toltec people, were the bearers of a mysterious legend that lives on today in
the cedar-scented deserts of New Mexico and Arizona. The legend, as many
of us know, is called "The Feathered Serpent." A snake, a bird, a man, a
magic boat ferrying a deity across the seas and skies, here is the archetype of
human brotherhood, and though the rapture of the feathered serpent is as
endless as the coils and feathers of its symbolic iconography, there is another
identity buried within—somehow, not surprisingly, a dog.

Quetzalcoatl, the feathered serpent deity, is a multidimensional, multi-
mythological man who appears in one of his incarnations bedecked in feathery
robes. Yet he has another presence, another name. This alter ego of Quetzalcoatl is called Xolotl, and he bears the face of a dog.

What kind of dog? Temple art shows a small, lemur-eyed dog whose
other name is Chihuahua, the state in northern Mexico where sculptures
representing him were first found. Xolotl is like Anubis, the jackal-headed
deity. Just as Anubis led the dead to the next world in Egypt, Xolotl performs
this same rite of passage in Mexico.

But how can such a small dog as the Chihuahua carry the weight of so
much mythology?

Not easily. For we know that dogs like them were sacrificed by the
Toltecs, and buried along with their masters. After the Toltec civilization

collapsed, another Mexican nation, the Chichimecs, took over. Their name, "*chichi*," means "a dog." So these were the People of the Dog.

After the "victory" of Hernando Cortés over the Aztec Empire in 1521, the prehistoric oral history of Mexico came to an end. And so did the mystery of gem-eyed canine gods. What remains, though, is a tiny dog that can sit in a soup bowl and trade places with a hot water bottle.

The Lore of the Dog

A graceful, alert, swift-moving little dog, the Chihuahua is one of the smallest members of the Canidae family. This is a well-balanced dog with a body perhaps longer than it is tall.

The well-rounded, apple-shaped head carries erect, pointed, batlike ears that sit very prominently on the face. The eyes are full, noticeably large, and black. Standing only 6 to 9 inches tall and weighing 2 to 5 pounds, Chihuahuas are strong given their diminutive proportions, and they're agile as well.

Their fur is smooth or long; the smooth coat is glossy and with a slight ruff on the neck. In the long-coated variety the fur is soft in texture with an undercoat; the ears in this version of the dog are fringed and the tail is plumelike. The coloration is widely varied—almost any color at all.

Chihuahuas have an alert terrier's temperament. Known for being both courageous and loyal, they are devoted family dogs. They prefer, though, the company of their own kind, and are not sociable among other dogs. Chihuahuas show a tincture of jealousy when their master or mistress is attentive to people outside the family. Moreover, they do not generally like strangers although they enjoy being the center of attention.

They are normally healthy, but it is necessary (because of their small body weight and thin coat) to keep them warm under intemperate conditions. These dogs also require daily exercise in order to stay healthy.

CHOW

The Laughing Dog of the Little Folk

JOHN BREDIN

SOME EXPERTS SAY that the word "*chowchow*" actually means bric-a-brac. They say that this is the term used to describe the contents of ships coming to Europe from the East. However, there are also those who believe the word "chow" is simply Cantonese/American slang for food. That seems likely, too, since the poor dog was fancied for his tender flesh as well as fine fur.

The Chow is undoubtedly one of the oldest recognizable dog breeds in the world. There's an early illustration of one on a Han Dynasty bas-relief, which places the dog at about 150 B.C. His ancestral home was either the Far North (Mongolia and Siberia) or northern China; take your pick, no one knows for certain.

The largest numbers of Chows, we do know, were found around Canton, where he was called "the Black-mouthed Dog." In Peking, however, the name of choice was "the Wolf or Bear Dog." A kennel of the Tang Dynasty (seventh century A.D.) shows that the popularity of Chows was unquestionable; housing for five thousand dogs and ten thousand huntsmen became the order of the era. Chows were first imported to England in the late nineteenth century and the breed started to be popular after Queen Victoria, "the Dog Queen" (so named for her love of Canidae), showed a special interest in them.

As an American import, the Chow arrived in 1903 and was given admittance to the American Kennel Club three years later in 1906.

THE ANIMAL BEHAVIORIST Konrad Lorenz once speculated that all lupus-blooded dogs (dogs that have a bit of the wolf in them) are of the one-master variety; that is, they show a preferred allegiance to one person only, much like the old wolf imprint myth in which the young animal attaches itself right away to the highest member of its society, the alpha or pack leader. Such a blood line is noticeably present in the wolf-faced Chow. In examining a variety of domestic breeds, the one which Lorenz believed was best qualified for wolf lineage was. the Chow. According to Dr. Michael W. Fox, "Lorenz later changed this notion of wolf-ancestry of 'one-master' breeds and jackal for more outgoing/sociable breeds." Dr. Fox believes "The reverse is more probable."

Be that as it may, the imprinting of the Chow, according to Lorenz, should take place as early as the first weeks of puppy ownership. For instance, he once bought his wife a Chow, as a gift, which his cousin kept for him one week prior to his wife's birthday. During that one week, the Chow irreversibly imprinted to his cousin.

In his classic study, *Man Meets Dog*, Lorenz tells the tale of Stasi, a female Chow-Alsatian mix, who bonds in a wolflike manner to the author. He describes Stasi as the love of his life. But trouble begins whenever Lorenz has to leave home on business. In his absence the dog becomes a terror in the neighborhood, killing chickens and living wild in the woods.

Whenever Lorenz is at home, however, Stasi is a model dog. Once, when he is leaving by train, she lowers her ears, ruffles her mane, and tries to board the already moving locomotive. Amazingly, the dog rushes the train and succeeds in getting on, but Lorenz is forced to put her off. She accepts his refusal with an ember of resignation in her eyes. Everything about this dog is wonderfully pure, as if she were all heart and no head, all love and no reason. All dogs, of course, fit into the mold of living in the moment and loving us without restraint, but Stasi was somehow different. The flaming golden red of her coat was her nature, all aflame.

Once, when returning to see Stasi after a long separation, Lorenz describes her in the following way: "Her hind legs gave way, her nose was directed skywards, something happened in her throat, and then the mental torture of months found outlet in the hair-raising yet beautiful tones of a wolf's howl."

For Stasi, her master is her life. Without Lorenz, her personality disintegrates. When hen murders, rabbit burglaries, and postman attacks mount up, Lorenz vows to do something, but he is then drafted into World War II and is sadly not present when Stasi's put into the Konigsberg Zoo.

There she peaceably shares a cage with a Siberian wolf, eventually having puppies, however, with a wild dingo.

Tragically, Stasi dies in another zoo during an air raid. Lorenz feels terrible about this, remembering her unqualified devotion: "Stasi spent rather less than half her six years of life in the company of her master, but nevertheless, she was the most faithful dog that I have ever known—and I have known a great many dogs."

Is it the blood of the wolf that makes this unbreakable bond? Some say that it is. Others comment that the Chow has an otherworldly quality, a mythic ingredient that is only vaguely understood by people today.

We have noticed the tail-curled, fairy world in the Chow's manner, but it's not only in the way that they look or act. Something in the Chow is of the mists; something ruff-furred and prehistoric. In Ireland, certain mounds are considered the secret homes of the fairy people, and round about them live their laughing guardians, who are none other than Chows.

In the following description by M. O. Howey in *The Cult of the Dog*, history, archaeology, and mythology share a moment of common ground, literally, if not figuratively:

> Fierce dogs which guarded the fairy mounds from intrusion by mortal men are often referred to in accounts of the fairy people. The materialistic explanation is to be found in the dogs of Chow type which were possessed by the Neolithic inhabitants of the desolate, untilled moorlands, who kept them to guard their dwellings and the sheep and cattle on which their living depended. These people lived in circular huts, partly sunken below the level of the surrounding ground and roofed with turf on which small bushes often grew, so that to the casual observer they appeared as small mounds or hillocks and were designated fairy hills. Skeletons of the dogs have been found on these Neolithic sites.

The Lore of the Dog

The Chow is a muscular, leonine dog with a stocky build and a mane-headed ruff; his bone structure is heavy and he is built fairly low to the ground. His head is large with a broad, flat skull and a short muzzle. The eyes—dark, small, and almond-shaped—are nearly lost in the lion's scowl that frequents the face of the dog.

The Chow's ears are upright, rounded, and smallish in proportion to the head. The tail curls and is carried high over the back. A unique feature, a rarity among dogs, is the Chow's blue-black tongue.

Chows have double-coated fur, abundant and dense on the outer coat with the undercoat soft and wooly. Coloration is red, black, and cinnamon. The Chow is generally 19 to 22 inches in height and weighs 44 to 55 pounds.

Chows enjoy singular ownership and have very strong personalities, including a will of iron. They are completely loyal and devoted to their family, and are, therefore, sometimes unfriendly and even aggressive toward strangers. It's important in Chow training to adopt this dog early. Imprinting takes place almost at the outset of adoption. The Chow's personality is dignified; some say the dog is without humor. Excellent hunting dogs, Chows were originally bred for hunting deer and bear. Their endurance is outstanding and their scent is as keen as their ability to track game. Chows were also bred to guard junks in China and as a result they are very good watchdogs.

COCKER SPANIEL

The Purloined Spanyell

BARBARA DAVIS

THE SPANIEL IS of Spanish descent, just as the name implies. The word "spaniel," probably from the French *"espaignol,"* means "spanish dog." Trained for the hunt in England and France some six hundred years ago, this effusive and affectionate dog gained the name "cocker" because of his skill in routing woodcocks from upland meadows and covered woodlands. Although the breed—we imagine even from the start—was singularly attractive and extremely friendly, it was not, in the late sixteenth century, designated as a "breed." At first, in eighteenth century England, there were two basics types: the land spaniel, used on land; and the water spaniel, used in the water. From our earliest records, the ebullient spaniel personality was abundantly present. What is the personality of a spaniel? Suffice to say that the dog is a warmer of hearts as well as of feet; a dog of unqualified jolliness, of tail-wagging excitability. A dog whose every move is said to be "spanielish."

In the early days, the spaniel was considered wild and untractable—the last thing a sportsman wanted. His volatile nature, his spanielness got the better of him, and on the hunt he actually frightened away his quarry, leaving the hunter quite empty-handed. Dog authority Edward C. Ash flatly states: "If they had not been so lovable and beautiful they would not have been kept at all!"

Ash goes on to say that the wild little spaniel ended up becoming "the maid of all work." This was because, though an upstart and a nuisance, the dog's nose was superior. No dog, Ash confides, was better for hawking; no dog finer for waterfowl. Add to this coursing, for the hares missed by the fleet greyhound were seldom overlooked by the ground-hugging spaniel.

Indeed, the spaniel's nose was so sharp that, according to one English huntsman, a man could spit upon a coin and hide it under a stone, and this crafty dog would soon sniff it out. Thus the spaniel achieved a large popularity in Europe, and in the seventeenth century all dogs were given the generic nomenclature of "spaniels." (See: cavalier King Charles spaniel.)

The Newfoundland, for instance, was called a "water spaniel." In eighteenth-century England, however, there were two distinct varieties, a larger and a smaller. These, in the order so cited, were the English springer spaniel, primarily used in hunting water fowl, and the English cocker spaniel, basically trained to hunt woodcock.

The English cocker spaniel was separated from the larger springer in 1892 when size became the dividing line between the breeds. During the nineteenth century the field cocker spaniels were the smaller and usually black-in-color variants of the two well-known hunting dogs. By breeding the field cocker spaniel with the English toy spaniel (perhaps the cavalier King Charles), English breeders produced a smaller cocker spaniel, which became the prototype for today's popular American breed.

An enthusiastic hunter like his English cousin, the American cocker has become a companion dog par excellence. He is smaller than the field cocker spaniel and may have longer legs, but essentially the old nose-to-the-earth attributes of the breed are still present.

THE ENGLISH POET Elizabeth Barrett Browning said of her cocker spaniel, Flush: "He loves me better than the sunlight without." This sincere remark contains a bit of irony since the poet rarely went outside with her dog. When Robert Browning was courting her, Flush nipped the kindly poet, whose presence dramatically altered the Victorian solitude of the Barrett household.

Virginia Woolf's spirited fictional treatment of Elizabeth Barrett's cocker spaniel is a good piece of canine portraiture. Based upon hearsay and folksay, the short story "Flush" is a brief, speculative tale; yet it does show some subtle aspects of the dog's nature.

Essentially, the story tells how Flush was placed second on Miss Barrett's roster of lovables, and how as a self-respecting cocker, the dog refused to be anybody's second. Long years of shared sensibility with Miss Barrett had made Flush a sensitive confidant:

He could read signs that nobody else could even see. He could tell by the touch of Miss Barrett's fingers that she was waiting for one thing only—for the postman's knock, for the letter on the tray. She would be stroking him perhaps with a light, regular movement; suddenly—there was the rap—her fingers constricted; he would be held in a vice while Wilson came upstairs. Then she took the letter and he was loosed and forgotten.

The love affair that utterly consumes Elizabeth Barrett and her handsome suitor, the English poet Robert Browning, is an anathema to the sensitive cocker spaniel. When Flush finds himself "brushed off with the flick of a hand," his jealous nature is enflamed. He makes two violent attempts to regain his mistress's favor, and to perhaps banish the newcomer. By biting Mr. Browning, however, he attains only his mistress's solicitude for the man, who is now designated by the dog as the Enemy.

Then Flush has a change of heart; he uses all the wit that has entered into his infinitely concentrated breeding to overcome his dilemma. Longing for the days of rice pudding and cream and the untrammeled hours of pats and gentle kisses, Flush changes course and tries a new tack. That is, if his mistress can fall into rapture over Mr. Browning, so can he—and does.

Simple as that, problem solved!

The hunter in him refused to believe that he couldn't catch his quarry, which, in this case, was Miss Barrett's heart. By loving Robert, Flush reclaims Elizabeth. And the three are, at last, joined in love.

Then without a word of warning, "in the midst of civilization, security and friendship, Flush is stolen," here the story's ended. We know nothing more of the dog whose famous owner has left us with a memoir and whose story was later embellished by Virginia Woolf. A clue as to the dog's disappearance, though, may be found in almost any handbook of dog characteristics. Flush, like most cockers, was sociable with strangers. So he probably went off with his kidnapper without so much as a bark.

As to motive, only a human cur would suspect the amiable, twice-bitten Mr. Browning, but then that affair is better left to a writer of mysteries.

The Lore of the Dog

The noteworthy American cocker is famous for having soulful eyes. Who could forget the almond eyes of Lady from Disney's *Lady and the Tramp*? Or Richard Nixon's famous cocker, Checkers, who helped to resurrect his faltering credibility in one of America's first televised speeches? People, too, have been given spaniel-like facial features by authors, such as the generally used 1930s literary device of "a woman with spaniel eyes." Naturally, these would be brown or hazel, and very large and moist.

The cocker's head is well-developed and rounded, the forehead smooth. The muzzle is broad, the jaws square, and the nose is either black or brown. The long ears hang down and are silken-haired.

This dog's coat can be silky, flat, or slightly wavy; it can become easily entangled on woodland romps. The coloration is black, red, liver, lemon, or any combination of these mixed with white. Physically, the cocker is as robust in body as in personality. The tail is carried in line with the top of the back or slightly higher; it is often docked. For the American cocker, shoulder height is normally 15 to 16 inches, with weight between 22 and 28 pounds. The English is 15 to 17 inches in height, weighing between 26 and 34 pounds.

The English version isn't as compact as the American, which has a heavier coat and more luxuriant feathering. The American cocker has a squarer head and muzzle, slightly shorter legs, and larger eyes.

The cocker spaniel is a cheerful little gamester, but this doesn't detract from his warm sociability. Overall, he is a cooperative dog with an eye for detail. His comportment is exuberant, indicated by enthusiastic tail-wagging.

As with many of the sporting dogs, this one needs regular exercise. Some say the cocker is all too amiable in nature, too willing to please to be a threatening watchdog. Not that he won't bark—he will. Some bark a lot, but what the dog really wants to do is follow his nose. If frustrated from nosing around, so to speak; or if not getting a normal amount of exercise, this sensitive dog may develop behavioral problems.

The coat, because of its fine fur and the dog's love of rambling, must be tended to regularly. Cockers seem to do well in the city, providing they have been trained to expect unfamiliar noises from an early age. Some say the English cocker is more temperamentally reliable because he has not been so finely bred as the American.

COLLIE

The Shepherd's Dog

JOHN BREDIN

THE COLLIE IS the canny dog of the Scottish Lowlands, a guardian of sheep whose ancestors are cited as the Newfoundland, the deerhound, and the borzoi. The smooth collie was once a drover's dog, used for driving cows and sheep to market. The rough collie was used mainly for guarding sheep in pastures. As early as the nineteenth century, dog fanciers took interest in the collie and began to keep written pedigrees. Although these were short, they can mostly be traced to one dog, Old Cockie, born in 1867. This ancestor dog, who resembled today's collie, was one of the first Scotch sheepdogs.

The name "collie" comes from *coalie*, or *coaly*, probably named for the black-faced sheep the dog herded in Scotland. It's possible, too, that the name was for the collie's once predominantly black color. In any event, the dog's sense of duty had made him a landmark breed long before authors and filmmakers praised the collie's inordinate love of family.

IT WAS QUEEN Victoria who brought the collie to the fore in the late 1800s. After this welcome introduction, the dog became the plaything of the royal and the rich. In America, nineteenth-century industrialist J. P. Morgan started a collie kennel and made the breed popular in this country. No longer in demand as a herder, today's collie is best known as a family dog. It is, in fact, one of the top five dogs associated with this role.

Authors, it seems, have long had a love affair with the picturesque long-haired dog whose name was either Lad or Lassie. Albert Payson Terhune (*Lad, A Dog*) was partly responsible for this, but the home-seeking collie was already an old oral tale when Eric Knight wrote *Lassie Come Home*.

"Literature and folklore," as Ted Patrick (*The Thinking Dog's Man*) explains, "abound in stories of heroic journeys made by dogs to return to homes from places far away, where they had been left or taken by their families." Sheila Burford's *The Incredible Journey* (the film is *Homeword Bound*) is about a pit bull, a golden retriever, and a Siamese cat that travel across Canada to get back home. Theirs is a record, as far as we know, of distance traversed to make it back to a familiar place.

How is it done? Animal psychologist and veterinarian Dr. Michael W. Fox suggests that dogs and other animals perceive time and season by reading the sun. What he calls "the dissonance between local (solar) and internal time (set by the sun's position at home)" is actually the animal's secret homing device, a kind of compass.

The "dissonance" of a lost dog could account for his seeking a path of harmonic movement back to home base. Thus, as Dr. Fox states, "the trans-located animal is able to find his square mile on the globe." He also notes that various animals possess an internal compass in their brains that gives them a geomagnetic direction sense.

In *Lassie Come Home* the dog's action is precipitated by a sense of duty, notably stronger in collies than in some other breeds.

> It was time to go for the boy! She wheeled and began trotting away—trotting as if she had to go but a few hundred yards. There was nothing to tell her that the rendezvous she would keep was hundreds of miles and scores of days away. There was only the plain, unadorned knowledge of the duty to be done. And she was going to do it as best she could.

Duty, collie-style, is not confined to human/dog relations, but also to other dogs. A myth from the Isle of Arran tells of two collies, an old and a young, who once lived together. They lived in the home of a butcher close to the sea.

One day the old collie was drowned and the young one found him lying on the beach. Shortly after, the young dog appeared at the butcher shop where he selected a piece of meat and headed out the door. When he got to the beach and found his dead friend, he put the meat by his open mouth. Some say that this was an inducement for the older to dog to wake from a deep sleep, but others, ourselves included, think otherwise.

Our opinion is that the young collie was giving his beloved a burial offering, a gift to take with him to the afterworld. Whatever view you may hold of this unusual incident, one thing should be clear: Collies are one of the most well-attuned breeds we have.

AMONG THE MANY myths of "Collie, come home" that we've read, there's a very special one featuring a collie named Shep, who appears in Ted Patrick's *The Thinking Dog's Man*. This dog once tended sheep in Central Park. Yes, Central Park, Manhattan. There were sheep there at the turn of the nineteenth century. They kept the grass trim and Shep kept the sheep trim and out of trouble.

The time came when old age warranted his retirement to the country. Across the Hudson River and forty miles upstream in New York State, Shep's new home, a farm, awaited him, and he was taken to it without anyone suspecting that such a dog was never meant for a life of country ease. This was a working dog and he liked to be about his flock, doing the work he'd been bred to do.

No sooner had he arrived than Shep said good-bye to the farm in the country and padded out of the pastures and paddocks, he pointed himself back toward Manhattan. One week later Shep turned up, "footsore, tired and grumpy, and checked into Central Park for duty. He had found his way off the farm, back along the road on the west side of the Hudson to the Weehawken ferry, across on the ferryboat, and up from the dock at Forty-second Street to Central Park."

Michael W. Fox might have a hard time explaining how Shep negotiated his ride across the Hudson River. After all, he had no money, no ticket, no hand to meet the ticket takers own. Shep had never come that way before; he'd never really been out of Central Park, yet he knew his way home and when he got there, he was literally embraced by his fold.

A SIMILAR STORY repeated itself on the TV sitcom *Seinfeld*. Elaine, who cannot sleep because of the neighbor's dog that is always barking, confides in Kramer, who subsequently steals the animal and takes it along the same route, perhaps, that Shep traveled the century before.

True to form, the little yipper—a Yorkshire terrier—trots back, and arrives, just as barky as ever, on her owner's doorstep. In her mouth, she has a little piece of tattered cloth bitten off from Kramer's coat, and this traces the dog snatcher to his lair. The unlucky Elaine now suffers the twin fate of stealing a dog, to no purpose, and listening, once again, to the maddening barks of the noisy terrier.

Ted Patrick, annoyed at what is often mistaken as occultism, rages against those who would claim that such stories prove that dogs have ESP. Based on his own experience the dog is "vastly more intelligent, more reasoning, more resourceful than man usually credits him with being." The myth, then, is not necessarily that dogs can or can't perform feats of homecoming grace, but that their manner of doing it is, and should remain, a mystery. Especially to humans who are lost most of the time.

The Lore of the Dog

There are two types of collie, rough-coated and smooth. These are impressive dogs, wide-chested and well-muscled at the loin. The tail is wide and fringed, flaglike, though not carried high. Collies are proud, beautifully furred, and bear the long-tapered muzzle that is their trademark. The skull, however, is flat and broad between the ears. The eyes are almond-shaped, medium-sized, and very expressive; so human in dimension, they've often earned this dog the commendation of "the ideal family companion."

The rough collie has an abundant outer coat, a soft inner coat; the smooth collie has short, dense, flat hair with a rich undercoat. Along with collie's lovely eyes and proud head, the ample coat is always deserving of mention: sable and white, tricolor, blue merle, and white. Overall, though, the dog's image is one of golden beauty. Often, too, there's a blaze at the forehead. The collie stands at a height of 22 to 26 inches and weighs 50 to 65 pounds.

Expression—not a fixed point like color or weight—is a thing of importance in the collie, and, perhaps, almost a characteristic. It reveals the dog's presence as much as the coat shows his fine breeding. Collies are noted for being high-strung and sensitive. They are loyal as well as extremely affectionate, and protective of children.

The collie is job-oriented to such a degree that even in play he will do "drills," such as crawling on all fours, as if approaching a sheep without frightening it. Exercise is important for a dog of this size and breeding.

CURLY-COATED RETRIEVER

The Crinkly Beauty

JOHN BREDIN

VISUALIZE BLACK CHAIN mail on a sleek, middle-sized water dog and you have a pretty accurate picture of the deft, tight-curled, crinkly beauty of the curly-coated retriever. Even if you've not heard of him, the dog has been around for almost a century and a half retrieving his best for a small but dedicated following. In fact, the curly-coated retriever was actually the first retriever thus classified in England. In the United States, the dog was first exhibited in 1907. With his solid black or liver coat gleaming in the sun, this dog is a most unusual and attractive member of the Canidae clan.

Among retrievers, he's long-legged, high-chested, lightly built—therefore, an excellent water dog, whose coat protects him from bramble and thicket, mud and foul weather. Nor is he limited to the hunt; curly-coated retrievers love to be with their family and friends, and are a most companionable addition to anyone's country retreat.

THE RARE AND unusual myth that celebrates the dog comes, naturally, from England and is of the specter variety.

There was once a weaver, they say, who worked hard and long at his loom until, one day, he died atop his own threads. That would have been the end of it, but he came back as a ghost to work the same ever-moving shuttle. People said they couldn't sleep for the chatter and clatter of the loom, and wouldn't someone go and investigate the old weaver's abandoned house and see what was going on there.

Someone did: the town minister, who was greatly put out by the event. "Why, look," he said, "what if all the prowling souls of the world decided to go back to work? Where would we be then?" No one had an answer, but no one wanted to look into the old house either. The minister was a brave and hardy gentleman, and fearless as far as that goes, and he went to the churchyard and there scooped up a handful of earth with his hand. Then he proceeded to the old weaver's house, and waited in the pale moonlight for the midnight hour to come.

When the clock struck twelve, the loom began to clatter and rattle, and the minister, fallen asleep underneath a mulberry tree, sat upright, wide awake. There, in the open window of the abandoned house, sitting in a pillar of moonlight, was the bent-backed weaver, working away at his forlorn and miserable nightly trade. "Ah, ha!" cried the minister, surprising the ghost, who turned a baleful eye in his direction. And it was then the agile minister sprang forward and pitched his handful of churchyard earth full in the face of the weaver-spirit—and the poor ghost lost his ethereal hold on whatever life he had, and changed forthwith into a large black curly-coated dog.

The minister took charge of the dog, then and there, and brought him to the rectory, where he handed him a nutshell, and said: "Dog, I want you to bail that pond!" But before giving the woeful dog that little bit of cast-off nut, he held it to the light to make certain there was a hole in it, and there was, and he handed it to the dog, and told him once again to bail the pond. They say that poor, crinkly beauty of a dog is there to this day, carrying water by the nutshell in his open mouth; bailing and pouring, bailing and pouring, to no avail all the livelong night.

The Lore of the Dog

One of the oldest duck hunters, the curly-coated retriever is strong, yet agile and elegant. The head is long, the ears small and drop, and the body well proportioned and large-chested. The tail is medium length and carried straight from the body. The coat is a mass of large curls that cover the whole dog. Some care needs to be taken in the grooming process because of the curly's tendency to pick up mud and sticks on his travels.

The dog is black or liver colored with sometimes a few white hairs. The height is 25 to 27 inches and the weight is 70 to 80 pounds.

This is a dog that needs plenty of exercise and an opportunity to swim on a regular basis. Curly-coated retrievers love water, and it isn't a good idea to keep them away from that which they love so much. Given the opportunity to retrieve, the dog will use as much gentleness with an inanimate object— a stick or a ball, for instance—as he would with a downed bird.

Curlies don't seem to enjoy living in a multi-animal household, and they can be quite unfriendly to other dogs. In spite of their independent nature, they aren't hard to train, and if bred for city life, they can easily make the necessary adjustment.

DACHSHUND

The Littlest Anubis

JOHN BREDIN

THE DACHSHUND, FIRST cultivated in Germany as a badger dog, goes back to fifteenth-century Europe. However, historical images date back to the dog cults of ancient Egypt and the Temple of Aphrodite. So the dachshund, or *teckel*, as he was known in Germany, was engraved upon the walls of a pharaoh's tomb five thousand years ago.

With his hound's nose and terrier's disposition, the dachshund was a German badger hunter's dream. As early as 1840 he was included in an all-breed stud book, and by 1888 the dachshund was a member of the Official Teckel Club. Early dachshunds were larger than today's breed because they had to fight a 25 to 40 pound adversary. In packs they were, and still are, used in parts of Germany to hunt wild boar. In addition, they can track deer and occasionally fox. Germans even bred smaller dachshunds to track rabbits and stoats.

Importation of dachshunds predates the Teckel Club of Germany, and, by 1958, this dog was among the four most popular breeds in America. Today, dachsys are still in the top ten.

MYTHOLOGICALLY, THE DACHSHUND is second cousin of Anubis (first cousin is said to be the Ibizan hound), the jackal-headed Egyptian god who guided the souls of the dead to the afterworld.

The long-nosed, dagger-eared deity, Anubis, has more than a little dachshund in his makeup, even though the dachsy's ears are turned down instead of up.

The Egyptian Book of the Dead describes Anubis as a dog-man (head of a dog, body of a man) who turned up at Memphis in ancient Egypt to become known as Anpu, or Anubis. Later he was mythologized as the son of the sorceress Isis in her marriage to her handsome brother Osiris.

Anubis was called upon to conduct the dead to an oasis in the desert, a kind of paradise. He was, therefore, the Deity of the Dead, the Master of Embalming, the Lord of the Track.

If this seems a bit much to put upon our little dachsy, consider that these dogs have the deepest affinity for tombs and tunnels—and, gardeners beware, dachsys will trowel anywhere to get at anything they want. They are exceedingly self-willed and fully enflamed with purpose and passion. In keeping with their ancient tradition, they function excellently as diggers, trackers, night watchers, and nurses. Their greatest quality, however, is devotion, the same spiritual potency found in the dog-headed god, who, when Osiris was murdered, stayed by his side, helped with the burial, and stayed on to make sure that all was well.

Recently, a dachshund was credited with helping a lost ten-year-old with Down's syndrome return to his home. The boy was playing in his yard when he saw two stray dogs, one of them a dachshund and the other a heeler of some kind, trot past him. He then followed them deep into a forest, where, as temperatures dropped into single digits, the two dogs stayed by the boy's side, sheltering him from the wind. For three days they kept their charge alive, but it was the dachsy's resonant bark that led a man on horseback to the youngster, whose only injury, as it turned out, was frost-bitten toes. The dogs were called "God's angels" by the mother of the child, who has rewarded the dachshund with a permanent home (the family is still looking for the stray heeler).

And so, the role of Anubis as evidenced here and in other sacred myths, is not about the deliverance of life after death, but the journey through the mysterious veils of life itself.

The Lore of the Dog

The dachshund has a low-slung body, jokingly described as "two dogs long and a half a dog high." However, he is really considered quite robust. He may be a hot dog at first glance, but owners will tell you how hardy he is on the run or on the dig.

The name in German is *dachs* (badger) *hund* (dog) and he has the honor of being the national dog of Germany. His low clearance, powerful, pistonlike legs, and loose skin make him ideal for underground routing and cornering of his foe. He is also not a bad fighter; dachshund jaws are strong.

The tail stands in line with the dog's back. Claws are down-curved, ideal for clawing roots and spading soil. The feet look slightly splayed, turning out when the dog is standing still. The classic dachshund is odorless, sleek, dark, low-to-the-ground, and ready for action. Dachshunds come in a variety of coats, colors, and sizes. The coat may be short-haired, wire-haired, long-haired. Colors range from red, black and tan, grey and white, dappled, and even harlequin.

The dog's size varies: A miniature dachshund may weigh 9 pounds and stand 5 inches at the shoulder. A normal size is 12 to 22 pounds with a height of 7 to 10 inches.

Dachshunds are sporting, companionable, cheerful, and excellent watchdogs. They are wonderful with children, as they are both affectionate and possessive.

Dachshunds are born comics, but also serious watchdogs. They are courageous all the way to foolhardy. Their stubborn streak is legion and they do not always obey orders. The dachshund may be difficult to house train. Males will often feel an abiding need for marking territory, frequently indoors.

The intensity of a dachshund is such that he will focus on any family-oriented activity with interest and commitment. Look out if your special love is gardening because dachshunds like to dig more than anything else on, or in, earth.

DALMATIAN

Saint Dominic's Dog

JOHN BREDIN

THE EGYPTIAN PHARAOHS had high regard for this spotted warrior, and so did the monks of the Dominican Order. Gypsies roving the Balkans owned and trained the dalmatian and, more recently, firemen used him as a mascot, celebrating his dapper appearance on their emblems and insignias. Versatile and adaptable, this handsome harlequin has dashed from country to country, from aura to era, and from the rise of one civilization to the fall of another. Always dancing with swift and confidant strides, the dalmatian is the Dog of Dogges, a Canidae so talented that he may even be capable of writing, or barking, his own history.

Little is known of the dal's Egyptian chariot days except that he was at home with wheels from the very start. Once called the Bengal Harrier, he was used to hunt hares. The Indian designation came appropriately from the fact that at some time early on, the dalmatian was an Indian hunting dog. This fits with the later importation from India to Europe, for the dog was frequently found (anywhere from 1400–1900) in the desultory bands of Romanies. The gypsies, of course, enjoyed the dal's easy company and his gift with horses, so once again he was a coach dog par excellence. His designated homes are as many and various as his spots and like his gypsy masters, the dog roamed about and made the wide world his familiar home.

Some authorities place him in Dalmatia, a part of west Yugoslavia, hence, the name. During the Balkan wars of 1912–1913, the dal was used as a messenger, primarily in Dalmatia. Some think that he shared bloodlines with the Istrian pointer, but he has also been linked with the hounds in England and was there known as a "Talbot Dog."

It was said of the breed, "That all white was considered excellent; so were the all black. But if the white hounds were spotted with black, experience tells us that they are never the best hare hunters."

How the dalmatian got lumped into the hound family, we don't really know. It's possible he wasn't a good tracker. The American Kennel Club tells us, however, that the dal could be anything he wanted to be from a sentinel in war to a draft dog, shepherd, ratter, firehouse mascot, trail dog, retriever, pointer, pack dog, and circus dog. So what we have is a dog of all trades. A dog so versatile that, if he wanted to, could even be a different breed altogether—a hound perhaps, though without the partiality of nose that hounds have at birth.

ONE OF THE dalmatian's most auspicious appearances in the realm of myth was in a celebrated dream that came to the mother of St. Dominic, the man who founded the Dominican Order.

The dream in which the dog appeared showed him carrying a torch with which to set the world on fire. The teachings of Dominic were thus symbolized by the dog dream, and the Order itself depicted the dalmatian in many different kinds of church art. The black and white coat of the dog turned into the colors used by the Order—white robe, white hood, and a black cloak thrown over these. The Dominicans were thus known as *Domini canes:* that is, the "dogs of God," with the black and white dog holding the burning torch as a symbol that the order would put witches and heretics to the fire.

Medieval artists seized the ideogram of the dal and it became the focus of many paintings. The dalmatian appears, in addition, in Tuscany on a triptych featuring St. Domino (Dominic) blessing a chalice. The dog indicates the saint's power over the disease of hydrophobia, or rabies. Naturally, this ties in with the mythology of dog breath being sacred and dog saliva being curative.

The image of Dominic's fiery torch has been borne along with the dal's good looks to the present day. What painting of a nineteenth-century firehouse doesn't have a dalmatian in it? Just as the European noble's coach was incomplete without a dalmatian, trotting with the horses or riding on the driver's box, so, too, the nineteenth-century fire truck always had an heroic fire dog, invariably a dalmatian. These dogs, brought to the New World by immigrants, joined the fire brigades in Boston in the 1800s, and spread from there across the East and West Coast. The gypsies had used them to chase away wolves and they were also employed as ratters in London's stables and firehouses. The multiple uses of the dalmatian sealed a bond with humankind, for when the dog wasn't ratting, he was prancing (dalmatians could easily keep up with coach horses), and when not acting as a fireman's friend, riding on the front seat of a fire engine, he was dashing into the flames—the fireman's savior.

The breed's primary appearance in a dog show was in Great Britain in 1860. The first American show appearance was in 1926, when the Dalmatian Club of America held its first National Specialty Show. Today, the dalmatian ranks high as a family dog. His alert mind and quiet reserve make him a sensible, friendly companion. Yet for those who seek his vast reservoir of other uses, he is only too willing to comply.

The Lore of the Dog

The markings are most distinctive in this athletically built dog: perfect coin-sized black spots on a classically clean white coat.

Dalmatians are medium sized and short coated. Their build is for long-distance endurance and it is well muscled with a large deep chest. Females are generally smaller than males and many dalmatians today are much larger than the accepted breed standard.

Although the spots are present (but not visible) at birth, the fur is pure white, unless patched. At about two weeks the spots begin to appear, and the coat is fully developed within one year. Patches, rather than distinct spots, disqualify the dal from the show ring; however, many owners find these patches to be attractive. The spots themselves range in size from a dime to a half dollar.

The average height is between 21 and 27 inches. The weight between 48 and 55 pounds.

Dalmatians are energetic and require a lot of exercise. They are people-oriented and do best in and around families. They are very sensitive, can be sulky when scolded, because of their long memory. When they desire attention or want to share happiness they can be boisterous. Although they do poorly as full-time outdoor dogs (their short hair does not allow them to deal well with weather extremes), they were bred to run for hours, and this they love to do.

Their temperament is exuberant and optimistic. A well-bred dal will be aloof with strangers, but neither shy nor aggressive. Dals are vocal—they coo, grunt, and will give a whistling yawn when attempting to avoid scolding. However, they only bark when necessary. They are intelligent and good at situation-recognition.

One noteworthy quality is a full-toothed smile, or, as it is known among breeders, a "smarl," a combination smile and snarl.

DANDIE DINMONT TERRIER

Auld Mustard and Auld Pepper

MARIAH FOX

Named from a novelist's fancy, this lovable dog has been called the "drollest of canine comedians." Indeed, that is what he is—a humorous dog of utmost seriousness, a dour dog of wry Scottish mien, whose hunting prowess against fox, badger, stoat, and otter became renowned in Europe; but not by the dog's actions alone. In 1815, the author who is credited with having invented the historical novel, Sir Walter Scott, wrote a book called *Guy Mannering* in which he featured a character by the name of Dandie Dinmont. The novel took off and so did the reputation of Mr. Dinmont's dogs, "Auld Pepper, Auld Mustard, Young Pepper and Young Mustard, and Little Pepper and Little Mustard." These were six spicy terriers of amazing dedication and gallantry. As Dandie Dinmont warrants in the novel, here were three generations of game little dogs, the scourge of "rottens, stots, weasels, tods and brocks." In translation, rats, stoats, weasels, foxes, and badgers.

Word at the time had it that Dandie, as well as his dogs, were authentic Highland creations. However, Scott himself denied it, stating unequivocally that Dinmont was drawn from "A dozen, at least, of stout Liddesdale yeoman" with whom he was acquainted. The dogs, though, were closer to the bone, as it were, for there was an actual gentleman who had, in good Scottish humor, given his terriers these comic, generic monikers—and these real dogs, were, according to Scott, legendary. Their color, as you might expect, was yellow and grayish black and they came from "a wild farm on the very edge of the Teviotdale mountains . . . where the rivers and brooks divide as they take their course to the Eastern and Western seas."

The style of Scott's work was romantic and thus somewhat inimitable; his characters were fashionable to such a degree that during the life of the novel many Dandie Dinmonts were seen strolling about the cafes of Europe, as well as the brooky hills of the English-Scottish borderlands. The dogs caused even more of a stir. In Scott's own words: "An English lady of high rank and fashion, being desirous to possess a brace of the celebrated Mustard and Pepper terriers, expressed her wishes in a letter which was literally addressed to Dandie Dinmont," but it reached, instead, the man who was thought to be his attractive model, Mr. James Davidson. Scott said Mr. Davidson was "justly proud of the application, and failed not to comply with a request which did him and his favorite attendants so much honor." Once again, it would seem that art does not imitate life so much as the reverse.

How six little "feists" could create such controversy is questionable and curious, but they did it with aplomb—to this very day; so the myth lives on. Interestingly, there is no meaty description in the novel that would do the tykes this kind of literary justice; they are a statement of fact, as permanent a part of the countryside as the rock cairns, the bristly briars, the patchy furze, the milkmaid and ale-drinking laird. So the blue rills glitter, the foxwoods shine and beckon, and the little dogs bark cheerily as the great mists of Scotland close over them. It is heady stuff, Scott's writing, even today.

The Lore of the Dog

The name Dandie Dinmont seems just perfect for this distinctive breed. Long like a dachshund with a silky topknot and bushy beard, forelegs noticeably shorter than hind legs, tail at a jaunty angle, this dog is a composite of several other members of the Canidae family. Authorities say the mixture of Scottish terrier, Skye terrier, and possibly even basset hound are combined in the breed. As early as 1700, this terrier ran the rats out of the border country between England and Scotland. But, as one writer said, "it required a century and a literary masterpiece for the Dandie to come by his name."

The Dandie has a rough double coat with hard and soft hair, crisp to the touch. His colors are mustard and pepper, which is to say, any color from dark ocher to cream, and from blue-grey to silver. Height is 8 to 11 inches, weight 14 to 24 pounds.

The dog's delightful nature is implied in Dandie Dinmont's praise of him. Unafraid, he said, of anything "wi' a hairy skin on't." Yet, in addition, we have come to know that the Dandie is a loving friend to children, an apartment pal, as well as a country companion, a jokester who will stop at nothing to get a laugh, and a dog who can gauge human moods better than a stand-up comic. Naturally, the Dandie Dinmont terrier is a great watchdog, for as they say, Rats beware, cats retire, Dandie's back in town.

DINGO

The Dog of the Magellanic Clouds

MARIAH FOX

Dingo bones dating back six thousand years have been unearthed in Australia, but this wild barkless dog is not necessarily a native of that country. Rather, he is related to the New Guinea Singing Dog and the Middle Eastern Pariah Dog, both of which may have descended from the Malaysian dhole, a foxlike distant relative.

In Australia, the dingo is commonly feared by white ranchers because he is known to slaughter sheep, just as wolves are said to attack such livestock in parts of the American West. However, the Aboriginal people have a special fondness for dingoes, even permitting them to sleep with their children and to act as their guardians.

The Karadjeri people of Northwest Australia speak of the two dingoes who, after they died, rose into the sky. There, they became men. Before attaining the height of the sky, however, they stopped to urinate—first one, then the other. The two cloudlike nebulae, for which this myth speaks, are the Magellan Clouds.

The so-called Common Dog that lives on the island of Jamaica resembles the Australian and/or African dingo. The following tale told to us by a Jamaican elder is of African origin, and, as he put it, told to him by "foreparents." It shows the alliance many so-called third world cultures have between women and dogs as opposed to the male-dominated dog relationship of Europe and America.

Once in the long ago, the story goes, a man was out walking in the forest when he came upon a snake trapped in a hunter's net. As the man had nothing against things that crawled upon the ground, he set the snake free. The snake thanked him by saying that he was now going to confer a special honor upon the man.

Then the snake raised himself to the level of the man and placed his tongue on the man's tongue. Softly, the snake inscribed something there, and then he did lightly put his tongue to the man's ear; and there was left some knowledge there, too.

Then the snake explained what he had done: His blessing, he said, would enable the man to understand the language of the animals. Moreover, he would be able to speak to them the way they spoke, and an understanding between them would grow and deepen. In time, the man might learn a great deal from the ways of the animal people.

The snake departed and the man, pleased with his new, but as yet untried, powers went on his way through the forest.

Sometime later, the man was riding his horse through the forest. Along with him, also riding on horseback, was his wife, who traveled a few paces behind him. Suddenly, the wife's horse whinnied loudly. The man, hearing this, burst out laughing.

"What's so funny?" the wife demanded.

The man said, "If you must know, your horse just said something very funny. She said, 'Two ride up front, but four ride behind.' "

"That doesn't make any sense," the wife replied. "Besides, how do you know what the horse is saying?"

"I have powers," said the man. Then he added, "Don't you see? Two ride up front—that's me and my horse. Four ride behind—that's you and yours."

The wife said, "Only two ride behind."

"Not so," said the man. "For you know that you are pregnant. So is your horse, which makes up four."

Now the man was well satisfied with his explanation, but the woman dismissed what he said because she believed that he had taken leave of his senses. Some more time passed, and, by and by, the man found that his wife was unmanageable.

As always, whenever he heard the words of the animal people, he commented on them. And, as always, his wife criticized him, and said he was crazy. One day, however, while wandering in the forest, the man met the snake once again.

"How are you coming along with your new speech and hearing?" the snake asked.

"Poorly," the man confessed. "Whatever I hear in the forest causes my wife much annoyance. She is greatly troubled with me and I fear there will be no more children under my roof."

"What a shame," the snake said. "But maybe I can point you in the right direction. Do you see that thatch roof over there?"

The man nodded.

"That place belongs to Rooster. Let him show you the way."

So without further ado, the snake slid off into the bush and disappeared. The man had nothing to lose, so he took the snake's advice and went to the rooster, but all he saw there was a bunch of hens. The rooster strode among them with dignity, head held high, spurred feet making puffs of dust in the soft earth.

The man was puzzled. Why had the snake wanted him to visit the rooster? But just then the rooster raised his beak and cried sharply, and all the hens jumped into a tree. They stayed there while the rooster strutted about, and they eyed him carefully. Finally, the rooster beckoned them to come down and join him.

"Why did you do that?" the man asked the rooster.

The rooster replied, "For no reason, really. It's just good training. My wives—and I have many, as you can see—do what I tell them to do. And they had better do so, otherwise I use these—" The rooster pointed to the razor-sharp spurs that he wore on his golden feet.

"I believe I see what you mean," the man said. He stroked his chin thoughtfully while the rooster added, "Of course, if you have but one wife, you needn't exercise your power, for she will obey your every word. On the other hand, when you have as many wives as I do, it's necessary to keep them in line."

When the man left rooster's yard, he thought: I have but one wife, and she runs me up a tree all by herself. What am I to do? But he vowed, as he walked home, that he would do something. So that evening he cut a switch and when his wife spoke to him in a demeaning manner, he winnowed the air with his wand, and, using a voice he had never used before, ordered her up a tree.

He was amazed when, without hesitation, she followed his instruction. For a while, then, the man exercised control over the woman. But the woman, they say, is smarter than the man, so it wasn't long before the man's wife found a dog to take her switchings for her.

The dog, being of good will, agreed, but on one condition. "You must always look after me and see that I do not starve," he told the woman. Then she told the dog that she had always controlled the food, both coming and going, preparing and cooking. The man, she said, was completely dependent upon her in this way. Therefore, since she held dominion over food, she would see to the dog's needs.

The dog, not fearing beatings but always hungry, was glad to hear this. And the two made a bond that was cast in stone. Now, when the man got mad at the wife, the dog stumbled between them, and caused the man to get angry at him. That is why they say the man kicks the dog when aiming for the cat. It is also why the dog likes the woman better than the man, but it does not explain why the man and the woman still do not get along.

The Lore of the Dog

This wild dog is the forerunner of Canidae's earliest pinpoint existence with humankind.

The dingo's broad head is pointed at the muzzle, the ears erect and moderately pointed. The face is wide awake and alert, and the ears, though smaller than the Cape Hunting Dog, stand out from the angular lines of the face.

Dingoes have lithe, well-boned, deep-chested bodies built for long-distance running. The tail, carried horizontal, is bushy and has a white tip. Color ranges from yellow-brown to light red to plain brown; in Australia there is also a whitish breed. Quite often, dingoes are white-pawed.

They are 22 inches at the shoulder and weigh as much as 60 to 80 pounds.

Although wild dogs, dingoes are semidomesticated and are known to be the pets of the Aboriginal people of Australia.

There is conflicting opinion on the dog's background and behavior. For instance, some say that dingoes, called *warrigaul* by the Aborigines, live with their families only until they leave to mate with their own kind. Other experts disagree, their contention being that the dogs stay for long periods of time, years, in fact, and become fully acculturated "house pets." There is some evidence that young dingoes are suckled by Aboriginal women. Said to be a "one-man dog," the dingo is rarely, if ever, struck by the hand of his master.

Since the dingo is not an official breed, little exists in print on them. We believe they are known to be excellent hunter's companions and fine guardians in the primary setting from which they originated, the Middle East, Africa, and Australia.

However, it must be emphasized that, apart from those breeds, which have been crossbred with other members of the Canidae family, the dingo is a wild animal with all of the predilections of his kind.

DOBERMAN PINSCHER

The Tax Collector's Dog

JOHN BREDIN

I<small>N THE LATE</small> nineteenth century a tax collector and dog catcher named Louis Dobermann decided to breed an aggressive terrier to protect him on his rounds. What he came up with, most likely, was a combination Rottweiler, Manchester terrier, Beauceron, and greyhound. Much later, another breeder, Otto Geller, helped to refine Dobermann's guard dog, and he was also the one who defined the first standard in 1900.

When the Doberman came to the United States some years after this, the breed was honed into the tense-muscled, feline "attack dog" that is well known today. Gone was Louis Dobermann's roughed-out, course-bodied, ill-tempered dog. Legend declares that this dog was "afraid of nothing and no one, including the devil himself."

Indeed, this early breed was so ferocious that according to reports it took a good deal of courage just to own one; even a two-month-old puppy, they say, would emit a scary growl.

Today's Doberman is a finely tuned and better balanced version of the earlier one. Still an expert fighter, still an alert guardian, the modern Dobie is responsive to commands rather than being a hair-trigger attack dog. Over the years, his history of police work, war service (which drastically reduced the breed's numbers), and guard-dog devotion gave the animal a prestigious dossier. Less well known but equally important is the fact that Dobermans are among the best guides for the blind. The Doberman Pinscher Club of America was formed in 1921 and did much to increase the dog's popularity in America where he commands a definite place in today's top ten most popular breeds.

DOBERMAN MYTHS OFTEN mirror this cool-eyed, quicksilver prowler. One famous tale is actually a rehash of the thirteenth-century Gelert ballad. The essence of the Gelert theme is that the dog's owner, a Welsh prince, returns home and sees an overturned cradle.

Puddles of blood lie beside it, and, nearby, the man's wolfhound has a blood-stained mouth. In haste—fearing the death of his son—the angry prince slays his dog before assessing the situation. This is the man's (and mankind's) undoing, for he turns to find a dead wolf on the other side of the room and his child, unhurt, underneath the upset cradle.

This same myth has journeyed over seven centuries to resurface with much variation in such an unlikely place as Las Vegas, Nevada.

In the new Gelert tale, a woman returning home from work finds her Doberman choking on something. Worried about the dog's welfare, she rushes him to the vet, who explains to her that she should go back home while he performs a tracheotomy.

No sooner does the woman arrive at her home than the phone rings. It's the vet telling her to leave the house immediately, and to call the police from a pay phone so they can investigate a burglary that has taken place on the premises.

The woman does as instructed, then she returns to the vet. She finds that her Doberman was choking on three human fingers that were deeply lodged in his throat. Moreover, when she calls the police again, they tell her that a burglar, who just happens to be missing three fingers, was apprehended in her apartment.

This same story traveled across America, being retold in countless ways.

Occasionally, the storyteller places the dog in the backseat of a car in the parking lot of a shopping mall. Sometimes the event takes place in a bedroom, adding a sexual nuance to the gruesome tale. However, the constant theme is that of an heroic dog and a punished intruder.

Eventually these urban legends became known as "The Choking Doberman," and they began to circulate in the 1980s in newspapers throughout the country. Often the myth was fashioned as fact, though the stories could never be fully corroborated.

In both "Gelert" myths, the true guardian is the dog. In each, as well, the dog's ferociousness is the target of some irony; the efforts of Gelert cost him his life, while the Doberman frequently dies from asphyxiation. The dog hero in each of the two tales is praised and turned into legend. The old folk-myth causes the listener to draw a breath. The new one draws forth a gasp—and there's the difference.

One could call the contemporary tale—for lack of a better word—disgusting. While the old Gelert myth surmounts the blood of the ironic event, the Choking Doberman tale (sorry) chokes on it.

This was not overlooked by journalists, who ran the Choking Doberman story with puns aplenty. Some referred to the incident as "putting the finger" on a crook. Others said, "You'll find this story pretty hard to swallow." Still others claimed the story revealed "hard-bitten truths." Basically, all of these myths suggest that we still put our faith in dogs, not men; and thankfully, we still have dogs to protect us from our worst intentions.

The Lore of the Dog

The exaggerated claims on Dobermans run in hyperbolic glee: the dogs are called catlike, cat-footed, with the disposition of a black panther. They are sleek, alert, vicious, dangerous dogs who have been compared to "loaded guns with hair triggers." They're known to have nerves of steel and steel-springed haunches.

These super-watchful athletic dogs are normally black and tan, as well as brown or blue. Of medium build and very muscular, they have straight forelegs and a tucked-up belly. Overall, the Doberman is clean lined and sleek.

The head is long, triangular, and the nose is pointed. The ears are usually dropped, but, in some countries, cropped. Erect ears, cropped to thin points, may be preferred; however, in England it is against the law to crop them. The tail is most often docked, accentuating hind-end muscularity.

Dobermans have short, glossy fur, silky to the touch. They stand 25 to 27 inches tall and weigh in at 44 to 57 pounds, though the weight can be much more.

The Doberman is easily disciplined and quick to learn. Though full of raw, animal energy, whose presence often provokes fear, this dog is born to be respectful and fulfills the old adage, "No bad dogs, just bad owners." The inquiring glance on the Doberman's face seems to be asking what it should do next. The dog is always awaiting a climatic command. Some have been so well trained that, even though food is set before them, they will not eat until told to do so. In addition, the command to stop eating will immediately bring a well-trained Doberman's head up.

Good-tempered, courageous, extremely athletic, and ardently disciplined are words that typically describe the dog's overall traits. To have a Doberman as companion, rather than exclusive guardian, one must devote time to early training in this regard. On the other hand, as guardian, the dog may be the best of the lot. Dobermans seem to sense the criminal at work and the crime is sometimes revealed to them before it is committed. The consciousness of the animal applies to machines as well as human beings. Cases have been cited in which a Doberman wouldn't rest, while on night duty, until his master turned off a certain machine that was due to become overheated. The dog whined in front of the machine until it was shut off.

Males and females have different temperaments. The male is aggressive and intelligent, but must be firmly disciplined or he may become unstable. Exercise plays an important part in this; without it, the dog may grow agitated. The female is more gentle, also a very fine guardian, and needs exercise as well.

Dobermans, generally, are not recommended for families with small children. For adults, it is suggested that the owners be good disciplinarians. A "dominant personality" seems to work best in Doberman training.

DOGUE DE BORDEAUX

The Dogue of Dogs

MARIAH FOX

THE DOGUE DE Bordeaux, or French Mastiff, is a well-established breed in France, and is now becoming popular throughout the world. The earliest Dogue de Bordeaux was a fierce descendant of the formidable Tibetan Mastiff. The American Kennel Club states: "Every partisan would like to claim the greatest antiquity for his particular sort of mastiff as well as to say the other sorts sprang from it." Cuneiform inscriptions, however, enable us to trace mastiffs back to 2000 or 3000 B.C. The Sumerian ideogram for dog is the same for servant, valet, and slave.

In addition, the British Museum has a Sumerian bowl, dating 3000 B.C., which shows a dog hunt in the marshes of Babylon. Bas-reliefs and Persian bronzes, from China to Great Britain, show great-shouldered, square-headed dogs of mastiff blood, chasing and cornering the wild ass and, armored and spike-collared, fighting alongside the legions of men. Obviously, the mastiff has his place in history, and, alongside the greyhound, possesses a bloodline of hunting and war going back to the earliest Metal Ages of man.

In Egypt, the influence of the Hyksos people during the Middle Empire introduced both the greyhound and, it is thought, the mastiff. The Egyptians freed themselves of the Hyksos, but they kept the mastiff. The Eighteenth Dynasty pharaoh, Tutankhamen, is depicted on a wooden casket standing upright in his chariot. He shoots arrows at Nubian soldiers, who are being harried by his Assyrian dogs.

So the mastiff, who was not so good at hunting water fowl or antelope, had a more specific assignment: to hunt men. This he did well, not by tracking them, but by fighting them in soldierly style. Here, then, was the ultimate soldier's dog, the devouring dog of myth, the magnificent, cream-coated canine, whose wrought-iron spiked collar was fearful to the fleeing enemy. (Henry VII used the same device on his mastiffs when they went into battle to protect their necks). While the cat may have had some precedence over the dog—though not, perhaps, by much—the killing of a dog in Egypt warranted the death penalty.

HISTORY VARIES ON how and where the Dogue de Bordeaux came to Europe, but the current theory is that Alexander the Great brought the dog from India to Greece about 300 B.C. The Greeks, it is said, introduced the mastiff to the Romans. However, Caesar, who wrote of the invasion of Britain in 55 B.C., describes the great dogs fighting next to their British masters.

In any case, the dogs were definitely employed to fight in the Roman Circus. Their combatants included, of course, men, but also bears, bulls, lions, and tigers. Much later, in the nineteenth century, the English themselves adopted a similar program. Their version of the Roman Circus was Westminster Pit, which contained some three hundred seats. The word "fancier," as in dog, is synonymous with the word bettor; once again, as in dog. Thus, even after such brutal events were outlawed in England (around 1835), the sport lived on.

The word Westminster was the equivalent of dog, while fighting dog was equal to mastiff. Although he was usually noted as a fighting dog, the mastiff enjoyed a two thousand–year popularity in England as, ironically, perhaps, a family dog. However, it was his fighting prowess, his legendary ferocity, that achieved this for him. People felt safe in this dog's company and accordingly treated him very well. Keeping mastiffs was compulsory for peasants, in order to keep down the "savage beast" population. Chaucer's *Knight's Tale* celebrates a mastiff described as a "white Alaunt." The word *alan* (wolfhound) comes from the Italian-French, and it is still used in English heraldry to depict the cropped-eared mastiff on a coat of arms.

THE MYTHOLOGY OF mastiffs is equally blurred by the hazy line of history. Herodotus tells of the founder of the Persian Empire, Cyrus the Great, who received a gift of a mastiff from the King of Albania. Pitting the mastiff against a bull, Cyrus found that the mastiff was disinclined to fight. So he had the dog killed. This enraged the king, who, in giving Cyrus another mastiff, warned him that the dog ought to fight worthy opponents. These, he said, were lions and elephants.

Eventually, the second mastiff did fight an elephant. The big-headed dog brought the elephant to the ground and would've killed the animal had it not been stopped. History or myth?

All we know is that Cyrus raised mastiffs, and he gave four towns in Babylon the responsibility of breeding and training them for battle. But whether or not a mastiff ever met an elephant in the ring is a hyperbolic sort of question.

The Greek myth of Cerberus tells of a mastiff-like dog who is posted at the gate of Hades. A monstrous watchdog, he carries, depending on the teller of the tale, anywhere between three and fifty heads, and he has "a voice of bronze."

Robert Graves in his mythological masterpiece *The White Goddess* describes him as a "cognate beast, with the usual triad of heads—lioness, lynx and sow." Usually Cerberus, a creature of the night, possesses a mouth dripping with serpents and black venom. Hercules fought with Cerberus, defeating him in a mighty stranglehold; but his great feat in subduing the dog was obtained by offering him a sweet honey cake, obviously fermented, because it had the effect of narcosis on the brute.

Another Greek mastiff myth tells of Hephaestus, whose golden creation was a great, man-high dog. Given to Rhea, the earth goddess, the golden dog was supposed to guard the infant Zeus. Later on, he (the dog) was stolen by Tantalus. The animal's theft caused the thief to receive a "tantalizing" eternal punishment: to be buried alive. The word "tantalize" actually stems from this ancient myth.

In the comic action film *Turner and Hooch,* the main character, played by Tom Hanks, is the inheritor of a murdered man's Dogue de Bordeaux. The dog teams up with Turner, a detective, and ultimately apprehends his master's murderer.

Even though the great dog dies at the end of the film, the viewer senses that such a dog would rather die in battle, defending what is right, than to waste away with the indignity of old age.

The Lore of the Dog

The massive Dogue has the face only a mother could love. The head is huge, and though square, it still seems like a wrecker's ball. Some descriptions render the head as if it were the only visible part of the body. The jowls hang down and are usually silvery with saliva.

The Dogue stands on short, muscular legs and has a lion's physique, complete with sparred ribs and catlike hindquarters.

The ears are relatively small and drop down. The tail is tapered and doesn't reach past the hock. The paws are leonine with strong toes and nails.

Colored fawn or in the tawny range, the coat is short, thick, and even, with white marks sometimes on the chest and feet and occasionally a black or red mask.

Height ranges from 23 to 26 inches with a weight up to 210 pounds.

The Dogue is a superior guardian with a formidable appearance. However, his true nature is one of steady and peaceful equanimity. His devotion without peer, a Dogue will gladly sacrifice his life for a loved one. Suspicious of strangers, the dog imprints, generally, to one master. However, after this loyalty, he is very loving of his master's family. Dogues are stoic and deal with pain as if it were only to be endured. He has dignity rather than gaiety, and his maxim is to always be watchful.

ENGLISH SPRINGER SPANIEL AND THE BRITTANY SPANIEL

The Sprung Spaniel

JOHN BREDIN

THE NAME "SPRINGER" comes from the dog's ability to crouch and spring forward, driving game into the open for the hunter. For the solitary hunter afoot, there is no better dog, and the springer is best used in wood or marsh, alone. Here is a dog of great energy, whose talent is not merely the art of flushing, but the searching that leads up to it.

The seventeenth-century text the "Art of Fowling" says: "To search is the perfectest character of the most perfectest spaniels." Translated into utilitarian terms, the springer is, without doubt, the dog of scent-superlative, addicted to the hunting of anything feathered. This means that he will pursue with unflagging passion, going into deep cover and springing the birds from the secrecy of their brambly hiding places. Once they fly, he freezes, the hunter shoots, and once given the command to retrieve, the whirly dog is in motion once again. Pointing and retrieving are two of his finest skills, though he is a wonderful water dog, loving the wade, the plunge, the swim.

Historically, the springer is the parent of all the other spaniels. In the

1800s, springers and cockers were born in the same litter, the only difference being their size and weight; any dog over 28 pounds was classified as a springer. Once the dog was officially adopted with a definite standard, the springer became a uniform breed, and, as the cocker was an indispensable house pet, the springer remained in the outdoors, a master of the working-hunting trade.

In 1902 the English Kennel Club recognized the springer spaniel as a distinct breed. Five years later he was introduced into North America and registered ten years after. It wasn't until 1927 that the springer was given official status by the American Kennel Club.

CERTAIN ODDITIES OF character have given birth to some rather curious springer myths, one of which is the story of the spaniel and the Pope.

It seems that a spaniel may have been responsible for the foundation of the Church of England. As the story goes, Henry VIII sent Lord Wiltshire as ambassador to Rome to obtain permission for his divorce from Catherine of Aragon. Upon arriving, the lord was ushered into the pope's presence, whereupon he knelt and prepared to kiss the pontiff's toe. To aid the lord in his beseechment, the pope raised his foot rather suddenly. At this point, Lord Wiltshire's devoted spaniel, crouching at his heel, sprang into the air and bit the pope's toe. Was it not a springer spaniel, crouching, springing, protecting—all the notable qualities of the finest hunt dog galvanized into action?

Count Gaston de Foix, writing in the 1300s, summed the spaniel disposition thusly: "They love their master well." Moreover, springers are noted for a special phobia: They may spring upon someone wearing an odd hat, wearing a strange perfume, or behaving in a manner unfitting—this is entirely up to spaniel discretion.

So the question remains: Did the pope merely offend the dog by threatening, as the spaniel's eye perceived it, his master's face? Or was it a subtlety of the pontiff's dress—his unusual headgear? We shall always wonder, and we shall never know.

In any case, poor Wiltshire had to return to England and tell the mercurial Henry that he'd been unable to get a grant from the pope because his dog had committed an indiscretion upon the pope's toe.

Ah, history, ah, myth—who knows which it is, or what it was, that really happened. All we know is what occurred after the fact, or fiction, as it were. To wit, Henry didn't get a divorce, but instead divorced England from Rome. And all because a noble member of the Canidae family was just doing his job.

Possible moral: Kiss not the foot of a stranger, no matter how mighty he/she might be. Or, kiss whatever foot you want, but make sure to leave your spaniel at home.

The Lore of the Dog

The English springer spaniel resembles the cocker spaniel, although he is definitely the parent of the two breeds. The most powerful of the hunting spaniels, the springer is deep-chested and has thrusting hindquarters, which provide the characteristic "spring."

The webbed feet, a trait of swimming dogs (otter hounds and New-foundlands, for example) and other water spaniels, enable springers to move swiftly in the water and smoothly across tidal and/or mud flats and river banks.

The white coat is marked with liver, black, tan, roan, or liver and tan. At the tail, legs, and throat, the glossy fur is well-feathered. The smooth coat is also weatherproof and thornproof, but gets easily tangled and must be brushed often.

The springer's wide rounded head, long ears, and wonderful, kind eyes give it a compassionate appearance, the look of the friend who will never leave and will always understand. According to most spaniel owners, this is nothing less than the truth. The average springer is 20 inches with a weight between 49 and 53 pounds.

The springer is friendly, and with training, an obedient companion for the hunt or the home. His training, however, must be sensitive and never harsh. Springers are unusually sensitive and shouldn't be treated with impatience. They need to be handled persuasively, not sharply. Their response to gentle authority will be returned with tractable behavior. They get along well with strangers and with children, but can develop phobias, such as exaggerated fears of objects or even of certain unexpected people. The list might include anything from an article of unfamiliar clothing to an unknown object.

The hunt-suspended springer is happiest when pleasing friends and family, but if not given occasional challenges and rewards, he may feel a little lost or despondent. Springers love any play that is retrieval-oriented, such as ball-chasing.

THE BRITTANY SPANIEL, a cousin of the English springer spaniel, comes from the province of Brittany in France. His ancestors, some say, ranged the Breton Coast in medieval times. The dog possesses two special traits. One, he has no tail; and two, he points like a setter. This is probably because many years of inbreeding had caused the line to weaken; however, around 1900 a French sportsman named Enaud introduced the blood of Italian and French pointers to strengthen the Brittany.

The Brittany spaniel is deep-chested and strong with the appearance of a small but vigorous hunter. The head is round, the muzzle short, and the alert eyes are set well into the head. The ears are drop, high-set, and fringed. The coat is fine but dense, and can be wavy or flat. Height is about 17 to 20 inches, weight 28 to 39 pounds.

Brittanies are white and orange, white and brown, white and black, liver and white, tricolor or roan. There is feathering on the front legs and on the hind legs to mid thigh.

Single-minded when it comes to hunting, the Brittany spaniel has earned the reputation of stubbornness. This quality, when combined with his other all-around talents, such as pointing and retrieving, has made him one of the most sought after bird-dogs in the hunting world.

THE SMOOTH AND THE WIRE-HAIRED FOX TERRIER

Terrar, Dog of Earth

JOHN BREDIN

JOHANNES CAIUS, THE Elizabethan authority on dogs, remarked that:

> Terrars, which hunteth the fox and the badger or greye only, whom we call terrars because they, after the manner and custome of Ferrets, in searching for the connies, creep into the grounde and by that means make afrayde, nyppe and byte the foxe and badger in such sort, that eyther they teare them in pieces with theyr teeth beying in the bosome of the earth, or else hayle and pulle them perforce out of their lurking angles, darke dongeons, and close caves. . . .

Ah, so true, one is tempted to say, so true, and so contemporary. For these dogs are little changed from what they once were, and what they were and are is nothing less, but certainly more than, a terror.

Historically, terriers were the dog of the common man. They originated in the British Isles, and in fact, Pliny the Elder mentioned in 55 B.C. that the Romans found "small dogs that would follow their quarry to ground." After most of the larger dogs in England had killed off predatory animals, as well as meat-bearing quarry, the people's love of the hunt did not diminish, even though their sources of hunting were almost gone from the land. Instead, smaller dogs were then employed to hunt smaller animals, and this became, once again, a national pastime. Each hamlet in the Isles during the eighteenth century had a favorite terrier to terrorize the rodents and burrowing pests of that community.

When colonialism became rampant and England sent the Union Jack across the varied seas, the little terriers went along for the ride, and, of course, later, for the hunt. Wherever this dog went, there appeared to be a quarry worth evicting, biting, hauling, pulling, and otherwise dismembering.

In the 1820s the Westminster Pit was an orgy of terrierlike activity. By glimmering candlelight, swift dogs were set upon hoards of rats, which were dispatched by the best of the breed. One famous terrier named Billy was famous for slaying and slinging one hundred rats in five and a half minutes. After England's first all-breed show at Newcastle in 1859, breeders began to concentrate on improving the terrier's looks. The fox terrier, in particular, benefited from this, growing stylishly longer of head and leg. However, many local huntsmen wouldn't risk losing the "terrar of the terrier" for anything, and they bred such closely related, older breeds as the Border, Lakeland, and Welsh terrier strictly for the hunt—and to hell with fashion.

The fox terrier's white fur originates from the practical use to which the dog was put in hunting foxes. Coming out of the earth, an ordinary terrier would be covered with dirt. Sometimes these terriers were mistaken for foxy quarry by the accompanying hounds, and the poor little dogs would be ripped apart by their own teammates. So, to counteract this canine confusion, breeders and hunters alike crossed the terrier with the foxhound, and thus the fox terrier was born, a dog of white fur, unmistakable on the field.

A fox terrier story came to us recently in the following form. We were informed by a friend that when he was growing up, his uncle had a most unusual fox terrier. Apparently, the dog would, on any occasion, be able to guess where a certain object was hidden.

The uncle hadn't trained the dog, per se, or given him any instructions in the matter. In fact, the whole enterprise began as a small half-hearted game. The man would place a domino under the couch. Then he would think where he'd placed it while his fox terrier, in another room, got the idea telepathically, and jumped up from where he was sitting to fetch the domino.

The dog was unfailing in his success. The hide and seek game got more and more baroque in style until there were all kinds of small objects hidden under many different pieces of furniture, all in odd rooms of the house. The dog, invariably, found them all. What made the game seem magnificent to the boy (our friend) was that his uncle never prepared the dog for the game; he just hid the stuff while his nephew stayed with the dog. Then he'd call his terrier and, together, they would commune silently for a moment. Suddenly, the dog would dash wildly away to unearth hidden pencils, spoons, spools, keys, and bottle caps.

Always, without fail, the dog knew where to go and what to do.

Was it a look, a twinkle, a clue, perhaps, in the uncle's eyes?

Our friend says no. The game was simple—just find and fetch.

The dog went out of the room, and with perfect terrier technique, went to earth and found his fox.

The Lore of the Dog

The texture of the coat is the only difference in the wire-haired and smooth fox terrier, but their similarity is legion—an aggressive terrier presence that can be triggered by the slightest movement or sound. However, these happy, curious creatures are intelligent and companionable and make excellent, if sometimes mischievous, friends.

A long pointed head with small V-shaped ears, flaps pointed forward, sits on a strong muscular body with a docked tail. The eyes are dark and circular. In the wire-haired variety, the coat is wiry and dense with a thick undercoat of softer hair. The face is adorned with a beard and mustache. The smooth-haired dog has straight, flat dense fur. The color is predominantly white with brindle red or liver markings. Height is about 15 inches, weight 16 to 18 pounds.

Since the great age of ratting, one hundred years ago, the fox terrier has been an outstanding family dog. These are sociable and affectionate animals, noted for their devotion to family, and equally watchful of household and home.

GERMAN SHEPHERD

The Dog of All Trades

JOHN BREDIN

ALTHOUGH THE ORIGIN of the German shepherd should include a cross with sheepherding dogs and wolves, most experts do not put this dog in the lupus category. In reality, the present day German shepherd was bred in the 1880s by a German cavalry officer, Max von Stephanitz. He was the one who crossed several European shepherds, in order to arrive at the great seeing-eye police pal—the dog of all trades. The first society for the breed was founded in Germany in 1899, and today, it remains one of the largest clubs of its kind in the world.

In the 1950s and '60s German shepherds were enormously popular in America. *Rin Tin Tin,* the TV serial, presented Rinty, the iconographic German shepherd whose heroism was the basis of the show. Faithfully, he watched over his young master, Rusty, the son of an officer in a U.S. Calvary unit. The wide interest in this program was partly the result of America's mesmerized Boy Scout nation, but it also had something to do with the dog's penetrating gaze and medallionlike stance.

Who knows how many millions of Scouts fell into those episodes every Saturday morning? Those who were blessed by owning a German shepherd invited their neighbors to join in homemade "Rinty scripts," which transformed sad suburban yards into the glittering cactus lands of Fort Apache.

Around the same time as *Rin Tin Tin,* a slim volume appeared that was to reshape what many people thought of as animal intelligence. The book is called *Kinship with All Life* by J. Allen Boone. Today, it is considered a classic of interspecies communication.

What Boone does is deceptively simple. As caretaker of the famous German shepherd, Strongheart, a celebrated acting dog in Hollywood, Boone raises a series of unfathomable questions—basically boiling down to one biggie: What is the meaning of life? This and many other similar queries are put to Strongheart, who, Boone tells us in his book, answers telepathically. "For the first time I understood how dumb a human can be in the presence of an intelligent animal," says Boone.

For Boone, the answers to his philosophical entreaties are learned the hard way—while trying to teach the dog how to be a proper human being. He fails in this attempt, but he succeeds in discovering that Strongheart is not, as he'd supposed, the mere summation of strategic training.

True, he is one of a long line of carefully bred, efficiently trained, blue-ribbon dogs from a major kennel in Germany, but Boone finds that Strongheart is much more than a dog with a quick mind. He is even more than a dog with a human mind.

As he says: "Then I knew that what I was actually being privileged to watch was not a dog expressing great qualities, but rather, great qualities expressing a dog."

So the roles of man and dog reverse; Boone turns into the student and Strongheart becomes the teacher. In the course of time, the dog that Boone was "babysitting" teaches *him* to read minds, to think, to see the arrangement of things in the universe without judgment, and to be more at home with himself.

Boone discovers that Strongheart can relax at any time, while, he, the inexorable human, cannot. However, he can learn; and so he does, with Strongheart's help. The dog gives the man the confidence to see things as they are, as faultless and illimitable, neither human nor animal in nature. Whether it's a romp at the beach, an afternoon nap, or the slow beauty of a sunset, Boone begins to discern that he has an inner eye, an ability to see "into" as well as "onto" the surface of things.

To be taught policework by a police dog would be one order of business (indeed, perhaps all police partners, humans and dogs, ought to learn from each other). But, to be taught metaphysics by a dog, an animal thought to be less than a chimpanzee, is something else again:

I had long been under the impression that while I lived in the upper levels of existence, all animals, not even excluding Strongheart, had to do their living on much lower and relatively unimportant mental and physical levels; and that between them and myself there could be certain rather limited service ties, but not much else.

In the end, Strongheart suggests through polite telepathy that he is tired of being read books, asked questions, and drawn into endless conversations. He wants to experience life, he says to Boone, on a firsthand or first-paw basis. He doesn't want to know anything about the thing; he wants to know the thing itself. Here, Boone realizes, the dog is much superior to the man.

D OG MYTHS, OF course, delve into the realm of animal intelligence in comic and portentous ways, but always, they assume that all people know that dogs began on Earth by having a close relationship with the primordial elements, the deities of wind, fire, and water, while Man was just coming to know them.

Myths tell us that Dog has teeth before Man. They explain that Dog knew the hunt before Man ever learned the art.

They say that Dog knows Fire, but that Man hasn't been blessed with knowledge of it yet.

Most importantly, the old myths imply that Dog's knowledge of God precedes Man's. These are the many truths taught by the cultural myths of indigenous people around the world. Dog is not an unranked citizen on the plane of existence in any of these myths; in fact, he is often a representative of "First Man."

If this is anthropologically credible, why, then, have we always insisted that dogs are inferior beings? Why have we treated them so?

Boone learns that dogs greatly surpass humans beings in the area of telepathy, and that we are what he calls "mental nudists." A dog can read us like an open book, though we have a harder time reading most dogs.

Dogs, kindly characters that they are, usually have the grace to keep silent about what they know, while clearly we are incapable of such beatitude. Dogs are quite certain of where they stand in relation to us, and we to them, as their so-called masters. But the truth is, they know us as we do not know them.

The Lore of the Dog

Large and powerfully built, the German shepherd also has an elongated frame with a fine, long, low tail that is slightly arched at the end. German shepherds have a dignified face which is triangular, with upright ears set against a dark wolflike muzzle. The eyes are almond-shaped and slightly slanted.

A thick, stiff outer coat covers a softer inner one; the length of coat varies with the dog.

The German shepherd's thighs are muscular and the hips are broad and well-placed for jumping and thrusting.

Colors range from black to tan to mixtures of these. There is usually a dark, or black, saddle. The dog is generally 23 to 25 inches in height and weighs 60 to 85 pounds.

The intelligence and resourcefulness of the German shepherd have long been admired. This breed has made remarkable contributions as a guard dog, sheep dog, companion dog, family dog, guide dog, rescue dog, and an army and police dog.

Beginning training for German shepherds is advisable at the age of ten weeks. Poor training of the dog in 1920s England was cited as one reason why German shepherds were unreliable as companions, but were nonetheless excellent guard dogs. Until the 1970s the breed was known in Great Britain as Alsatian, or Alsatian wolf dog, because of anti-German sentiment.

Although German shepherds are best known as service dogs, they are also great family pets and have a deserved reputation for not only being serious, but also playful within the context of the family.

GERMAN SHORT-HAIRED POINTER

The Perfect Pointer

JOHN BREDIN

IN ENGLAND, IN 1650, hunting dogs were not gun dogs and pointers were not pointers—yet. This was quite simply because a practical firing weapon hadn't been invented. The world awaited the sportsman's gun, but while it waited, feathered game was sprung for the hawk and ground animals were caught by the net. Naturally, hounds and spaniels were sought for each of these activities; however, with the invention of the sporting gun around 1680, a new dog came to the fore. This remarkable animal was the pointer.

The delicate art of pointing—how it began and what thought was placed upon it—is not fully known, but the gun had so much to do with the dog's development that one might say, "they grew up together."

When on the hunt a sportsman had to get his firing-piece ready; he had to see that the priming was properly in place and the pan held the powder. When these two were in good order, the hunter would then think about raising his gun and firing it.

First however, he must think of his dog, for the pointer's stance was everything, and it held the key to a successful hunt. Besides being a compass, pointing toward the game that the hunter sought, the dog was a barometer of patience and perseverance.

Standing and waiting, waiting and standing—these were the dog's order of the day. The pointer, as much by habit as by preference, developed a stance of such telling virtue that the hunter could read it like a road map; in it was distance, velocity, value and kind, all things the hunter needed to know. Some pointers would stand in place for as long as two hours until the game was flushed upward and a shot was fired. Here was a dog that probably wished to bound into the thicket instead of stand before it as if mounted on a board. So, what held him, what froze him in place?

It's been suggested that pointers suffer from a kind of hypnotic restraint, causing them to prolong the moment before springing. This may seem far-fetched to some, but in any case, the solitary huntsman needed a dog that would move slowly and methodically along with him, a dog responsive to inner and outer messages of almost psychic exactitude. The pointer was a perfect candidate for this and he became the favorite of German nobles and poachers, the latter of whom used him mostly at night, when the dogs carried lanterns fastened to the top of their heads.

The pointer hunts by scent, by smelling the game, then assuming the rigid, nose-lifted, tail-high position of the classic point. That isn't all; at the same time the dog's body freezes and his head and tail go up, he raises his front foot ever so lightly.

If the front foot is up but the tail isn't raised, the dog may still be scenting but not truly pointing. In order for the true point to happen, there has to be union between all of the dog's physical responses.

The final—and most critical—signal is "the tremble." Over the full length of the pointer's body there flexes vibrational tremor, so that the whole dog quivers with expectation, particularly his nose.

This is the pièce de résistance, the consummation of the pointer's train-ing and being. It's also the precise moment he achieves his rightful point.

James Watson's *The Dog Book* contains an eighteenth-century poem by a poet named Gay describing the pointer's art as a thing of beauty:

> *See how the well-taught pointer leads the way:*
> *The scent grows warm; he stops; he springs the prey;*
> *The fluttering coveys from the stubble rise,*
> *And on swift wing divide the sounding skies;*
> *The scattering lead pursues the certain sight,*
> *And death in thunder overtakes their flight.*

The Complete Sportsman published in England in 1689, by Thomas Fair-fax, makes mention of the ritual that precedes the fowler's raised piece. Here we find the ritual that ranks as high as the art of the shoot itself: "Go early into the field," he recommends, "take with you some rum in a wicker bottle that will hold about a gill; this will keep out or expel wind, cure the gripes, and give you spirit when fatigued; but do not take too much, for too much will make your sight unsteady. When you have got your gun, a turn screw, worm and flints ready, call your pointers."

So the perfect point of the dog is equal in measure to the moment of readiness in the man; both, it would seem, have a point in them, and these must work, in turn, to the timing of an autumn dance. The hunt itself is as important in every respect as the outcome, the whole thing being a kind of seasonal symphony rising toward that sudden, but expected, thunderclap of the gun.

THE GERMAN SHORT-HAIRED pointer—as an ineluctable breed, won through a perfect union of man and nature—is subject to question. It is thought that he came from the mixed blood of the legendary Spanish pointer (who was reputed to hold a point for twelve hours) and the St. Hubert hound. The pointer of 1600, the result of these two lines, was a bit heavier and stouter than today's dog. Some years later, the English pointer and the Italian pointer were mixed, and thus the German pointer of 1860 came about. This dog had greater speed, a better nose, and was a finer tracker and retriever. Some say that the English foxhound was added to the line, giving the animal quickness of foot, as well as patience afoot.

The German short-haired pointer of today, if pure bred, comes from such fine original stock, and has not changed at all from his nineteenth-century predecessor.

In America, the so-called plantocracy gave the pointer some extra point-ers, which may account, at times, for members of the breed resembling some of their legendary handlers. A pointer that acts rangy and unruly will suddenly whip around, straighten up, and point like the North Star. As Charles Gray, the author of *Dawgs*, described it, "The tail and muzzle aloft, like a violin string had been stretched from the tail to the back of the head, and somebody had reached down and pulled it taut."

A young breakaway dog that has his work ahead of him, but who flies low, skimming the alfalfa like a swallow, suddenly comes to a full point "so hot it smokes." This is not only just what the doctor ordered, but just what the trainer needs to win a championship.

This is a discovery dog, a figure of style and steadiness, a ground-quarterer, who knows his business and won't let anything (like a distracting deer or a beckoning gulley) break his trance. Young and untrained though he may be, his blood is fired for the one-eyed moment of truth with God's birds, and he knows the autumnal dance without having had many seasons to perfect it.

Some dogs have the point down before they begin, others never really learn it properly, though they try. The difference between a true point and a false one is like the nautical error that grounds a ship; it can be heard as well as seen.

The skimming style, the whirl, the simultaneous raise of nose, ear, and tail is something so akin to art, it cannot be described without metaphors. It is an effort of generations cut to a single, self-styled stroke that would be easy if it weren't so hard. Having seen it, "it's not forgot."

The Lore of the Dog

The German short-haired pointer is lean and clean, sturdy and symmetrical, designed for the hunt. The back is short and level. The horizontally carried tail is usually docked. The broad head is set upon sloping muscular shoulders; the muzzle is long but not pointed. The nose, brown and prominent, is a noticeable feature of the face. Brown eyes and long brown drop ears are normal for the breed.

The coat is short and thick with colors of solid chestnut, chestnut with small white markings, dark chestnut roan with chestnut head and markings, white with chestnut mask, markings and speckles, or black with any of the other combinations.

Height is 21 to 25 inches and weight is from 45 to 75 pounds.

Every hunting capability is joined in the versatile makeup of the intelligent pointer. He can track, point, and retrieve in all kinds of weather and terrain. Yet, in spite of the sportsman's training in the breed, the pointer also makes a fine watchdog. However, it is not strictly a family pet, for the dog is too energetic and needs an athletic guardian whose need for exercise is as great as his own. For this reason, he may also be unsuitable for the city. Pointers are friendly but their enormous exuberance may allow for problems in any small, confined environment. A frustrated pointer can become an annoying barker and chewer. Training should begin at eight months, if the owner's preference is for hunting.

GOLDEN RETRIEVER

Lord Tweedmouth's Golden

BARBARA DAVIS

THERE IS A widely circulated myth surrounding the genesis of the golden retriever. Six circus-performing Russian trackers were ancestors of the breed in England, and the story goes that Lord Tweedmouth so admired the troupe of performing dogs that he purchased all of them and bred them with a bloodhound to reduce their size. Truth or myth? We'll never know.

Most experts agree, however, that the true origin of the dog was the Tweed water spaniel and either a small Newfoundland or a flat-coated retriever. Record books from Lord Tweedmouth's estate in the nineteenth century in Scotland prove that yellow puppies were bred from Nous, the Lord's first yellow retriever. And so we have consensus on the golden.

The dog became popular in England at the end of the nineteenth century and some were brought to the United States and Canada in the 1890s. The first registration by the American Kennel Club was in 1925 and the Golden Retriever Club was founded in 1928. Today, the golden retriever is one of the most popular dogs in guiding the blind and assisting the physically challenged.

LIKE MANY DOGS that have a reasonable and rational mind, a preference for good deeds, and a love of fondling sticks, the golden retriever has a reputation for getting into predicaments and, at the same time, finding a way to get out of them. Golden retrievers love offering someone a helpful paw, even if it entails a distressing moment for themselves. They are unselfish and unrestrained in their love of companionship and their offering of guidance. Some of these brave goldens have even gone beyond the pale to be of service, as the following myth demonstrates.

There is a young woman who works for a firm in Great Britain whose sole purpose is to investigate the rumors of haunted houses. According to Ms. Dallens:

> We were inspecting the ruins of a mansion on a lake in northern Ontario, which had caught fire and burned down in 1921. The reason for our visit was that denizens of a nearby town complained of hearing ghostly dog howls on the premises of the old estate. Whenever anyone visited the area, no dogs were seen. Nor were there any stray dogs in the small town itself, and all the local dogs were fully accounted for and normally pent up after dusk. So what was making the howling at night? Wolves was the first thought; then coyotes; lastly wind in the pines. Yet none of these explanations seemed quite right. A complete investigation of what was left of the building and the grounds revealed nothing unusual, and no dog, wolf, or coyote scat was found anywhere nearby.
>
> Interviews with townspeople who had lived near the mansion at the time of the fire revealed nothing out of the ordinary until an elderly woman was found, who had a most unusual tale to tell:
>
> " 'My grandmother was living on the old estate, which, at the turn of the century, was being used as a nursing facility. Grandmother was completely incapacitated, confined to bed and wheelchair. Blind and infirm, she was entirely dependent upon helpers to move her about. However, she insisted that her dog Kelly was the one who did these things for her. No one knew what dog she was talking about but the nurses at the home got used to her insistence and paid it no mind. One night there was a great fire— no one knows how or why it started—and the bottom two floors were consumed in flame, and the top floor was choked with smoke trapping the residents who slept there, including my grandmother.

By the time the firetruck got out to the lake, the building was gone, collapsed. Nobody lived through the disaster, except one person: my grandmother. Amazingly, the firemen found Grandmother, sitting out in the ferns, safe and sound. Those ferns by the lake were ten feet high in places, and those firemen had to really look to find her, but find her they did—they were led to her, they said, by the sound of a howling dog.

" 'Now, no one can prove or disprove a thing, but the way Grandmother told it, her faithful golden retriever, Kelly, woke her up and pulled her out of bed. Then, dragging her by her nightshirt, he pulled her across the floor and got her down the stairs before they burned up. This must have been long before the bottom floors were raging, when the place was just full of smoke. Grandmother told me, time and time again, how Kelly would coax her along, and how, by holding onto his collar (she still had the use of her hands and forearms), she could move along like an inchworm. Being so low and scrunched on the floor, she was able to breathe some fresh air coming in through the outside entranceway, and she didn't inhale any of the smoke that must have been just a foot over her head.

" 'So, when the firemen found her, pretty as a daisy, stretched out in the ferns, you can imagine what they thought. Naturally, they figured she was dead. Some said that she'd been saved, as well, by a nurse on the third floor, who, after getting her safely down the stairs and away from the house, went back up there to rescue others, but then perished in the flames when the stairs fell away. No one knows, or will ever know, what really happened, but they say you can still hear the ghostly howls of Kelly out in the bracken and the ferns. I can't speak about it myself, for I've never heard them, nor anything like them. As to the dog, she did have one once, my mother confirmed that. It was a golden retriever that couldn't be trained to hunt, so it was given to my grandmother when she was first confined to a wheelchair, as a gift from a disgruntled hunter.' "

Golden Retrievers, many owners say, will go out of their way to help a human in distress. However, few have passed beyond the pale to return and save someone; or perhaps such events are too fantastical to be recorded until quite recently. As an oral tradition, however, ghost dogs go back to human-kind's earliest beginnings.

The Lore of the Dog

The golden retriever is a sound, well-put-together dog, symmetrical and strong with a broad skull, drop ears and a straight muzzle. The fore and hindquarters are muscular and well-proportioned.

The coat is dense and water-repellent, with a good undercoat. It may be straight or wavy and has feathering on the legs. The rich golden color comes in various shades, but the feathering can be of a lighter hue.

Standing between 21 and 24 inches in height, the golden retriever is 55 to 75 pounds in weight.

This is a very active dog whose kindly face is the subject of greeting cards and advertisements. Known to be a fine retriever—an "obsessed retriever" to some—he loves to run and fetch anything, from a stick to a stone. The retriever also has a highly developed scenting ability. Even-tempered, affable, and well-mannered, the golden retriever is another of those dogs that falls into the "best friend" category. They are excellent with children, very patient even with infants; they can be chewed on, sat on and ridden on without complaint. Their friendliness is legendary, making them perhaps less likely guard dogs than other breeds. However, this shouldn't rule out their being trained for this purpose, as golden retrievers are very intelligent and like to learn.

GORDON SETTER

The Duke of Gordon's Black-and-Tan

MARIAH FOX

Bred by the Duke of Gordon in the 1820s, the Gordon setter's roots may go back much farther than that; in 1620, for example, a popular "black and fallow setting dog" was described by Markham in Scotland. However, the story that clings to the heather even now is about a highland shepherd's dog; a black-and-tan collie, which the Duke of Gordon crossed with the setters of his own Gordon Castle.

In 1842 George Blunt brought a pair of setters from Castle Gordon to America and one of these was given as a present to the great American orator and statesman Daniel Webster, the man who out-argued the Devil in the courtroom. After this, more of these dogs were imported from Great Britain and the Scandinavian countries, and the Gordon strain was thus introduced to the world.

Today's Gordon setters are beautifully built shooting dogs with gorgeous markings befitting their heathery lineage on the Scottish moors. Considered a most pettable dog, they're known for being clean and fine and showing no signs of irritability, shyness, or viciousness of any kind.

Well known as a guard dog, the Gordon's famous "bird sense" becomes applicable common sense when working devotedly with children of all ages. The following story comes from a small town in West Texas where one particular Gordon made a name for himself in the 1920s.

According to the tale, a crazy and unsatisfied dog owner sends a gun-frightened Gordon to a seasoned dog trainer with a note that reads, "If you can't make a gun dog out of him, I'll personally show up and shoot him dead."

The trainer dismisses the note, but tries hard anyway to train the dog—all to no avail. This Gordon has been beaten into submission, and there's no way to break his fear of guns, or of any violent action, for that matter. In terms of the hunt, the dog is useless.

On the other hand, true to the Gordon's nature, he's an excellent "kid's dog," and the trainer's boy falls in love with him. When the trainer sees this, he makes an offer to the owner to buy the dog, but the man stubbornly refuses. What's more, he makes another threat: "I'm going to come over and put the dog out of his misery if he doesn't learn to point."

The following afternoon, the trainer's son falls off the back porch into the path of a seven-foot diamondback rattlesnake. Fortunately, the father is there, gun in hand, but as the snake strikes—and misses—so does the man. Sand spurts behind the snake, the rattler rolls to the side, coiling again to strike.

Just then, the Gordon setter appears out of nowhere, he leaps into the whirring coils, and when the dust settles down, the Gordon has killed the snake.

The story might stop here—with the boy okay and the Gordon unbitten and the snake stretched out, dead. But the tale's bettered by one final little touch, the arrival of the curmudgeonly owner, who's threatened to kill the dog.

Climbing out of the truck, the owner says he's going to shoot the dog right on the spot—unless the animal has learned to point. At this very moment, the Gordon drops the lifeless snake, and, for the first time in his life, he does what his Scottish ancestors were taught to do the century before—he points—directly at the shotgun-toting owner, who then lowers his gun and leaves, never to return. The story, whether fact or fiction, clearly shows that *this* Gordon Setter was first, a family dog, and second, a hunter's dog. What was bred in the bone came out in the flesh because the dog adored his new family, especially the young boy.

The Lore of the Dog

The Gordon setter is large, heavy-boned, and flat coated; more massive than the Irish setter. Bold-eyed and black of coat, except for the red-gold (or mahogany) tracery. This added color on chest, muzzle, over the eyes, inside the hind legs, forelegs, and around the rump gives the dog a distinctive Gordon look against the russet sedges of the fall season. The contrasting color splashes aid a hunter whose eye may be beset by sunlight and shadow. The dog stands out well in snow and the blues and grays of eventide.

Descriptive writers have gone berserk over the poetry of the Gordon's lineage and upstanding physical virtues. Ralph Kirk, author of *Six Breeds*, says, "The dog has the bones of a colt and the furnishings of a Dane, and a face full of teeth to make a cougar shiver his whiskers loose."

The blackness of the Gordon's coat contradicts the simple edict that white is the absence of color and black is the presence; for, with the Gordon setter, his black coat seems to "gleam, glint, sparkle and flame." It is said that his red Irish cousin's coat cannot match the Gordon's for its blazing blackness.

The legs are feathered with black and mahogany-tan silky fur. The tail is rather short and carried horizontally, or just under the line of the back.

The ears are dropped and covered with fine, shiny feathers.

The size of the dog varies geographically, according to the kinds of game the Gordon is being trained to point. He may vary from 23 to 27 inches in height and 45 to 70 pounds in weight.

The Gordon's been called "a dog with a mind of his own: Scotch." Negative commentaries range from the following: too big, too slow, wrong color, not wide enough, no range, strong-willed, and hard to train. Some critics have even complained that the dog is easily cowed and not courageous in the field.

The American Kennel Club, however, states that, though the Gordon is perhaps a slow-quarterer, and works very close to the gun, his virtue of being a one-man shooting dog is unquestioned. With the right trainer or master, the Gordon will be an eager worker with a fine memory that requires no retraining. Not only is the dog devoted to the hunter who loves him, but also the family that surrounds the hunter, which makes him an excellent guard dog. His so-called willfulness is the product of a mind that works as well as his hunting prowess. If confined without regular exercise, the Gordon may become high-strung and hard to handle.

GREAT DANE

The Deutschlander's Dane

JOHN BREDIN

OF THE GREAT Dane one asks Hamlet's question—"To be, or not to be"?—because this breed is not Dane at all, but Deutsche. French naturalist George Buffon mistakenly called the dog Grand Danois, but why the English decided to adopt the name, aside from the power and euphony of the words, is still a mystery. There is, moreover, no reason to connect the dog to Denmark, for he was initially bred in Germany, and is still called Deutsche Dogge there. The Great Dane actually resembles a cross between a number of different breeds, including the Irish wolfhound, the greyhound, the mastiff. The Molossian face—the Apollo of Dogs—appears etched on Greek coins from 39 B.C., but even before that it was cleanly chiseled on Egyptian monuments and tombs, making it a majestic and massive square-jawed face to remember.

The modern Dane, bred as above, was a tracker of Medieval boar; and not only was the dog a great sight-and-scent hound, but he was also a be-dazzling in-fighter. Great Danes would dance around the straight-charging boar, and then dizzy them with tricky feints and false passes. When the boar was weary, the Danes closed in, not to kill but to hold with crushing jaws.

The elegance of the Dane promoted him from hunt status to lead coach dog. The English nobility used him thus, and his French name, Grand Danois, fits this dog's delightfully rhythmic pace. So the Harlequin Great Dane preceded the pomp of carriage and horse, heralding the coming of lords and ladies, and no equipage, it was said, was without the neat two-stepping Dane. Today, that same high-forehead prance is visible in the breed, even when taken on a short walk around the block.

He is revered in literature as a dog of undoglike virtue, the expressive nobility often breaks into clownish comedy putting him in a category all his own.

One reason why the Great Dane is a dog of many faces is that his sight is more sensitive than his scent, and he seems to be "sighting" all the time. The famous poise and alertness of the dog is attributed to this. The sightfulness of the Giant Dane may have given him a reputation for second-sight.

Myths suggest that the Dane's vision is also used to sight spirits. In Teutonic mythology, all dogs have "feral vision," a special kind of eyesight enabling them to be spirit-sighted. An old Germanic tale tells us that dogs would not attack the warrior-hero and deity, Odin when he traveled in disguise among men, but they could, without difficulty, see the death goddess, Hel, whenever she passed by. According to the folklorist Jacob Grimm, when a dog witnessed a vision and howled, a man could look between the dog's ears and see whatever apparition the dog was having. This belief is echoed today in the Caribbean where obeah men still douse their eyes in "dog-matter" to attain spirit-visions or to see *duppies* (ghosts).

Anyone owning a Great Dane knows that they are always seeing something that isn't there, or in deference to the breed, they're seeing that which we as humans can't see. This mysterious quality, as shown by a quizzical and bewildering stare, is comical, and has been satirized in tabloid cartoons like "Marmaduke" and "Scooby-Doo," both of which poke fun at the Danes's discomfiture when seeing things that "aren't there"—namely ghosts. Scooby is famous for running upright like a man, dodging monsters and mayhem and leaping into Shaggy's arms for protection.

Another Dane trait is to adore all other creatures great and small—with special emphasis on the latter. Some years ago, the talk of the town in Denver was the unique friendship between a Great Dane and a common house mouse, barely bigger than the dog's nose.

We have seen Danes befriend birds as well as bees, and one we know grew up in the company of a dachshund (like the Disney film *The Ugly Dachshund*) and thinks he is just an overgrown *teckel*.

The cartoonish lovability of the Great Dane goes back to a decoration on the Babylonian harp of Ur. Here one can see an ancient comic strip, not unlike "Marmaduke," in which the Great Dane is shown walking on his hind legs and talking like a man. The attribute of speech has followed the Great Dane through the centuries. From the golden halls of Assyrian kings to the gray suburbs of America, Great Danes have always been great "talkers."

Wilt Chamberlain, the legendary seven-foot basketball player, once kept a brace of Great Danes. "I'm a big man and I like big dogs." His preference got him kicked out of his apartment on Central Park West. The dogs kept growing until, as Wilt said, "Only one of us could get into the elevator." When other tenants complained, Wilt shipped out. Big is what you get with these huge dogs. Big-hearted and big-minded, they're completely unaware of their own great big bulk, but that's what makes them in no degree small.

The Lore of the Dog

Few dogs carry themselves as does the Dane. His large square face is equipped with deep, dark, expressive eyes, capable of much emotion and intelligence. He has high, strong, sloping shoulders and leonine hindquarters that give him the lithe movements for which he is known. Danes don't jump so much as spring; they feint, whirl, and leap with athletic ease. It is as if their joints were made of well-oiled ball bearings. Nothing could be less true, however, for these wonderfully agile dogs often have ligament and sinew trouble; and they can break their tail by flinging it against something hard.

The Great Dane's smooth, short hair comes in a variety of colors: black, blue, brindle, fawn, and harlequin.

He stands 28 to 32 inches at the shoulder and can weigh anywhere from 100 to 120 pounds.

Perhaps the centuries-old tradition of guarding princes has given the Great Dane his countenance of noblesse oblige. No matter, he has it; and he has earned it. Like some other members of the upper-class canine family, Danes can be much embarrassed by their actions, especially when inappropriate. For all their great size, they are adroit and particular about eating and drinking—some will not eat at floor level, while others refuse to drink anything but tap water fresh from the source. They disdain bad manners and do not like to be told they are doing something wrong; innately they seem to know how to act.

Yet the Great Dane is not so reserved and composed that he can't have a good time. He likes nothing more than a good romp; in fact, he loves to wrestle about the floor with a master so inclined.

He has a good sense of humor—some say he actually laughs. The bark of a Dane is pronounced, very round and full. While not aggressive, he is also far from timid, as his size should warrant, but he barks more threateningly than he bites. Nonetheless, the Great Dane is an admirable watchdog and his lion's bark-roar should be enough to send shivers up a prowler's spine. Overall, though, these dogs are extremely lovable, tractable creatures who cannot imagine that their size should prevent them from such small-dog pastimes as curling up on the couch.

GREAT PYRENEES

The White-furred Lord

JOHN BREDIN

THE GREAT PYRENEES comes most recently from those legendary mountains on the border of France and Spain, but his ancient past goes back to the Bronze Age more than three thousand years ago. His ancestors were from Central Asia or Siberia and his fame was depicted by Babylonians and the Court of King Louis XIV. He has been described as "an animated snowdrift," a dog whose lineage was perfected in centuries of high mountain isolation that made him a shepherd's friend. There, in the Great Pyrenees that gave him his name, this dog watched over his flocks of sheep. He was called the Pyrenean Wolfhound or Bearhound because of his courage when such predators threatened his flocks. The French called him "*Patou*," a generic name for the breed meaning "shepherd"; translated this became Anglicized as "the Dog of the Shepherd of the Pyrenees." The French are also credited with bringing the dog down from mountains to the farm, where, when they were not pulling carts or doing other menial chores, they were accustomed to sleeping in open doorways, a practice which got them the nickname of "matdogs."

In the seventeenth century, Basque fishermen brought some of these mighty dogs with them to Newfoundland, where, some say, they were bred with an unknown local retriever to become the Newfoundland. The Pyrenees blood is also known to have some St. Bernard in it. General Lafayette in the mid–1800s enjoyed the dogs and gave a pair to an American friend, and thus they came to America; yet it wasn't until 1933 that the American Kennel Club recognized them as a breed. Because of his size and strength, the Great Pyrenees has always found work as a pack-carrier; border smugglers used him in his native mountain region and the U.S. military used him in the service of the war effort during both World Wars.

ONE OF THE dog's most outstanding features is his guardian nature. He stands alone among many pack dogs in that he'd rather watch a flock, or guard a child, than do anything else. His bark has the ring and resonance of authority, his posture proves him to have been an excellent logo for King Louis, but his preference, like Ferdinand the Bull, is to sit still and gaze and just smell the flowers.

Jon Huntress, a teacher and author, told us:

> Some years ago while my wife, Cherie, and our little boy Jesse were living in the village of Tesuque, New Mexico, we had an unusual experience with our Great Pyrenees whose name was Steppenwolf. Stepper, as he was called, used to follow Jesse around like a great white, ever-shifting cloud of snow. Wherever Jesse went, Stepper was sure to follow. One evening we went out for dinner and Jesse remained in the care of our friend, Mida. Now, Mida's kids and Jesse got into some trouble while exploring the acequia that runs through the middle of Mida's and our own property. This is the Mother Ditch, so-called by the Spanish settlers, who, following Indian custom, brought irrigation water to their crops by a series of manmade waterways, the largest of them being the great acequia, the Mother Ditch. It was into this swift, green-running water that Jesse fell and was almost swallowed up and drowned—something that happens to at least one person each year in Northern New Mexico—but Stepper was there to save him. Mida heard the big dog barking and when she arrived, Stepper was holding Jesse up by his jacket.

We remember Steppenwolf quite well and recall how he was lord of the frosted-stubble and field in that pretty little valley of Tesuque. In the mornings when the fog was still hanging on the plain, Stepper moved about slowly, going in between the old crooked rows of twisted apple trees that were planted there in the 1800s. There were times when the dog and the fog were indistinguishable. Then the great dog would appear out of the sparkling, sunstruck mist, his huge ears shining with feathers of firelit dew.

He was Jesse's faithful guardian, Stepper was, a watchful lord of his
pasture and all that transpired within it. But he wasn't around when, far from
his ken, Jesse died in an automobile accident a short time later. According to
Jon, Jesse had awakened from a dream shortly before the crash:

> "Mommy," he announced, "I'm going to become a bird."
> Cherie said softly, "Jesse, I want you to stay with us and be
> our little boy."
> But Jesse replied, "I will be a bird, Mommy. But when you
> call to me, I will fly down and be your little boy."

Not far from the Huntress house lives the famous Santero, Ben Ortega,
who is best known for his carvings of St. Francis. If you go there today and
walk the fields that Stepper once roamed, you might chance to see, moving
in and out of the wreaths of fog, the Great Pyrenees, the white-furred lord
of Tesuque passing regally under the bent and lowering limbs. You might
see, too, a little boy running ahead of him, and disappearing into the old apple
trees. But if you really want to see something extraordinary, you must arrive
there in the fall of the year when the trees are beginning to go bare. In one
tree, gnarled like one of Ben Ortega's saints, you will see an astonishing sight.
That tree will be full of singing birds of all shapes, sizes and colors. And there
will always be one who will fly at the window of the little house, pecking at
the glass to get in. We know, for we have seen it with our own eyes.

The Lore of the Dog

The Great Pyrenees is born of mountain stock and his body shows it: big
lungs, large back, broad chest. The head is bearlike, big, and wedge-shaped.
The nose is black, the eyes brown and wide-set; small triangular ears decorate
the handsome, massive head. The tail is long and plumed, and curled at the
tip.

Most Great Pyrenees have a flat, snowy coat, but this isn't always the
case; some have sandy color in their fur. The coat's designed for bad weather
and the fur may be thick or slightly wavy. The feet are short and compact;
double dewclaws are common on the feathered hind legs. The height is 28
to 32 inches, the weight 110 to 125 pounds.

The Great Pyrenees is not an emotive dog, given to bursts of enthusiasm,
but he is good-natured and affectionate, and his extraordinary sense of fidelity

and guardianship gained him great popularity among the French nobility of the eighteenth century.

Edmond S. Bordeaux, author of *Messengers from Ancient Civilizations*, tells of the Great Pyrenees with which he grew up. He explains, much as Jon Huntress did, that this is a special breed, given to protecting children. He is told by his grandmother that "it is no small thing to be adopted by a Pyrenean Mountain Dog, as he is the King of all dogs. She said I must always prove my worthiness by always taking good care of Nuage when I was here in the summer, and in return, I would have a friend more faithful than ever. . . ."

The dog, Nuage, saves Bordeaux's life more than once, and every summer the two are inseparable companions of the Dordogne Forest. When he grows up and becomes a writer, the dog is still following him around. He writes: "I entered my room and sat at my desk. . . . Nuage of my childhood, now very old but still very dignified and erect, followed me in and took his place, as usual, under my chair. I kicked off my shoes and tousled his ear with my toe, and he made a contended sound and went to sleep. I worked for several hours. Finally I got up, being careful not to disturb Nuage with the chair, but Nuage had died in his sleep—there in his favorite place, at my feet."

The Great Pyrenees is a dedicated guardian, a steadfast companion of children, a life-saver in more ways than one.

GREYHOUND AND WHIPPETT

The Courser of the Nile

JOHN BREDIN

HE HOT SANDS of the Valley of the Nile were home to the greyhound, for the pharaohs maintained great kennels as their royal sport. Throughout Persia, Greece, Rome, and northern Europe, the greyhound—and his quarry, the bounding hare—has coursed. According to many sources, the greyhound came to the British Isles through the Phoenicians or the Celts.

In any case, their popularity with royalty throughout the world seems to have been, and to be, de rigueur. Illuminated manuscripts from the twelfth century show greyhounds under the great tables; and it's known that nobles went to church with hawk and hound. Thus the patient greyhound, who had to forbear Roman orgy, became acquainted as well with medieval liturgy.

In America the greyhound appears courtesy of the Spanish explorers in the early 1500s. George Armstrong Custer, the ill-fated fool of the Little Bighorn, owned a pack of forty greyhounds in the 1870s. Well he knew that these sight hounds were as good at scenting as seeing, but he must not have used them on the day that he lost his golden locks on the battlefield.

The Indians who saw these fleet-footed dogs admired them for their great gift, and the Comanches called them *"nukasari,"* the run-off dog. Among the Indians of South America, particularly the Mojo people of eastern

Bolivia and the Madeira headwaters, the greyhound was used as a hunt dog; this was when the first Jesuits visited them and saw the dog in action.

THE REPUTATION OF the greyhound as a courser, or running, dog began as early as the late 1500s in Great Britain. Homesteaders in the American West began to race them in the nineteenth century, but only as a result of the dogs' first use, as harriers. Once people saw them run after rabbits, they boasted of their ability to beat other dogs at the running game.

Today's greyhound racing, chasing after a mechanical bunny, didn't become widely popular in this country until the 1920s. Though they were once killed at retirement age—sometimes after only a single year on the track—there is presently an active and successful national adoption program.

MANY A GREAT greyhound myth, handed down over the centuries in verse or song, cannot be verified, but merely admired. There's one instance, though, in which an old English rhyme about a greyhound that chased a stag until both the dog and the deer dropped dead from exhaustion, was proven to happen.

It's a rare case of mythology turning back into history, and with proof to boot. The story is here told by noted dog author Edward C. Ash, who tracked its origin back to fourteenth-century Scotland:

> Edward Balliol, King of Scotland, enjoyed coursing stags in a private park when one day, a stag hard-pressed, jumped the wooden pales out of the park and ran away. After it went one of the greyhounds and the King and the Court for 30 miles as the crow flies . . . at Redkirk the stag turned back. Never had there been such a hunt as this before! The stag, utterly exhausted, reached the park palings; desperately it tried to jump back into the park. It succeeded and fell down on the other side, and there it died. Along came the greyhound; it could hardly keep its feet. It came to the palings and attempted to scale them, and fell back dead.

There the story retold by Ash would not end but just begin, because as he explains, the king vowed that the event of that day should never be forgotten. Thus they cut off the stag's antlers and fastened them upon a young oak tree, close to the tragic scene.

Over the years the expanding bark swallowed the horns, but the fabled tree became known as the Hartshorn Tree. People would not forget what happened there, so they erected another set of horns and still another tree, and so on down the ages until any vestige of the horns was gone. And yet a little rhyme still remained:

Hercules killed Hart agreese
And Hart a'greese killed Hercules

It was up to Ash to solve the mystery of the myth by finding some reference, somewhere, to those famous oak-eaten horns. "I wrote to Red-kirk, but the letter came back marked 'no such place.' " Finally, by sleuthing through some ancient letters, he finds the proof that he is looking for. The letter written in 1731 tells of finding the Hartshorn Tree: "The horn of a large deer found in the heart of an oak fixed in the timber with large iron clamps." The eighteenth-century author goes on to say that the trees in the wood of Whinfield Park were large, some thirteen feet in diameter.

So the myth that came down the centuries was finally pinned down, not by an iron clamp alone, but by the printed word.

In the *Metamorphoses* by the Roman poet Ovid, the greyhound appears "quick-footed," "swift running" over the "high hanging cliffs," and going "where roads were difficult / Or no roads at all; they still sped on." The dogs of the epic poem are in pursuit of their own beloved master, Actaeon, who has been changed into a stag by Diana. His punishment comes about because he has spied Diana in a state of undress, and had the temerity to stare at her. Thus his life ends with his own dogs, who cannot recognize him even though he is piteously calling out to them, tearing him apart.

The loyalty of this hound is legendary (which makes the Ovid tale all the more ironic, as he himself knew). In "Tristan and Isolde," the great Irish love story, there is a greyhound named Hodain. Tristan gives the dog to Isolde to comfort her, and according to the tale, after Tristan's departure, Hodain runs no more, but crouches at Isolde's side and bites any man who comes near her.

Another Irish myth shows greyhound devotion mixed with the theme of bitter love, in which these high-spirited dogs are often the unwitting accessory. In the seventh-century Irish tale of King Roman of Leinster, the king, thinking that his son is having an affair with his young wife, kills him at the table. The son's loyal greyhounds stay by his side, neither eating nor drinking, while the father, who realizes his awful error, mourns his boy for three days and nights at the supper chair where he has been slain. The dogs figure importantly in this classic ballad, for theirs is the inheritance of grief.

Other Irish myths depict the greyhound as having a potency of magic, and a special talent for the lifting of grief. This may come, in part, from their extraordinary prowess afoot. It is said on the Isle of Man that only a black greyhound—without a single white hair upon it—can overtake and catch a witch.

Somehow, the royal greyhound has a mythical reputation for being at the right place at the wrong time, and for having a sorrowing fixation. Perhaps it is that their masters' passions are larger than life and they, being so prodigiously fleet of foot, can outrun anything except death itself. So, at the foot of the dead, they are sentenced by their great love, to halt and wait.

The Lore of the Dog

The word "greyhound" in English is synonymous with "swift." The dog's features are, even in repose, ones of motion: whipcord leg, steel-springed haunch, inverted, sculpted belly, arched neck, cat-clean feet. No doubt that this fine canine was specially designed for cutting down the competition. The fifteenth century *Book of St. Albans* characterizes the greyhound as well as it can be done: "Headed like a snake, necked like a drake; backed like a beam; sided like a bream; tailed like a rat, footed like a cat."

They come in all colors of short, shiny, sleek fur. However, they may, at one time, have lived up to their once prevalent color.

They stand 26 to 30 inches at the shoulder and weigh between 60 and 70 pounds.

The greyhound, whose chiseled face and regal demeanor reflect his upbringing, is thought to be vain. Perhaps as a result of long service to kings and queens, the aristocratic greyhound may appear somewhat aloof, and is often reserved even with family members. However, the greyhound is loyal and loving, a creature of comfort and comportment. His baronial bearing is a study of equanimity, a compass of composure. The greyhound knows manners because he practically invented them. This isn't surprising when one realizes the dog has been winning races, as well as favors, for over fifty centuries.

THE WHIPPET, WHO has been called a "small greyhound" is not an ancient breed, except by partial bloodline. The dog was developed by the miners in northern England as a poor man's greyhound. Because of the dog's smaller stature, which was possibly the result of crossbreeding the Italian greyhound with terrier stock, the whippet was, and is, less expensive to breed and to keep. A commoner's greyhound, then, a dog of consummate speed, the whippet is also surprisingly strong for his slight build.

"Whippet," according to some sources, means "to move quickly," and derives from the expression "to whip it." Other sources say that the dog's name sprang from the Old English word "whappet," which meant "small, yapping dog." This latter definition does not seem appropriate, for these are not noted to be barky, although they are good watchdogs.

Whippets came to America with the immigrants who came to New England to work in the textile mills, and had a preference for racing these dogs. And what a dog of speed these sprinters are—they can cover a 200-yard straightaway in 11½ seconds (a speed of 35 miles per hour).

This is a most symmetrical animal, giving the impression of sturdiness and strength, as well as comely beauty. The head tapers to a dagger point, the eyes are oval and dancingly alive. The dog's ears are rose-shaped and small. The loins are well-tucked-up, the legs straight and solid, but very narrow, like those of a racehorse. The tail is long and tapered. Whippets have fine short fur and they come in all colors. They are 18 to 22 inches in height and 18 to 28 pounds in weight.

The Italian greyhound, from which the whippet was most probably bred, looks like him and has many of his characteristics. Among these are the poetically visual standards of skin and body. According to Edward C. Ash writers from the nineteenth century said "the skin so delicate, a heavy hand could damage it." These were, the writers said, dogs which "could be held to the sun and seen right through." Ash also quotes a Dublin owner as stating his dog was "a vast soul in a little carcass."

In whippet racing, there were special trainers whose job it was to pitch the dog at the outset of the race. They had to throw them with such precision and grace, that the small dogs, called "little greyhounds," landed afoot and already agallop. In motion, they move like birds, like banners, like the wind with the sun passing through it.

IRISH SETTER

The Big Red Dog

MARIAH FOX

THE IRISH SETTER began as a hunting dog, whose dashing russet form was used in tandem with the flight of the falcon and the flash of the net. The way it worked was, the hunter threw a dragnet over both the quarry and the dog. The job of the early setter was to hold a point upon his belly. While the dog was earthbound and motionless, the hunter cast his net and caught his quarry, usually woodcocks.

The patient dog was often struck by the weights tied to the net as it was being cast. What came of this danger, practically speaking, was a new kind of crouch for the well-trained hunting dog; it was a maneuver both in self-defense and in support of the hunter. Such was the practice during the Middle Ages in Europe.

The breed known today comes from a red and white dog whose ancestors were English setters, spaniels, and pointers, with some Gordons thrown in. The solid red Irish setter appeared for the first time in Ireland in the nineteenth century. The Gaelic *madradh ruadh,* or "red dog," was bred primarily for his strong color. However, in creating so red a dog, the breeders lost some endurance which originally made the setter stand out as a bird dog. The new strain, a fatal beauty, "for the bench only," was a mistake in that it produced an animal whose character was dulled by too much breeding.

IN THE UNITED States and the British Isles, the Irish setter was glorified in shows, raising cries of admiration from aristocrats and plebeians alike. The first Irish setters made their U.S. debut in 1875 and they were a success in both show and field. Stepping high like a drum major, his silk coat gleaming like a chestnut, the Irish setter set records for the breed.

In the 1950s, Irish setters were synonymous with playing cards, as every home had a set where the dogs were featured on the top side of the card. They were also a standard item for the amateur oil painter, who painted by following the numbers. And a country home in the fifties without a setter was not really a proper country home.

ONE OF THE most common myths of the dog is the one not about a man but a boy soon to become one. In stories of this genre, the youth, reaching beyond the span of his years, undertakes a man's task with a confident dog as his mentor. *Rin Tin Tin* and *Lassie Come Home* each feature this bittersweet song of youth; the reaching out for manhood by learning canine courage and unspoken, or unspeakable, love.

An unforgettable tale of boys and dogs was the book *Big Red* by Jim Kjelgaard. Boys growing up usually have a hard time looking up to conventional heroes; it's the offbeat ones that draw their attention, and often, their devotion. Dogs and young people have a similar emotional makeup, especially those youngsters between the ages of nine and twelve.

Big Red is a chestnut of a tale about a chestnut dog whose love knows no bounds; neither does his courage. Danny, the young protagonist, is supposed to learn how to train Irish setters for show, and this he does admirably, faring well in a man's world, where words and worldliness are judged by other men.

Danny's particular rite of passage occurs first in the world of show where he trains Big Red and wins a blue ribbon. However, the heart of the story—the anxious theme of youth at the testing edge of manhood—comes later when Danny and Big Red try to track down the killer bear known as Old Majesty. Danny must keep his head and save Big Red from the claws of the angry bear. The dog, it appears, would rather point and play at hunting than face the dreaded bear; after all, he's a setter and not a hound. As Kjelgaard writes, "Red never had been a trailing dog, and would not now become one. But if he could catch the body scent of Old Majesty, and was urged to the attack, he would chase the big bear and bring it to bay." Danny is forced to wage a battle of wits, as well as woodcraft, for, while stalking the bear during the night, the trail turns around and the bear comes up stalking him. Fear rules, and Danny's manhood is put to the test.

What happens then is nameless and it comes suddenly upon the boy. The bear, dreamlike, is caught in Danny's flashlight beam. He hovers before the boy, "something huge and black . . . the wind blowing out of the valley eddied around it, curling the long hair that hung from its belly. . . . Old Majesty was a monstrous thing, an animated mass of something that had no more life than a stone or a rock, and upon which bullets had no effect. Wide-eyed, Danny saw it within thirty, then twenty feet of him, and in that moment he knew that he would have died if it had not been for Red."

When the Irish setter finally locks with the bear, the boy falters, fear-stricken. However, seeing Red in a life-and-death struggle renews Danny's courage and he bravely kills the bear with his rifle.

It's at this moment that the setter's instinct is exemplified: Big Red, after the fatal shot rings clear, won't "molest or disgrace a fallen enemy." He won't attack Old Majesty again. Every inch of the story is, of course, patently familiar and some would say it contains a bit of Mark Twain's flapdoodle, tear-jerk prose. On the other hand, Danny might just as well be Beowulf and Old Majesty, Grendel. The story is awfully old; and whether Twain or Faulkner influenced it doesn't much matter because it really harkens back to the camp-fires of youth. The handsome Irish setter is proof that dogs often transcend breeding. And that individual animals are exactly like people in that their character is frequently indistinguishable from the love they give when love is given to them.

The Lore of the Dog

The Irish setter's bloodred mahogany color, long neck and lean head, straight and strong front legs with flowing symmetrical feathering make him the burnished beauty of a crisp fall day. The chest is deep, the ribs well spread. The long loins have a nice tuck-up before the strong rear legs. The tail extends slightly downward when in motion, and has a gentle wave. Altogether, there is no gun dog more representative of the northern woods with their leaves changing color and the taut apple chill of a morning where, out of a fog-banked field, two hunters are coming into view, dogs at their sides. The setter ripples with unfettered joy at the mere thought of going out of doors. The combination of explosive gambol and misty russet fur that is straight, flat, silky, and fine, set against the dog's classic lines, make him the hunter's companion of American paintings. When motionless, the front legs and feet, as well as the rear legs, are perpendicular. The neck is stretched up and forward, head and muzzle parallel with the ground, the plumed tail sloping gently downward.

The somewhat almond-shaped eyes have an earnest, alive look and the wet nose senses which way the wind is blowing even inside a room.

Height is 25 to 27 inches and weight is 60 to 70 pounds.

An Irish dog with impish humor is the setter. Yet, properly trained, he is eminently well-disciplined. The humor lies behind the deep eyes and has its special place when the dog is not working.

When on the hunt, there is an aristocratic nervousness, honed to the flight of birds. A fast-tracker, the setter weaves rapidly from right to left, even on the sidewalk of a city. He is a coiled spring, set to fire.

Such fine sporting dogs need plenty of exercise; confinement does not suit the breed at all.

In addition, human contact rounds out the dog's disposition. When not socialized, his naturally outgoing personality doesn't develop properly, and he may become surly or sour.

The Irish setter is slow to train, but sweet with children and gentle with people in general. Energetic, splashy with feeling, the Irish setter loves to be about and adores positive reinforcement. If not given to the hunt, or some likely work ethic, the dog needs a daily regimen of running—something upon which positive reinforcement can be specifically measured. Irish setters seem to have a craving for intimate ownership, and while this may be said for most breeds, the Irish setter, true to his poetical origin, does not take well to owners lacking in empathy. He flourishes with gestures of sentiment and affection, but this must not be given inappropriately, or falsely, or it will be immediately detected. Here is a dog who is keen to the soft word, but who will jump to the shout, provided the person meting out the discipline is worthy of the call.

IRISH TERRIER

The Terriblest Terrier

MARIAH FOX

DAREDEVIL, WATER WIZARD, hunter of rat and rouser of lion, the true fighting Irish terrier has no equal for size or glory. His lineage is long as well with a bloodline stretching two thousand years and an ancestor—a wire-haired, black-and-tan curmudgeon known as the Old English terrier. Although this worthy is now extinct, his blood still bristles and burns in the lion-hearted Irish terrier.

The first showing of an Irish terrier was in Glasgow, in 1875, and it was in the late nineteenth century that the breed became popular in the British Isles. Brought to America shortly thereafter, people of all walks of life began to enjoy this dog's energetic, diehard character. One human occupation, however, seems to have had a special fascination with him—and for all terriers, actually.

We refer to writers, those terriers of humanity, whose need for doing what they do—nobody knows why—is so terrierlike as to exceed compulsion and to become some kind of nervous religion. The comparison is obvious, if not odious. Terriers go at their particular order of work with one-minded, fiendish relish, and writers seem to have copied this sacramental fury.

In fact, writers are fond of saying that they go after an idea "like a terrier worrying a rat." The writer Roger Caras might be describing another of his trade when he lays down the law of terrierness: "Terriers are generally but not always smallish dogs with a fire inside that simply cannot be quenched. They are scrappy, playful, sometimes hyperactive, generally exceedingly loyal characters."

In one of his essays, "A Boston Terrier," E. B. White quotes an ad that says, ". . . when a dog's nerves tire, he obeys his instincts—he relaxes." White adds: "This, I admit, is true. But I should like to call attention to the fact that it sometimes takes days, even weeks, before a dog's nerves tire. In the case of terriers, it can run into months."

He then launches into a salty memoir of one of his favorite Boston terriers, and from that to a boyhood memory of a fox terrier. The literature of terriers is generally about dogs that "go to earth," and so we have here the summation of all terrier/writer obsessions—that of the Stone Supreme, as White wryly calls it.

Here is an anthem to writers with terriers, terriers with writers, and those of us who are just terrier-types. White writes:

> He kept it with him day and night, slept with it, ate with it, played with it, analyzed it, took it on little trips (you would often see him three blocks from home, trotting along on some shady errand, his stone safe in his jaws). He used to lie by the hour on the porch of his house, chewing the stone with an expression half tender, half petulant. When he slept he merely enjoyed a muscular suspension: his nerves were still up and around, adjusting the bedclothes, tossing and turning.
>
> He permitted people to throw the stone for him and people would. But if the stone lodged somewhere he couldn't get to he raised such an uproar that it was absolutely necessary that the stone be returned for the public peace. His absorption was so great it brought wrinkles to his face and he grew old before his time. I think he used to worry that someone was going to pitch the stone into a lake or a bog, where it would be irretrievable. He wore off every tooth in his jaw, wore them right down to the gums, and they became mere brown vestigial bumps. His breath was awful (he panted night and day) and his eyes were alight with unearthly zeal. He died in a fight with another dog. I have always suspected it was because he tried to hold the stone in his mouth all through the battle. . . . He was a paragon of nervous tension, from the moment he first laid eyes on his slimy little stone till the hour of his death.

The Lore of the Dog

The Irish terrier has a deep muscular chest, giving him stamina for the chase. The body is fairly long with a straight strong back and muscular, slightly arched loins. The tail is generally docked, but not too short, and well-furred. His powerful jaws make him one of the best vermin destroyers.

The dense wiry outer coat is colored red or wheaten, and the undercoat is soft and fine.

The small ears are triangular and there is ample fire in the dark eyes. The head is narrow between the ears, wrinkle free; the muzzle is well formed and finely chiseled. The height is 18 to 19 inches and the weight is 25 to 27 pounds.

This miniature Irish wolfhound is really a diminutive of his grand old Irish counterpart. In temperament the Irish terrier is both protector and companion extraordinaire. According to the American Kennel Club, there is no terrier "hardier or more adaptable . . . equally at home on the country estate, in the city apartment, or in camp; he thrives in the northland or in the tropics."

This natural water-dog is also a trainable gun-dog, and on his own, he will kill all kinds of small game and vermin. The dog is the quintessence of physical sturdiness and incorruptible character. A born guardian, he is wonderful with children. He likes to play and to work, and is just as passionate about one as the other. In fact, to an Irish terrier work and play are on the same order of business. There is no mistaking his military manner, however, his deep stare, or his competence in any affair that calls upon his allegiance.

IRISH WOLFHOUND AND SCOTTISH DEERHOUND

Prince Llewellyn's Dog

MARIAH FOX

CANINE HISTORY, IT would appear, was written with the wolfhound in mind. For example, this dog was present in Rome at the Imperial Circus, A.D. 391. Clan leaders in Ireland used him in battle, and he fought courageously beside his warrior-masters. Christopher Columbus brought wolfhounds on his fourth voyage, and they traveled to Panama with him. In Ireland, the wolfhound extirpated the wolf and thus put himself out of a job. By the 1780s there were no more wolves or elk in Ireland, and the wolfhound began to languish as a breed for lack of purpose.

By the early nineteenth century, this great dog was all but gone. It was then that Captain G. A. Graham decided to bring back these gifted sighthounds, which he did by crossing the Scottish deerhound, the Great Dane, and the borzoi with the last of the Irish wolfhounds.

Although it took him twenty-three years to perfect the breed, Graham was able to do so successfully. Brought to the American West, the wolfhound took up his old pastime of wolf hunting and he was also sent out against the coyote. Today he is revered more for his elegance and proud bearing than for his hunting skill, which has been much less in demand.

———

THE MOST FAMOUS wolfhound myth spawned an equally famous Welsh proverb: "To repent as deeply as the man who killed his dog." The thirteenth-century folktale, from which the saying transpired, tells of a prince, Llewellyn, whose favorite wolfhound was named Gelert.

One day the prince was hunting, and he noticed that Gelert was not at his side. Returning home immediately, the prince was greeted at the door by his wolfhound, who had a blood-reddened mouth. Inside the prince saw his son's cradle overturned, and the house in disarray.

Now, thinking his dog had killed his son, Llewelyn drew his sword and plunged it into Gelert's heart—then he heard an infant's cry from underneath the cradle. At the same time, he caught sight of the torn shape of a dead wolf off in the corner of the hall.

Llewelyn built a stately tomb for his dog under a nearby tree, and so it was that the village of Beddgelert, which means Gelert's Grave, received both a name and a saying that have lived through the ages.

ANOTHER WOLFHOUND MYTH comes from Norway, or possibly Iceland, where there are records of wolfhounds being given away by the Roman conquerors. In the early ninth century, a king called Eystein was run out of his kingdom. From abroad he assembled an army and re-took his palace. Then, since he did not feel his former subjects to be loyal to him, he offered them two alternate rulers: one his slave, the other his dog.

The people chose the dog, a wolfhound, and the dog-king lived royally, and the people honored and loved him. He reigned for three years, imprinting decrees and orders with his paw. His subjects agreed that things were no better, but no worse, than before. In this they were content, for they knew that the dog-king was neither deceitful nor corrupt, and he could neither be lied to nor bribed.

Then one day, while napping in a meadow where there were many sheep grazing, the dog-king saw a wolf pack approach and he rushed to the sheep's rescue. In the fight that followed, he lost his life. Naturally, his subjects were full of sorrow for what had happened. They gave the dog-king a great funeral, and they buried him in a place which is known to this day as "The Hill of Sorrow."

PATRICK MACALPERN, AN English slave who, in the fifth century, became St. Patrick, owed it all to wolfhounds. One night in a dream he saw a ship waiting to take him home. Making his way to the coast to find it, he was refused passage, but then seemingly without reason, was asked aboard. The ship was carrying more than one hundred stolen Irish wolfhounds to the European market, and they were wild and raging against their abductors.

Patrick, however, had an immediate calming affect on them, which the surprised shipmaster welcomed. Upon reaching the Continent, they made their way inland without food, and over a period of twenty-eight days of travail, both men and dogs were dying in equal numbers of starvation. The shipmaster taunted Patrick to pray for food, saying, "If your god is that great, he will come to your aid."

Patrick replied, "Turn to Him and He will turn to you," and he then began to pray and, miraculously, a herd of swine crossed their path. Immediately, the starved men killed them and they and their dogs were fed. When Patrick returned to Ireland years later to preach Christianity, he met Prince Dichu, who at first was going to kill the strange, white-robed saint. He straightaway set his dogs upon Patrick, but the animals merely whimpered at the young saint's feet. The prince, seeing how his own dogs loved Patrick, was deeply touched. From that moment on, Saint Patrick's mission in Ireland began, and Prince Dichu was his fondest ally.

THE WOLFHOUND IN all of these tales shows an abiding love of human beings. But some say the dog's truest obedience is to blood and he must do that which he was born to do. As the wise Aesop wrote, "What is bred in the bone will come out in the flesh." Only in the tales of transcendance, those that raise both man and dog above their fixed station on earth and give to each the power of divinity, is the dog free from the dictates of the blood.

The Lore of the Dog

This commanding, galloping hound is rough-coated and powerfully built. Larger than a mastiff and almost as graceful as a greyhound, it's also as docile as a spaniel. Yet the crush of the wolfhounds's jaws is said to be even greater than that of its bred-in-the-bone enemy, the wolf. Often described as shaggy-browed, the wolfhound's misty appearance calls up feudal lords and firesides, cataracts and leafy glens. The harsh coat, wiry under the eyes and jaw, was made to withstand wet weather. It comes in gray, brindle, red, and black and white. Standing 30 to 32 inches in height, the wolfhound weighs 105 to 120 pounds.

While the wolfhound is a ferocious hunter, he is very gentle around people. The old Gaelic slogan applies: "Gentle when stroked / Fierce when provoked." Curiously, however, this dog is too gentle to be a ferocious watchdog. He enjoys human companionship, but because of his great size and ranginess, he's not easily managed in tight quarters. The wolfhound has a natural preference for countryside that affords him good running, and, when that isn't available, a room with a view.

THE COUSIN OF the wolfhound, the deerhound, is a focal point of Isak Dinesen's novel *Out of Africa*. Some say this dog was the forerunner of the Irish wolfhound; others contest this opinion, saying it's the other way around. Dinesen states flatly that her only dogs were deerhounds and their lean-shadowed silhouettes were the very essence of African grandeur personified into a domestic animal, which, nonetheless, seems half-wild. She describes in unmatched prose how her deerhounds were dark gray against the sombre green of her highland coffee farm near Nairobi.

As she elevates their statuesque shapes, she explains that these noble dogs turn landscape into tapestry and tapestry into landscape. Theirs, she says, is a "feudal atmosphere," and she praises their "gallant and generous character." Her most lavish praise is reserved, however, for the deerhound's great sense of humor. Apparently a laugh on a deerhound's face follows the dog into sleep, where, Dinesen reports, "they continue to chuckle at human folly."

Phoenician traders may have brought greyhounds with them to Great Britain at about 1000 B.C. and these light-haired dogs would probably have needed to develop an extra layer of fur in order to be hardy in their newer, colder environment. Therefore, the deerhound—light of limb and characteristically greyhound in appearance—was, most likely, a breed that came from Phoenician, or Middle Eastern, stock. Once known as the Royal Dog of Scotland, the deerhound was not available to anyone under the rank of an earl. When the clan system collapsed in Scotland, the common man began to hunt deer and the Royal Dog became a plebeian hunting animal. Nevertheless, the lines of grace and grandeur remained in the blood and breeding of the dog, and there is, as Dinesen says, nothing finer to see than a deerhound in angular, arrowlike flight across the green sward.

Deerhounds are deep-chested, long-legged, and muscular. The head is broad and big with a pointed muzzle and small ears, set high but folded toward the back of the head. The jaws and neck of this hunter are like the Irish wolfhound—exceedingly strong, able to pull down a fleeing buck. The coat of the deerhound is shaggy and coarse, stiff to the touch; long on the body and legs and softer on the head and belly. The colors are grey, grey-blue, brindle, yellow, or rust. A long curved, scimitar tail lends the dog a classic, medieval beauty. The deerhound stands 28 to 32 inches and weighs 85 to 110 pounds.

Characteristics of the breed: wolfhounds are noted to be great protectors and hunters, and they are very, very fond of children. However, if you own one, it is almost a necessity to have large quarters and a good area for the dog to run. Sir Walter Scott, in describing the Scottish deerhound, called it "the most perfect creature in the world." This is, indeed, a dog of mythic size and artistry, a creature at home on tapestries and stained glass, against winter skies and waving grass.

JACK RUSSELL TERRIER

Parson Russell's Ratter

THE JACK RUSSELL terrier takes his name from the Reverend John Russell, who bred one of the finest terriers for working fox in Devonshire, England, in the 1800s. The good reverend's passion for hunting foxes may have been secondary to his passion for the pulpit; but it's possible that the two merged in his mind, for in the nineteenth century devil chasing and fox hunting were not that far apart.

At any rate, this flamboyant man with a penchant for the ethereal and the earthly had more than a little influence on the character of his one-minded, mercurial little dog. For there's a lot of legacy packed into such a compact member of the Canidae tribe.

Today, owners of the Jack Russell may disagree on fine points, but they form a quorum on the dog's aggression (with their own breed and with other dogs), hunterly skill, and the animal's unequivocal sense of humor. Jack Russells love to hunt and let nothing stand in their way when the opportunity avails itself. Having located the burrow of a ground squirrel, for example, the dog is bound to go underground and stay down under for days at a time.

No one knows how Reverend John did it—if, in fact, he did anything, but the present breed has a fiercely independent focus. Curiously, there seems even today a tangential connection between men of the cloth and men of the hunt. In terms of mythology, there is a further connection: The St. Hubert hounds were raised in a monastery, and in the British Isles the Wild Hunt became known as the Hunt of St. Hubert.

Parson Russell taught his dogs to hunt with an evangelical vehemence. It was work he wanted from them, unselfish work, not namby-pamby play. The dogs operated as members of a pack and there was a religious zeal in their kind of hunting, which has been passed on into the present century. According to Alice Winston Carney, researcher and Jack Russell breeder, "The ancestors of today's Jack Russell had to be carried on little platforms (on the groom's back) when they went on fox hunts. The reason was that the dog, if not carried, would run until the pads wore off."

Dog author Edward C. Ash adds: "In the olden days they liked a long-legged terrier, able to run with the hunt, but such a terrier found it difficult to get to the fox. Others preferred small terriers, which they carried on the saddle. Hard-bitten little souls, with a peculiarly blunt view of pain. They helped to hold on to the saddle with their small feet, sitting there half asleep, dreaming of foxes."

There are more inferences of the Jack Russell's link to the underground, some of which portend a deeper psychic connection to human consciousness. Any Jack Russell owner knows that the bouncy little dog is a clown, possessing a love of fun and trickery that rivals a leprechaun. When not working, Jack Russells love to play the fool.

No surprise then that a dog resembling the Jack Russell adorns the eighteenth-century Marseille tarot deck; or that the smiling dog's companion is the Fool. The card shows a Jack Russell leaping with forepaws extended, trying to hug the Fool's leg. But the expression on his face suggests that he is also trying to tell the Fool something; perhaps something important.

As court jester to the king, the Fool has a privileged position—one of poking fun, using the double-edged sword of truth and folly to make certain his political points—and they are always sharp—are known to everyone.

Turning back to Greco-Roman times and before that to ancient Egypt, the Fool was a man of influence in the world of the occult. He is part of the collective unconscious and represents the urge to play and to persevere; to be reckless and to be whimsical, but always to keep a careful measure of things as they are, or were, or will be.

The Fool was a chief historian, a kind of sacred clerk and his history goes back to Thoth, the Egyptian moon god. Thoth, keeper of the divine archives, watched over all arts and sciences of man, including magic, hieroglyphics, arithmetic, geography, geometry, astronomy, soothsaying, medicine, surgery, music, and the written word.

Interestingly, Thoth is a figure of duality with the body of an ape and the head of a dog. In other words, a bestial man ruled by a divine dog.

———

THE RELATIONSHIP BETWEEN the Fool and his dog in Shakespearian times is yet another archetype. Portraits of court jesters usually included a dog; the two are court siblings, each an animal of a certain kind. Thus, in many tarot decks we see the dog not nipping or barking at the jester's heels but earnestly trying to tell him something. One reason for this image is that the link between the Fool and the dog is, symbolically, an active relationship between the conscious and the unconscious mind. The Fool himself is an instinctual man, while his dog, being even more primal, lends greater power to his actions. Together, they show humankind how to achieve harmonic balance.

In some tarot decks, the Fool is depicted as a young man setting off on a journey. Though blindfolded, his inner eye is clear, and this is because he sees through the eye of his dog. The Fool, as it has been written, is a member of humanity who "remains behind and therefore has the original wholeness of nature." In this way the dog seems a natural companion to the Fool.

AMERICAN INDIAN TRIBES, the Lakota Sioux and the Hopi Pueblo, to name just two, celebrate the clown as a sacred member of their society. And it's no coincidence that dogs also figure prominently in their mythology. In the Sioux Fraternal Society of the Heyoka (or Clown), the sacrificial dog is meant to carry prayers for health and long life to all relations.

The Hopi, in one of their great migration myths, tell of a young man who goes on an arduous journey. On his way he meets an elder in the underground (the human unconscious). This old man offers him two dogs, a male and a female (in other words, two aspects of the human psyche).

The elder says, "Remember this well, my son. Take good care of these dogs; do not mistreat them. Whoever mistreats them will have rheumatism in the knees: That is the way dogs defend themselves."

Myths that feature the dog-at-the-knees-of-man are a permanent part of the journeying motif of human consciousness. So it is the dog—and often a little dog at that—who, when our passive, secular vision fails us and we can see no other alternative, offers us his own bright eye into the sacred nature of all things above and below.

The Lore of the Dog

The name "Jack Russell terrier" is often used today to describe a variety of white-and-brown terrier-type dogs. However, the Parson Jack Russell of England is a long-legged version of the American short-legged dog.

The breed also comes with three different coats: smooth, broken, or rough. All of these shed, but the smooth coat seems to shed the most. The Jack Russell is either all white or white with black or tan markings. The tail is short and upright and docked.

In addition to being well-muscled, the Jack Russell is also well proportioned for his size, standing between 10 and 15 inches (weight unspecified). His cheerful, feisty face makes him desirable in commercials and films, where his presence implies both mischief and intelligence.

Many owners start the primer by stating, "Terriers are trouble; Jack Russell terriers are double trouble." Or, "Something about them makes them not want to mind." Elizabeth Brownridge and Terri Batzer, in their Internet feature "Terrible Terriers, an Accident Waiting to Happen," have put together a series of cautionary tales that assess how terrorizing this preoccupied terrier can be:

> It is generally accepted that the word "terrier" is derived from the Latin word *terra,* meaning earth, and that the name was applied to those dogs who entered "earths" to engage their quarry. But another theory was put forward that the world "terrier" was derived from "terrorized" and, given the instinctive aggressive behavior that is sometimes visible in our terriers, this seems highly possible.

Such aggression, others say, is the result of bred-for-hunt lineage. While there are still some who claim that the dog is a Jekyll and Hyde personality— sweet one moment, monstrous the next. One thing is clear: If the gate is left open, the Jack Russell will go. And, one might add, get into trouble.

What trouble? It's not uncommon for them to hunt down chickens, rodents, other dogs, cats, and anything else that intrigues or suits their fancy. The worst of it is that Jack Russells frequently kill their own kind. In other words, if left to their own devices, they may attack one another at will. The result can often be deadly. The killing of co–house pets and housemates is something to be avoided at all costs. When, for instance, two- or three-month-old pups are mistakenly kenneled with adult terriers, the outcome is usually dire.

As one breeder writes, "Jack Russells function on the nine-time-out-of-ten principle; and they can count!" By this she means if you, the owner, trust him to behave on the tenth temptation, forget it. It has further been said that the Jack Russell has such an uncanny personality that he/she may be less a dog than a cat in a doglike body.

Researcher and Jack Russell breeder, Alice Winston Carney asks, "Are they good pets? Oh, yes. But for everyone? Definitely not. Jacks are for people who want an energetic companion. However, they must be willing to live with both unpredictability and irascibility. For here is an animal protector who has the personality of a leprechaun."

KOMONDOR

The Dog Lord of the Southern Steppes

MARIAH FOX

THE NAME "KOMONDOR" comes from the Hungarian word for "serene." In Sumerian it is *Ku Mund Ur* which means "Lord of the Dogs." Legend tells us that the dog himself came from wolf cubs reared by tenth-century shepherds. History confirms that he is a descendent of the Aftscharka, a dog of the southern steppes.

Some insist that he was discovered by Germans and imported to the prairies of Hungary, where he became associated with the Hungarian herd, both sheep and cattle. His impenetrable coat was a formidable barrier against the fang and claw of predators that tried to pilfer his herd.

The main early breeders of komondors were the migrant Magyars of Hungary, and they've been breeding them for over a thousand years, keeping the line as pure as possible by not allowing them to be crossbred. Another point of view is that the komondor was once bred with the kuvasz (a direct translation of the Turkish word *kawasz* is "armed guard of the nobility").

Whatever view is taken, we know the komondor is a Hungarian dog and one whose lineage extends back to the lost land of Sumer, or Sumeria, and whose American Kennel Club ordination occurred in 1937.

THERE ARE A great many myths about sheepdogs. One of our favorites, captured in a Warner Brothers cartoon, features the good-natured sheepdog and the sneaky but failure-ridden wolf, who hopelessly tries to outwit him. The story line is not unlike that other perennial wonder, featuring Wile E. Coyote and the Road Runner.

Whether komondor or Old English sheepdog, Ralph exhibits the classic traits of the breed. Nonchalant at all times, he pretends not to see that which he truly sees and his presence is a white cloud of beneficence over his flock, saving them from the most insidious of lupine tricks. He does this with an economy of gesture, a faint raising of the eyebrows (which he hasn't got), and with the glacial composure that komondors and Old English sheepdogs seem to possess.

The burlesque of the sheepdog and the wolf, though humorous, is biblical in origin. As quoted in Matthew, chapter 10, verse 16: "Behold I send you forth as sheep in the midst of wolves; be ye therefore wise as serpents, and harmless as doves." That description fits the komondor quite well. Not only were sheepdogs employed in biblical times, but the book of Job mentions "the dogs of my flock."

The Lore of the Dog

The komondor's armored coat is his most outstanding physical feature. The strands are corded and separated, eight to ten inches in length, and the coat itself is always white, or off-white. This woolly robe, dense and double-coated, shields the dog against knifing winds and predatory teeth. The weight of the coat is impressive, consisting of 2,000 single cords weighing as much as 15 pounds. Heavy boned, the komondor is 25 inches tall, or taller, and 125 pounds in weight.

He has superb eyesight, despite the hair in his eyes, and the komondor is one of the best guard dogs there is. That shaggy baggy coat comes in handy in a fight. Groomed for show, he's evidently shag-handsome, yet in a field, watching over his flock, he looks like an outcropping of rock—or just another sheep.

The Komondor has been used for police work because his looks deceive and he's very responsive. He's also excellent as a companion dog—wary of strangers, always on the lookout, invariably gentle with his family.

Some experts do not recommend the komondor for children; not because of his temperament, but because of his burliness. Temperamentally, the komondor is high on the list of laid-back dogs. They need special treatment with regard to that amazing waterfall coat, and their size requires more than a small apartment to move around in. One owner who lives in and enjoys open spaces says that "this rugged outdoor dog is fun to have around in rough weather because he doesn't mind it."

That's because he doesn't feel it.

KUVASZ

The Hungarian Horsemen's Dog

MARIAH FOX

THE KUVASZ (PRONOUNCED *koo-vahss*) dog of old Hungary, by way of Sumeria, may be the oldest world breed. An ancient list of belongings from two Sumerian families includes the name *Ku Assa*, the old form of *kuvasz*. Excavated in the Sumerian cities of Kisch, Ugarit and Ur are the clay boards upon which the list is inscribed. This is proof enough that the kuvasz was as important a part of Sumerian life as the indispensable horse. In fact, the stem word for dog was "ku;" the root word for horse was "assa." So the kuvasz was undoubtedly a horse dog, a horseman's dog, a dog of horse herds.

In the great migration of the Hungarian tribes from the ancient civilization of Sumeria to the Carpathian Mountains, the people carried on horseback their language, their music, and their religion. And traveling along with them across the endless plateaus and rivers were, of course, their beautiful white dogs, their kuvaszok.

For almost a thousand years the name of the Ku Assa appears again and again, until the Hungarians conquered the Hungarian basin. Then, for almost six hundred years, there is not one word about the dog's existence. Did the breed die out or did the people just stop writing about them?

Actually, the Sumerian migrants who'd given up the travail of travel now became the incipient nation of Hungarians. Adding to their settled way of life was the adoption of a new religion, Christianity, and the casting out of the old pagan ways; so out went the old Gaia earth-mother religion.

In doing so, the people gave up their former way of writing, and therefore such written words as "Ku Assa," slipped away—but were not forgotten. Indeed, it took another six hundred years for the common man to begin to write his own ancient language. By then, the lovely Sumerian hieroglyphic—the oldest written iconography on earth—was lost. But after all that time, the words were still in the people's memory. They didn't quite know how to write them, but they remembered them.

And their wonderful white dogs—what of them? These were not lost either. They, too, were present and as legendary as the word Ararat or Ur. By and large, the Word and the Dog came up the centuries together, the working heritage of another time, but not one that was destined to fade away.

One thing that changed was the dog's ownership. In the past he'd been a commoner's dog, but starting in the fifteenth century, the kuvasz was favored and bred by the nobility. His job changed from sheep-watching to castle-guarding—he looked over large estates and helped to hunt big game; and in both of these occupations, he became indispensable.

King Mathias I of Hungary developed a large pack and his kuvaszok kennels supplied puppies to noblemen and visiting dignitaries. The king was never seen without his dog and, at table, the abundant kuvasz fur was used as a royal napkin.

ONE REASON WHY the kuvasz is such a good watchdog is that his early training wasn't as a herder as much as a watcher of herds. One might imagine him sitting with paws folded under a tree, staring intently at a vast herd of horses. So, as a watcher of men, the dog's intention and disposition was the same. He worked with his eyes, and he missed nothing that moved and little that didn't.

A myth of the Sumerian past is that of the Dog Star. As a symbol of fidelity, the dog had no peer; and the same was said of the steadfast star which bore that name. Sirius, the brightest star in the heavens, appears in almost every religion of antiquity. So timely and unfailing was the appearance of Sirius that, when it was seen, the people knew that the equinox was upon them. In time the grateful affection for this star grew into adoration, for Sirius told the people of Egypt that the Nile was going to to overflow in late summer. Once they saw the faithful star, they knew it was time to move their flocks and herds to higher pastures. Then, from on high, they would watch the great river course the valley and nourish another year's crops.

To travelers upon the trail, the Dog Star was a lantern, a beacon against the darkness that surrounded them. Mohammed called God "the Lord of the Dog Star."

Some ancient civilizations—Greek and Roman, for example—saw the coming of the star as the onset of madness, the dawning of "dog days," a term still in use today. What this meant was that the Dog Star, which came during the hot months of July and August, was bound to herald more heat. This, of course, could be destructive to crops.

SUCKLING PUPPIES WERE sacrificed during dog days to ensure that the Dog Star was propitiated in the proper way. But just as the Ides of March mean change, the dog days mean hot, hellish pressures brought down on human heads.

The sex of the Dog Star is usually male, but the Egyptians believed that Isis dwelt within this constellation, and naturally, she ruled as a goddess—the queen of the fixed stars and of heaven. Isis's power on earth regulated the flow of water, and great temples were erected in her honor.

In the Assyrian Creation Myth, the Dog Star is one of the twelve significant stellar signs. In Navajo mythology, it is the star known as Coyote. Bringer of rain and manager / mismanager of water, Coyote on earth makes floods and manipulates misfortunes that, in the end, affect positive change. His reigning cycle, the thirteenth month of the Navajo calendar, occurs between winter and spring, and is a time of quiet change.

All in all, the Dog Star is a messianic myth, giving a heavenly hero to the earthly body. And in each of these heroes and prophets, from Mohammed to Ulysses, there resides a dog, who, whether holy or hellish, kindly or mad, keeps an eye out for humanity.

The Lore of the Dog

The kuvasz is a broad-backed, light-footed, sturdily built dog with snowy fur that is thick and wavy everywhere except on his head and feet. The ears lie close to the broad, flat skull, and the dog's long nose gives him a look of nobility. The dark brown eyes are almond-shaped, as Hungarian as his bloodline.

The white, or ivory, coat is another tribute to the breed's aristocratic lineage.

The Kuvasz Fanciers of America explain that in North America two different breeds of kuvaszok seem to exist. This is due, they say, to a confusion created by some European breeders, who, having no exact idea of what the ancient, aristocratic dog really looked like, came up with a version which somewhat resembled the Great Pyrenees. The correct kuvasz has a wolflike appearance, wavy coat, lean but muscular build, and refined head.

Kuvaszok range between 24 and 28 inches in height and weigh between 70 and 90 pounds.

Here is a dog whose devotions are several: Kuvaszok can be trained to be excellent flock-guardians, or fine house-guardians; indeed, they can be both.

Owners say that the dog needs consistent early training in either of these pursuits, though. For they have a stubborn streak, and without training, they become overly watchful and possessive. Once used to watch over entire villages in Hungary, they seem to want to do the same in a suburban neighborhood. So an owner has got to be a careful disciplinarian, especially during the dog's first six weeks of training. Given that a normal kuvasz has such training, the dog may still wish to bark at things that seem out of the ordinary to him—anything from joggers to flags that flap in the wind.

Kuvaszok also imprint to the strongest member of the family, and will test each one to be sure, shifting his alliance if a family member is too submissive. For this reason, they do not respect children, necessarily, as their superiors. Once again, training is everything.

LABRADOR RETRIEVER

Saint John's Water Dog

MARIAH FOX

N O ONE KNOWS exactly why the Labrador retriever is called by this name, since the dog didn't come from Labrador, but rather from Newfoundland, where he's known as the St. John's Water Dog. His connection to Labrador seems, at best, to be highly circumstantial: coming from England in the early 1800s, these powerful, short-haired dogs were used to carry catches of fish and broken nets and tackle off the bleak shores of coastal Labrador. British sportsmen, seeing such an adept swimmer, recognized the animal's potential as an agile land-and-water retriever, and so it was that the Earl of Malmsbury, one of the earliest owners of the dog, coined the name Labrador retriever, and wrote of them as being "otter-tailed and oil-coated."

This original breed, however, died out in Newfoundland because of a heavy dog tax and quarantine law. Fortunately for us there were enough dogs in England to nurture the versatile, salty swimmer back into sufficient numbers for breeding, since no dog has such a gifted nose for bracken, warren, and the odd inclement climate of waterfowl.

Today's Lab lovers still praise the dog's extrasensory nose, his short-legged, solidly built, saltwater-cast shining coated face and form. He is a rough all-around shooting dog and a superior water dog, but one shouldn't forget the Lab's easy way with children, and his friendship to outdoorsman and indoorsman alike.

The breed was first recognized by the English Kennel Club in 1903 and by the American Kennel Club in 1917.

As WATER DOGS, Labs have many myths and legends surrounding their life on the cod banks and coastal regions of the world. Sometimes these stories have an otherworldly ring to them; dog visits from the grave are not beyond the spoken revery of the fisherman, whose long days and nights upon the sea are cause for equally deep reflections on the meaning of life.

The following tale of author and Lab breeder Kathleen Osgood concerns her husband, Larry, a fisherman from Key West, who had a special Lab named Wester. As is often the case with Labs, who seem to like animal friends as well as human companions, Wester became best friends with Kathleen's cat, Starshine.

After sixteen years of inseparable friendship with the cat, Wester developed cancer and died, and Starshine fell into a state of complete despondency. After moping about the house, the cat finally took to sleeping all night on Wester's grave. Larry wasn't taking the loss of his old friend any better than Starshine was, so Kathleen got a female Lab pup in the hope of cheering everyone up. They named the pup Windy.

Well, Larry's disposition may have improved along with Kathleen's, but Starshine, whose days were spent hanging out with the new pup, still spent every night on Wester's grave. During the day, though, she perked up and, according to Kathleen, it became clear that the devoted old cat was teaching the newcomer all of Wester's peculiar ways. If cats could talk, she said, that pup would've had his ears burned off with Wester tales, but as it was, somehow Starshine passed on the flame of Wester's greatness.

One evening at sunset, Larry pulled up to the dock in his fishing boat. Looking up from his fishing nets, he saw a sight that stopped his heart. For there on the dock sat Larry's mother, who had died the year before. And next to her sat Wester.

She waved and smiled, and Wester thumped his tail.

Drawing near the dock, Larry rubbed his eyes. Could it really be? Or had he been on the water too long, his eyes burned from the sea glare?

But, no, it was really there. As he studied their faces Larry saw his mother and Wester slowly fading from sight; his mother's arm around the dog's neck, the two of them growing fainter. She was smiling and fading, as was grey-muzzled Wester, both of them going into the golden afterglow of a Key West sunset.

Kathleen and Larry have spoken many times of the vision on the dock that day and they've decided that they were "holding on to Wester a bit too hard." They realized Wester was in a place he loved, along with Larry's mother, and it was time, they thought, to let go of Wester, let him fade away into the Key West night, as they knew he must. So they did—they let go.

The next morning Starshine was asleep on Wester's grave, as usual, but when Kathleen tried to wake her up, she found that the old cat wasn't asleep. She'd followed Wester into the light and now they were all together— Wester, Starshine, and Larry's mom—together at last.

The Lore of the Dog

These wide-chested, heavyset dogs are light-footed and agile on either land or water, but they're especially beautiful to watch around and in the water. Nothing gives them more pleasure than swimming, head aloft, feet whirring like a paddle-wheeler.

The Lab's face is comely—the head wide and strong jawed. The ears are set far back and hang close to the dog's cheeks. The heavy yet smooth coat sheds water, as if it had an oil base. The colors range from black or yellow to chocolate or liver; always a solid color, though, with maybe a light spot somewhere on the chest.

The distinctive tail is round, tapering from a wide base and covered with short, thick fur. Labs use their tail as a rudder in the water, and it works well for them.

This solidly built dog is well protected against foul weather. In fact, they enjoy a good nor'easter, a good bit of weather to test their sails.

The Lab is one of the best retrievers of any breed, working easily on both land and water. However, the dog's high shoulders and bulky body (standing 21 to 24 inches tall and weighing 55 to 75 pounds) keep him from going into the dense cover that a spaniel, for instance, will penetrate with ease.

Labs would rather be wet than not, and one trainer, Kathleen Osgood, commented that one of her dogs "drinks with her feet in the water and her head under water, up to her ears." Another of her trainees "wasn't dry ten days of his seven years. At the age of five weeks, he jumped ship and swam for shore, a distance of five hundred yards, before we picked him up in our boat. With their otterlike tails, Labs are the most natural swimmers; and with their oiled overcoats and down undercoats, they can stay in the water for very long periods of time without getting water-logged."

These sweet, loving, kind, loyal dogs do not insist on one owner or a single master. Rather, they enjoy the role of family protector, their affection spreading warmly over a variety of family members of equal importance.

Young Labs, it would seem, often enjoy the relationship of an older mentor, usually another Lab. This "Dutch Uncle" companion sometimes offers tutelage of some sort, but sometimes it's just a good friendly influence that "helps to keep the lid on."

Labs really enjoys having a steady job. Jobless, they fatten up in their older, or indolent, years (Labs generally have huge appetites), but if kept busy they'll stay trim and fit, especially if there's water around. Genetically, the Lab is bred to hunt and retrieve; however, as a popular household dog, he needs to be given tasks that replace the hunt. One Lab we know spent all of his days collecting sticks from a nearby pond. He swam into the water, retrieved the stick, climbed out, shook himself off, and placed the sacred staff upon his ever-mounting pile. Sometimes he would go to his wooden mound to survey the wealth of sticks. When some were missing, he seemed, incalculably, to know about it.

LHASA APSO

The Barking Lion Sentinel Dog

MARIAH FOX

MANY NAMES AND many uses are associated with this ancient dog, whose birthplace was probably India, China, and Tibet, and, most likely, in that order. The dog, who is often identified with Buddhism and the Dalai Lama, may have followed the old rounds of the Buddhist patriarchs. Just as Buddhism went from India to China and thence to Japan and the rest of the world, so, too, did this little dog follow in the footsteps of Bodhi-dharma, the patriarch who brought holiness out of a cave in India and bestowed it upon the world, or so the myth goes. Some say the Pekinese was the official Lion Dog, others claim that the Lhasa apso was, indeed, the dog of this title. Both, in our estimation, were bred for the same exalted purpose: to watch over an emperor or a lama.

With the abandonment of the Buddhist faith in China during the Ming Dynasty (1368), the Lion Dog lost its position of honor, and according to M. O. Howey, author of *The Cults of the Dog,*

> Edicts forbidding them to be bred in the Temple of the Imperial Ancestors were issued and very strictly enforced. Yet they did not become extinct, for priests, eunuchs, and women about the court protected and sheltered the little creatures. So, when in 1644 the Manchu conquest placed that dynasty on the throne, and the La-mas were reinstated in their sacred office, the Lion Dog resumed

its important position in the religious life of China. Tibet was reconquered and the Dalai Lama, as head of the Buddhist religion, became the temporal, as well as the spiritual, ruler of that country under the suzerainty of China.

It was thus that the relationship between the lamas and the Lhasa apso became a fact rather than a myth. And so, there existed two little Lion Dogs, one in Peking, the Pekingese; and one in the mountains of Tibet, the Lhasa apso. The latter, since only males were given as gifts by the Dalai Lama, remained a pure strain, unbred beyond the mountains of his origin. These sacred animals had a spiritual identity with the Lion of the Sakyas, the Lord Buddha himself. In fact, according to Ms. Howey, "The beautiful little creatures are trained to turn the prayer wheels for the Lamas. Because of this, they are popularly known as Prayer Dogs."

In addition to Prayer Dog, the Lhasa apso is also known as the Chrysanthemum Dog, owing possibly to his bright, flowerlike face and fur. The name Lion Dog also refers—like the pug and the Peke—to the icon of golden mane, the leonine ruff. *Rapso,* in Tibetan, means "goatlike"; if this indeed refers to the apso's coat, we are uncertain, but the dog's nickname, *apso seng kye,* means "barking lion sentinel dog." In England, he was known as the Talisman Dog, in view of his bringing of good luck to any and all who might come to own him. This comes from the fact that some Tibetans believe him to be a reincarnated lama, who has not yet ascended to heaven. Thus, a spiritually potent being, and, some say, "a lucky dog."

As ONE OF the oldest dogs on earth, the Lhaso apso probably dates back to 800 B.C. and was bred by mixing the Tibetan terrier and the Tibetan spaniel. Over the centuries the dogs were raised in monasteries in the remotest mountain retreats of Tibet; the people who were permitted to have them, aside from the lamas themselves, were occasional Chinese dignitaries. Therefore, the little Lhasa apso became a rarity and his preference for heights, holy chants, thin mountain air, and monastic ceremony was bred into the solitude of his life among the monks. The Sherpa guide who accompanied Sir Edmund Hillary to the top of Mount Everest obtained his first breeding stock of little dogs from a monastery in Tibet. The first of the breed to enter the United States was brought in by American dog breeders, Mr. and Mrs. C. S. Cutting, who received them directly from the thirteenth Dalai Lama in 1933. Owning a male and female as foundation stock, the Cuttings began Hamilton Farms Lhasas in Gladstone, New Jersey. Two years later the Lhasa apso was accepted by the American Kennel Club.

ANIMALS IN THE Buddhistic pantheon are neither high nor low, in comparison with human beings. Everything in Buddhism is affected by the law of karma, the idea that the life you lead lives on after you die. Death, then, is merely a state of rebirth, an awakening into another life, which is informed and shaped by the one prior to it. Dogs in the old Buddhist tales are in a constant state of satori, or watchfulness. Humans can, it is believed, attain this themselves, but it is difficult and not an easy path for the average person. What is a dog, then, but a passport to satori? For, given the dog's eyes and ears, the animal's constant awakened attention to those things around him, he is what the Buddhists sometimes call a "realized being."

No dog is more realized, in this sense, than the Lhasa apso. Lhasas were used to guard the inner court of the Dalai Lama, whereas the large Tibetan mastiff blockaded the main gates and doorways. It is said that "when a Lhasa apso looks in the mirror he sees a lion." And, when he looks at a person, he immediately knows whether he is looking at a friend or a foe. The acute hearing and quick reflex of the Lhasa is present at all times. One wouldn't think this dog could outmatch the sizeable power and portent of a mastiff, and yet, the old myths tell of chambers guarded by mastiffs being broached. But no one entered a room where a Lhasa was posted without being observed. Like the monks who raised them, the Lhasa has an iron-willed constitution. Time is of the essence to them, and this, too, could be related to the many formal ceremonial gatherings and the inviolate order of the day that these ritually bound dogs attended in Tibet.

Chevy Schutz, a Lhasa owner, writes about her dog Muffin:

> Any schedule, once started, will be followed. She has a timepiece in her head that is keyed to the U.S. Naval Observatories Atomic Clock. Vitamins must be offered by 7:00 A.M. Morning treats are 9:00 A.M. Failure to conform will initiate a full-fledged campaign. First, a high bark from across the room, followed by paws on your lap. No petting! Reach for her and she will back up, give you another excited bark while lowering the front of her body to the floor to challenge you. Muffin is territorial, possessive, loving, dependent, and independent, with the jumping and balancing abilities of a mountain goat.

All of the above qualities may be the inadvertent result of this dog's breeding in a place of profound and irrevocable order. The goat-jumping aptitude may also be one reason why the dog was named, or qualified, as

"Rapso," the goat-haired one. Once again, as the Lhasa's job was to guard certain members of the Tibetan Monasteries' elite corps, this dog shows an obsessiveness when it comes to guarding her preferential people.

Says Chevy Schutz, "Muffin is extremely possessive of her family. We first recognized her protective attributes when I had pneumonia. The doctor said I should lay across the bed and have my husband tap me on the back to help my lungs. He rapped me twice with the flat of his hand and Muffin appeared. Two more raps and Muffin was on the bed. My husband raised his hand to tap me again, and Muffin's front feet were on my back with her head under and pressing against his hand. A warning growl came from her throat and every tooth in her mouth was showing."

Nor was this Lhasa content only to guard her people; she also made it her business to guard her "courtyard" with the furor of a territorial lion. "Although Muffin is older now, her guarding instincts have not diminished. She will wake up from a sound sleep, dart outside and go after anything on four legs that dares to enter her territory, whether rat, raccoon, cat, Marsh hare—nothing walks in her yard. The whole neighborhood dreads mango season when she chases and trees raccoon raiders diligently, all night, every night."

So the dog that once watched over the sleep of the Dalai Lama now waits for recalcitrant raccoons. Yes, there is something of the sage in these mystic dogs, and it is not just their mantralike name, Lhasa apso.

The Lore of the Dog

The Lhasa, at first glance, is an unusual dog: The coat is heavy and straight and parted down the middle of the head and back, so that the fur is like a curtain. The head is large for the compact body and decorated with mustache and beard. The ears are drop and heavily feathered; the tail curls over the back. Altogether, the dog appears to be a masterful monk or a mage, wrapped in floor-length robe, and on his way to some secret ceremony.

The coloration of the Lhasa is variable: gold, sandy, honey, dark grizzle, slate, smoke, part-color, black, white, and brown. Only these colors are acceptable for purebreds in the United States, according to the American Kennel Club, but in Canada all colors qualify. Height is 9 to 11 inches; weight ranges from 12 to 18 pounds.

Although not immediately recognized for physical strength, these dogs are athletic and well-muscled, not delicate at all, and they can hold their own with most other dogs. They are quite assertive and territorial. Possessive of their human families, Lhasas always keep watch for interlopers. Their acute sense of hearing has given them a reputation for being extraordinary watch-dogs. On walks, the Lhasa apso has good endurance and does not tire easily. In Tibet, the dog was accustomed to very high altitudes and was said to be a barometer for avalanches.

The American Lhasa Apso Club has the following recommendation for ownership: "We do not recommend the Lhasa for families with children under the age of three. This is because of the small size of a Lhasa puppy, who can possibly be hurt by a child falling on him." They also state that the dog is "seldom a pet, but rather a companion; often a clown, but never a fool." Lhasas are neither deliberately stubborn or willful, but they know what they want and when they want it, and they are addicted to schedules and timelines—sometimes their own—and they do not like to have their preferences subverted. These are dogs of both dependency and independence, and there is a balance between the two which they seem to want meted out on a daily basis.

MALAMUTE

The Freight Dog of the Mahlemiut

SID HAUSMAN

THE MALAMUTE IS a dog bred by the Mahlemiut, members of the Inuit people of Alaska. Their main residence was the upper part of the Anvik river region, but these people were known to have traversed a large part of the northern landscape. The dogs themselves became well known around the time of the Klondike gold rush in 1896, when they were used to pull sleds heavily stocked with cargo. The Indians had formerly used them for hauling food, but their later use was much more strenuous. However, as freighting or draft dogs, the malamute was enormously successful because of his great and powerful body. He could pull huge sleds over a long distance and remain at a steady, dignified pace the entire time.

According to kennel experts, "the malamute is a domesticated purebred dog, and has been for many centuries." However, there is disagreement about this, and to deny the influence of wolf blood in the breed is a bit like stating that the Great Dane has no mastiff in him. Yet the kennelers are right in that much ado over the wolfiness of some of the Alaskan Canidae has given them an uncomfortable, and disputable, reputation. Romance in dog literature and depiction on the silver screen has also added to the misinformation of the breed. For instance, this passage on Nordic dogs from Cecil G. Trew's *The Story of the Dog and His Uses to Mankind* is classic: "What the horse is to us, and the camel to the Arab, such, and even more, is the dog to the children of the ice deserts of the forlorn and frozen regions of the North. His strength, speed and endurance alone enable that lonely race to traverse those trackless wastes shrouded in nature's pall of eternal snows, where a gale is much dreaded by the Esquimaux as the simoon by the Bedouins in the sandy deserts of Arabia.''

Yet another passage in the same book quotes a northern traveler, a Dr. Kane, who takes pity on his dogs because of the lack of light, the dismal temperature: "It then occurred to me how very dreary and forlorn must these poor animals be . . . living in darkness, howling at an accidental light, as if it reminded them of the moon—and with nothing, either of instinct or sensation, to tell them of the passing hours, or to explain the long-lost daylight."

Human ruminations about dog feelings are misleading at best, but there seems to be an overload of anthropomorphism when it comes to dogs of the "lonely northland." What do we know? And what do they tell us that we cannot understand? Malamutes are real talkers, and the noise they make comes from, it would seem, a wish to speak in some human vernacular. They're not barkers, generally, but they can, as the kennel folks say, "howl the roof off a house." Yet it is in their insistent *"woo, woo, woo"* kind of talking that they try to communicate to humans in the best, and perhaps, imitative, way they know.

Or maybe it was the other way around: We learned to talk from them. Indeed, among the many dog myths of Alaska, there is one that seems to fit the malamute. The story goes that while the native people often ate wolf flesh in times of great hunger, the flesh of the dogs was exempted from the cooking pot. The reason for this is found in an old myth that tells of the Creator Bird, who by skimming the waters with his wing caused the earth to rise up from the depths of the sea. This was, they say, how the earth began. Then Creator Bird went on to create all living things, with the exception of Man, who was born of the dog. This is why the Athapaskan people, who live north of the Arctic Circle in Yukon Territory, abhor dog flesh. You cannot eat that which you are, or that which you come from. (The ceremonial eating of dogs, however, was practiced by other Indian people, notably the Tsimshian, much farther south along the northwest coast, whose eating of live dogs by spirit-possessed dancers was an anathema to early explorers and missionaries.)

Perhaps the reason for the Native American reverence of the malamute rests upon his strong back and his infinite goodwill to help humanity. Certainly no pack dog is more friendly, more family-oriented, more gentle, more intuitive, and more talkative than the malamute of the Mahlemiut.

The Lore of the Dog

The sweet-faced and pretty-voiced malamute is a large, powerful, Arctic dog. The largest of the sled dogs, he is wide in the head, broad-backed, and barrel-chested. The beautifully almond-shaped eyes are an outstanding feature of the face. The ears are triangular and upright, the tail is curled over the back. The soft and thick fur feels like the softest raccoon fur to the touch. The coat is light grey and white, or black and white. The height is 23 to 28 inches and the weight is 85 to 125 pounds.

One surprising feature of the malamute that makes him a pleasure to have indoors, as well as outdoors, is the fact that his fur is odorless. It sheds hugely twice a year, but in between, when the dog is in the house, you won't smell him at all.

These dogs are excellent with children and all other family members. They're not of the watchdog mentality, though, and aren't put off by new-comers and strangers. They don't bark, but they do howl. The way they seem to talk to people is both charming and interesting from a linguistic perspective.

As freighting animals, the malamutes were considered champion of the Arctic breeds, and today they closely maintain their original form and function as the ultimate freight dog. The Indians first used them for hauling food in the winter and belongings in the summer. The thing for us to remember now is that these dogs always were used to other dogs in a pack situation, and, in order to be successful in their work, they needed to be cooperative.

Today's malamute is no less of a worker, a hauler of packs, or even a member of the pack. All of these roles are present in the breed. The family that owns one will notice how well he behaves in concert with both people and animals. He enjoys living with an extended family; and if he hasn't one, he may try to attract, or create, one of his own.

The work ethic is deeply bred in malamutes. They are working dogs, first and foremost, and they seem to demand a good, sensible job or task, so that they can perform at their best level. They are usually unhappy when confined to a backyard or a pen, and given nothing to do. Malamutes are great hiking, traveling, camping, trail-and-companion dogs. Although, if al-lowed to roam, they will sometimes get into trouble.

This breed enjoys supervision and training, the earlier the better.

MALTESE

The Ancient Dogge of Malta

MARIAH FOX

C HARLES DARWIN PUT the origin of the Maltese at 600 B.C., and so here again is one of earth's oldest candidates for Canidea status, a tiny Maltese malted with a swirl of names that dazzle and confuse—Maltese terrier, Maltese Lion dog, Ye Ancient Dogge of Malta, Melitaie dog, Roman Ladies' dog, the Shock dog, the Comforter, the Spaniel Gentle, the bichon.

Each of these doughty names carries with it a petite histoire of the dog that was bundled and bartered along the Mediterranean trade routes of the Old World.

The Melitaie dog, for instance. Melitaie, the ancient name for Malta, tells us that the little traveler came from the island that bears his name.

The name "Comforter" derives from the dog's use as a hot water bottle and as an extractor of pain and illness drawn out of, and away from, the stomach.

The Shock dog was an English name of the eighteenth century given because of the Maltese's fur, which stood out in shocks when the dog wasn't bathed or groomed. But the name may also refer to the shocking state of the dog's uncomely fur, rather than the texture of it.

These are just a few of the tiny dog's appellations; its origins, of course, journey the globe. It has been stated that the Maltese is not an islander at all, but rather a mountain-born dog, starting out in Switzerland. Descended from a spitz type, bred for turf and marsh, the Maltese was then taken to the south, arriving on the old trading island of Malta.

However, there is also evidence that the Maltese was worshiped by the ancient Egyptians, and perhaps brought to Malta by Phoenician sailors. Aristotle (384–322 B.C.) believed the dog to have been on the island of Malta during his lifetime. Such dates and suppositions are now blurred with the passage of time.

W HAT WE DO know about the Maltese is that this tiny fellow has held a lion's pose in literature for a good twenty-eight centuries, during which time he has been lionized for his virtues, not his controversial and sketchy background.

An aristocrat by circumstance, and later by manner, the Maltese has lived with the rich and famous ever since he first slept on a velvet pillow. This position hasn't always garnered him an easy life, however. For some of his fondest families were those lords and ladies destined to die by hanging, guillotine, gibbet, and dagger.

On October 16, 1793, for example, the day of Queen Marie Antoinette's beheading, her pet Maltese leaped from the Saint Michele Bridge into the Seine where he died. So goes the old tale—but tradition also tells of the Maltese tucked into the petticoats of Mary Queen of Scots (Mary Stuart) during her 1587 beheading by order of Elizabeth I. The dog survived the untimely death of his flame-haired mistress, but later died of grief.

Aldrovandus, sometime before 1607, wrote an early history of the breed in Latin, and he recorded two major breeds: one with a short and one with a long coat. He also said that one Maltese sold for what would, by today's standards, be a five-figure price.

Eighteenth-century dogs were as small as squirrels and spent much of their time burrowed in the billowed sleeves and ample bosoms of their mistresses' clothes. Later, this became a matter of poor taste, and it completely fell from fashion.

By the 1800s the Maltese was a showpiece, spawning other showy and tributary breeds, such as the bichon frise and the Little Lion dog of France.

In 1830, however, the dog was all but extinct in England, and this prompted Queen Victoria to purchase two members of the breed in the Philippine Islands. By the time the voyage had returned them to England, the dogs' coats were in such bad repair that "presentation to the Queen was deemed impossible." She settled, sometime later, for two of their offspring.

In 1877 the Maltese was exhibited at Westminster in the United States, and in 1888 two females, Snips and Topsy, were officially accepted into the American Kennel Club. The present era, sometimes called the Golden Age of the Maltese, continues to see the rising popularity of the dog, whose official status is now among the top thirty.

Given the fame and history of the Maltese, one would think that the accompanying myths would be almost inexhaustible. Such is not the case. Looking high and low, one finds only tiny, footnotes, or if you prefer, pawprints.

There is, though, one fine myth in which a maltese plays a diminutive but responsible role. The story (from Rome, A.D. 160) involves a grieving widower whose wife appears before him as a ghost.

In tears, the widower throws himself upon the ghost, but she stands back and laments: "As the custom is, you burned all of my garments in the funeral pyre—all but one."

The unfortunate husband begs to know which garment this is, but before she can answer, his Maltese, lying under the sofa, begins to bark, chasing away the spirit-wife, who quickly vanishes.

The widower bends down to berate the dog, and there under the couch is his wife's golden sandal. We will never know whether the dog was barking at the ghost, the sandal, or both, but the golden item was later burned—setting the matter, and the spirit, finally to rest.

Another Roman myth deals with the Stoic philosopher, whose patroness begs him to care for her Maltese dog. He accepts—but not without many protestations, being too old, too selfish, and too set in his ways.

Finally, riding to his home in a crowded carriage with the dog stuffed into his cloak, the hoary-headed philosopher begins to philosophize. His lips move to speak and quick as a snake, the Maltese flicks his tongue at the Stoic's beard. There is no frolic in this action, however, for the dog spies a goodly amount of food tucked away in the wad of chin fur there.

This happens later in the evening, too, while the sage is once again pontificating on his favorite theme. Sharp as a ferret the brazen dog dives into the wagging white floss. But this time, according to the tale, he takes the liberty of "marking the man's mantle," as the storyteller so delicately phrased the little dog's lifting his leg and peeing in the Stoic's beard.

Dog authors, hearing this story, have since exonerated the cleanly little dog, saying that his comportment is better than the spaniel's or the barbet's.

They say that his breath is nicer and his snort less grotesque, and his desire to please far surpasses his willingness to displease.

Nonetheless, the beard-wagger's tale remains as is, Maltese-marked for all time.

A FINAL TAIL-TO-FOOT-NOTE, from the Greek writer Aelian: "Epaminodus, on his return from Lacedaemon, was summoned to a court of law to answer a charge involving the penalty of death, because he had continued the command of the Theban army four months longer than he was legally authorized to do. . . ." Finally acquitted of the charges, Epaminodus left the courtroom and was met by a Maltese, who immediately fawned over him. Said the outraged leader, "This animal is grateful for the good I have wrought, but the Thebans, to whom I have rendered the greatest service, would put me to death." How or why these small, life-saving dogs always appear at such moments is as curious as Destiny itself. The fact is, though, they're there.

The Lore of the Dog

The Maltese is a tiny dog covered with long silky, snow-white fur, parted in the middle from nose to tail. The fur can be as much as nine inches long. The head is proportionate to the rest of the body, which is square, with a well-set tail folded up in back.

The eyes are round and black. Ears are triangular and wide-set. Height is 8 to 10 inches; weight can range from 4 to 9 pounds.

Sprightly, intelligent, and gently mannered—yet unafraid of anything—this is the Maltese.

They are great companions and "healing dogs" because they stay with people for long periods of time without growing restless. Some live as many as nineteen years and the average Maltese is rarely sick.

Practical needs include the regular attention that must be paid to his coat, which, if uncombed, can end up being badly matted. Daily brushing is highly recommended. The Maltese listens well to instruction—having, "theater in the blood"; however, they have a will of their own, and can be obstreperous.

MASTIFF (ENGLISH BULLMASTIFF, BULLMASTIFF, NEAPOLITAN)

The Massive Molossian of the East

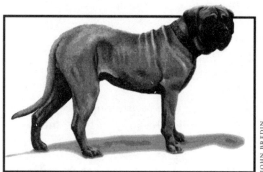

JOHN BREDIN

THE MOLOSSIAN DOG was first seen in ancient Greece and Rome. Some say this was the Tibetan mastiff, brought to Greece by Alexander the Great. But it is believed today that the Molossian dog was brought to England by sixth-century Phoenician sailors, and that this animal then became the ancestor of the English mastiff. Great-shouldered and shag-furred, the towering Molossian bore a build and a name that matched his massivity. He was called Alan, Dogue, and Bandog, but the name that stuck, perhaps because of its phonetical size and the French word *massif,* was "mastiff."

Marco Polo commented, on first seeing one, "But you see they have in this province a large breed of dogs, so fierce and bold that two of them together will attack a lion. So every man who goes a journey takes with him a couple of those dogs, and when a lion appears they have at him with the greatest boldness, and the lion turns on them, but can't touch them for they are very deft at eschewing his blows." Thus was the Molossian of the East described in the land of the Great Khan, the Orient.

GREAT BRITAIN, ABOUNDING in the hound, used the large dog for hunting and bull-baiting, favoring it for the latter. Of course, the mastiff was the very emblem of the "Dogs of War." The expression, and the dog as an auxiliary of war, is as old as the concept of military dispute. This goes back to the time of biblical battles and the Assyrians, Gauls, and the war dogs of Attila the Hun. A dog belonging to King Charles V of Spain wore armor, a coat of mail with an undergarment of purest velvet. In medieval England, he strode upon the field, unclad, as a boar hunter's companion. Journals make mention of the mastiff on various coasts of the New World: Jamaica knew of him, for he was unleashed upon the Arawak; Florida found out about him, as he was set upon the fleeing Indians by Ponce de Leon. One story tells of a Native American woman, who, in trying to outrun a mastiff, gave up because she knew it was no use. Sitting down, she awaited her death. She did not know of the great dog's nobility, however, for he was trained not to harm a seated person.

DOG MASCOTS, FOLLOWING the creed of the Dogs of War, were employed with marching men in World War II by Belgium, Italy, Germany and Great Britain. A New Zealand regiment reported of its favorite mascot: "News of the death of Major, bullmastiff mascot of an infantry battalion recently returned to New Zealand after fourteen months service in Fiji, will be received with regret by members of the Kiwi Division. . . . It was a common sight to see Major leading the battalion through the streets of Suva, along dusty roads at Nausori or over the hills at Namaka. Clandestinely brought to New Zealand, he soon became acclimatized and was with the battalion on its long treks. He was at the battle of the Kaimais. . . . Major was buried with military honors . . . on the summit of a green hill overlooking a parade ground. He remained a soldier even in death."

The dogs of war achieved a kind of rank as well as ceremonial burial status. On one European campaign, during line-up, there was a dog that barked "Sir." Another that took away the fallen flag from his dead master and brought it back to his infantry's side. These stories are endless, but one that particularly stands out concerns General George Washington. One evening, during the Revolutionary War, the general was in his tent having dinner when a large and strange dog, presumably a mastiff, entered it. The dog looked hungry, and upon examining the animal's collar, he saw that it belonged to his adversary, the English General Howe. Ordering him to be well fed, General Washington then had the dog returned to enemy lines under a flag of truce. General Howe returned this kindness with a well-wrought letter, explaining how fond he was of his canine friend.

GEORGIA STORYTELLER O. Victor Miller tells of a fabulous backwoods boar hunt in which a dog that combines the mastiff, the bulldog, and the hound tracks a 200-pound boar into a Georgia swamp. But first he sets the mood by explaining the ancient origin of the hunt itself:

> Hunting wild hogs is a time-honored avocation. Prehistoric cave paintings in Altimara, Spain, depicting the wild boar testify that our Stone Age forebears hunted piney woods rooters some 30,000 years ago. Boar hogs figure prominently in ancient Egyptian, Greek, and Roman mythology. Venus's boyfriend, Adonis, for example, was killed by a wild boar. From drops of his blood sprang up red flowers, anemones, which the same hog probably rooted up later. Book 11 of Homer's *Iliad* likens the surrounded Odysseus to the lather-jawed boar that hunters hem up to their own peril, and the same Odysseus (Book 9) is recognized while having his back scrubbed by a maidservant who remembers a tusk scar on the warrior's thigh.
>
> The boar figured prominently in Europe, where medieval hunters on horseback chased them with hounds, and Columbus probably introduced the first swine to the New World. Spanish explorers brought swine herds to Florida and South Georgia, where some ran off into the swamp and reverted to type, begetting the tribe of boar hogs southwest Georgia sportsmen love to chase.

The bullmastiff, as gamekeeper's assistant, was used to chase poachers as well as the garden-ruining European boar. According to Jan Wiener, a Czechoslovakian author, there was nothing in Europe to compare, in size, weight, and truculence, to this particular species of wild animal: "The boar was deadly. If you didn't kill him with one shot, he would certainly run right over you, ripping you apart with his tusks." O. Victor Miller, stating it a little differently, remarked, "A stricken boar hog can peel your leg like a banana by tossing his head sideways." But, Miller watched in utter fascination as the great dog Foots latched onto a giant Georgia swamp boar:

Foots had his powerful jaws locked onto the ear of a bristling 200-pound razorback. They were spinning with such whirlwind fury that I could hardly tell the hog from the dog and turf from the fur they were kicking up, raising a fuss like a thunder squall through a rusty windmill. I squatted on my haunches, duck walking in close enough to fill the frame of my camera. "Get back!" ordered Norman, snatching a .357 from his shoulder holster. I stayed in close clicking pictures, secure in the knowledge that the hog was too busy with Foots to come after me. Then Foots suddenly lost his grip on the hog's ear, and I still am unable to accurately reconstruct exactly what followed. My last clear thought was my delight in the close-up pictures I was taking without a zoom lens.

"Watch out, he's loose!" warned Norman, jumping back. Before I could fully appreciate the gravity of the situation, the hog was magnified into two baleful black eyes, a slotted snout and a lathering mouth that brandished bright tusks. I suddenly realized with awful clarity that the magnified picture I saw wasn't the result of a telephoto lens. The boar has rushed out of focus toward me, fogging my single reflex lens with foul breath, too close for a man on haunches to outrun. Then there was a blank space, a dead zone, and the next thing I knew I was standing alone in the woods listening to the echoes of an unearthly sound that could've only issued from my own throat. The mayhem had removed to the creek, where Foots caught the hog again, resuming the foray in splashing water until the ruckus was silenced by the crack of Norman's pistol. And it was over.

"Well, I never saw anything quite like that," Norman said. "When the big hog shook Foots loose and went bristling after you, why, you just bristled back at him and hopped clean over hog, dog and all. From a flat foot squat, I mean. You about as froggish a full grown fellow as I've ever seen. If there'd been a giraffe running behind that hog and Foots, you would've cleared him too."

The Lore of the Dog

There are several members in the mastiff family besides the English mastiff. These are the French Dogue de Bordeaux; the Italian Neapolitan; the English bullmastiff. Each one is a descendant of the mastiff of the East, the Molossian.

The most widely used of all the breeds is the English variety, but the others are becoming more popular all the time.

In writing of the English mastiff, the first thing that comes to mind is his great size. No member of the Canidae group is bigger boned, though there are some, the wolfhound to name one, who are taller at the shoulder.

This dog is big! And he carries a large rectangular head, heavy, muscular shoulders, and a great wide chest. The fur is short and dense; the color varies—apricot fawn, silver fawn, plain fawn, dark fawn. The muzzle and small drop ears are black. The feet are wide, round, and arched. Minimum height is 30 inches, with weight between 175 and 190 pounds.

THE ENGLISH BULLMASTIFF, recognized by the English Kennel Club in the early 1920s, was bred by crossing mastiffs and bulldogs. A combination of the two dogs, he is smaller than the English mastiff but larger than the English bulldog. According to Roger Caras in *A Celebration of Dogs*:

> . . . the bulldog-mastiff cross produced a dog of enormous power. It was first called the gamekeeper's night dog and later that was changed to bullmastiff. It was quickly recognized as a separate breed. In those days of night patrol the dog was preferred in the darkest colors possible, black being very much preferred. That made it, of course, more difficult to see. That is not the case today. The bullmastiff was bred and trained to attack in a unique way. It wasn't supposed to bite, not really, just keep the gamekeeper's adversary off his feet. The bullmastiff hits hard, and if the foe tries to stand, the dog tries to hit again. It is an inexorable force.

The English bullmastiff has a large square head with a broad nose, wide nostrils, and strong teeth. The muzzle is black. The eyes are dark and set on either side of a deep furrow. Overall, the face is judicious, thoughtful, calm, tenacious, courageous, and, sometimes, when he's not at work, consummately bored. The coat is short and thick and comes in all shades of red fawn and brindle. The ears are triangular and carried back and to the side. Height is 24 to 26 inches and weight is 100 to 120 pounds.

THE NEAPOLITAN MASTIFF is the Italian version of the Molassian of the East. Attrition from a combination of poor breeding practices and life during the Middle Ages nearly demolished the breed. Sicilian kings brought it back by mixing the Dogue de Bordeaux with local mastiffs. By the Second

World War, the breed was again in danger of extinction. Careful breeding by just a few enthusiasts, however, reintroduced the bloodline again. Today's powerful-looking dog has a big head with pronounced dewlaps that fall to his neck. The ears are small and docked; the eyes dark. The body is wide and muscular, the tail docked to about one third its length. The coat is short, thick, and comes in black, blue, grey, brindle, and fawn. Height is 25 to 29 inches and weight is between 110 and 160 pounds.

The French mastiff, or Dogue de Bordeaux, is covered in a separate chapter.

ALTHOUGH ORIGINALLY BRED for ferocity, today's mastiff is not a dog of war, but of peace. The ancient genetics, though, are there, and given encouragement, will emerge as the best house-and-body guard dog there is. Mastiffs make excellent child guardians as well because they love children, and they do not mind being roughed-up by them. Their patience, like the Great Dane, is legion. But it must be noted that in fairly recent times, the French and Italian mastiffs were dropped from the line of police work because they were considered too ferocious to handle. Mastiffs of all breeds require regular exercise and freedom from confinement.

NEWFOUNDLAND

Lord Byron's Boatswain

JOHN BREDIN

SOME SAY THE Newfoundland was brought to the country that bears his name by the Vikings. Others argue that when Newfoundland became a possession of Great Britain, the Tibetan mastiff was brought and bred with the local bear dogs there. Then, to complicate matters, there are those who claim that Labrador retrievers from Labrador swam the Strait of Belle Isle, or crossed on foot when the water was frozen, and, once again, bred with the local Canidae. A final argument might be that the Newfoundland's ancestors are the Great Pyrenees, who were brought to Newfoundland by Basque fishermen.

Today most experts agree that the Newfoundland was bred in Newfoundland to help men with salt water fishing, sea rescue, and house guarding. They are still used for each of these, but also for pack-carrying and cart-dragging as well.

The dog's double-coat is extra thick, ideal for shedding water and keeping out the cold. These two factors make them well suited to swimming in the cold northern waters of the Atlantic.

The bravery of Newfoundlands as ship's dogs is legendary and there are many recorded accounts of their heroism at sea. Napoleon himself was once nearly drowned when leaving Elba. The Newfoundland, who snatched him from dark Elban waters, unwittingly altered the history of the world.

Another famous Newf during a raging winter storm is credited with saving one hundred people off the coast of Newfoundland. He braved the white-capped waves and blizzardlike winds to fetch a lifeline back to shore so that a ship could be stabilized.

Seaman, the historic Newf of the Lewis and Clark expedition, ensured the journey's success on more than one occasion. Although he howled over the "farosity" of summer mosquitoes, he bore the needled barbs of the prickly pear in pained silence. Seaman cost Meriwether Lewis twenty dollars in St. Louis, not a small expense for the year 1803, but the dog proved worth his weight in silver, or, as a Shawnee barterer figured it, beaver skins. Lewis was offered three of these venerable pelts for his dog and, naturally, he refused.

In May 1805, Seaman's worth increased incalculably when a crazed buffalo crashed into the explorers' camp "and was within eighteen inches of the heads of some of the men who lay sleeping. . . ." The confused animal blundered around the camp, crushing gunstocks and bending rifle barrels with his enormous hooves, but the buffalo didn't kill a single explorer because Seaman rushed out and forced him to change his course. Both Lewis and Clark testified in their journals that they owed life and limb, and those of their party, to their guardian. A fitting tribute to this great dog was the gesture of Lewis that commemorates this Newfoundland's name: a northern tributary of the Blackfoot River was called Seaman's Creek in his honor.

O N A P R I L 1 4 , 1912, when the *Titanic* went to its freezing grave in the iceberg-haunted North Atlantic, the first officer's large black Newfoundland patrolled the icy waters around the area where the ship went down, barking a beleaguered call for the master who wouldn't appear. Christopher Bland (*Dogs USA*) writes of this moment in history:

> Soon after, the SS *Carpathian,* which had been notified earlier of the *Titanic*'s predicament, steamed into the disaster site. In its haste to locate survivors, the *Carpathian* sped directly toward the fourth lifeboat, oblivious to its presence on the black ocean. The *Titanic*'s passengers, exhausted and weak from exposure, were mute in their protest as the ship came on. Rigel, who was paddling ahead of the fourth lifeboat, sent up a continuous bark which alerted the Captain of the *Carpathian*. The order to stop all engines was immediately given and the gangway was lowered. Rigel then guided the lifeboat through the darkness to safety. Upon being brought on board the *Carpathian*, Rigel appeared little affected by his ordeal

and stood against the rail to bark for his lost master until he was taken below for food and medical attention.

Perhaps no words celebrate the greatness of the Newfoundland better than the lyrics of this nineteenth century children's song:

> *I am the noble Newfoundland*
> *My voice is loud and deep;*
> *I keep watch all through the night*
> *While other people sleep.*

The Lore of the Dog

Newfoundlands seem square instead of long and round, with their massive head, short muzzle, and thick neck. Their eyes, small and bearlike, intimate their lineage with the Viking Bear Dogs of long ago.

The ears are small, triangular, and hang down close to the head; when wet, they become frizzy. The coat is heavy and coarse, wavy, and just a bit oily to the touch. Buried in fur, the Newfoundland looks seafaring, and, in fact, the coat could be a sailor's peacoat, heavy about the collar. Usually black, this coat may also be a bronze color. There is a special kind of breed, a Landseer, which is black and white.

Average height is 26 to 28 inches, with an average weight of 120 to 150 pounds. It is not uncommon, however, to see dogs much larger than this.

An outstanding feature of Newfoundlands are their usually webbed feet, used to travel over marsh and shore. There's probably no better swimmer in rough or forbidding seas than this great, galumphing water dog, whose history, like that of the St. Bernard, includes thousands of saved lives.

The Newfoundland's noted for being a compassionate dog, and as Lord Byron once wrote: ". . . beauty without vanity, courage without ferocity, and all the Virtues of Man without the Vices."

He was referring to a dog for whom he built a monument on his estate at Newstead Abbey in England. This Newfoundland was honored like a man.

Some say the personality of the Newf is pastry sweet. For these empathic dogs would rather suffer themselves than see a human being experience discomfort. Life's burdens are but a token to them, considering the gladness they get out of being with their family. They are entirely oriented around the selfless desire to serve.

When unable to be of service, they may become solitary and sad-faced, as if waiting for the moment of opportunity when they might be called upon to perform a brave and important deed.

The Newfoundland is very good with children and exceptional with children who happen to be near water.

OLD ENGLISH SHEEPDOG

The Original Shaggy Dog

JOHN BREDIN

THE OLD ENGLISH sheepdog goes back at least one hundred and fifty years, for as the American Kennel Club states, he is "no mere upstart." However, there's an obscurity in his origin that still leaves something to the imagination. For instance, some say the dog has a bit of Scottish bearded collie in him, while others swear his ancestor is the Russian Owtchar. There is even an American Indian lineage for the dog. On the Fort Belknap Reservation in Montana, the Gros Ventre tribe once celebrated the "Shaggy Dog Dance." It appears that once, long ago, during the people's ancient migration, they left a shaggy dog behind at their old camp. One old man realized what had happened and so he waited for the dog. That night, the two of them slept alone in their own camp, and the dog said to the man in a dream, "You have been kind to me, so I will now give you a sacred dance."

A painting of Gainsborough's and the engravings made from it in 1771 match up well with Walt Disney's galumphing haywagon of a dog, made popular in book, film, comic strip, and popular joke in the early 1960s.

However, the official history of Bobtail, as he's affectionately called in Great Britain, probably begins in the eighteenth century, where he became a drover's dog, whose job it was to drive sheep and cattle to market. In this respect, he differed from his komondor cousin, much of whose time was spent as shepherd rather than drover.

Since these dogs were tax-exempt because of their working status, the owners bobbed their tails to prove their occupation. Thus the fond name Bobtail and, subsequently, the word "curtail." The lack of a tail as a rudderlike appurtenance seems to have had no adverse effect on this dog's driving ability, however, and it also gave us a functional vocabulary word.

The Old English Sheepdog Club of America began in 1904, but the dog had a slow climb to popularity in this country. Fanciers, it appears, thought Bobtail was too big, too bumbly, too furry, and even too ephemeral. Although his virtues far outweighed his faults, he was labeled "excessive."

In time, though, things came around for him as people began to realize that the dog's personable manner was his most outstanding trait. Americans found out soon enough that Bobtail was neither a wanderer nor a sprawler. He was neither dull-witted nor rambunctious. Size notwithstanding, Bobtail began to appeal to the public fancy. He became a creature of cuteness, who was now the large target of small jokes.

If this had fallen on any other dog, it might have lessened his stature, but in Bobtail's case, it pumped it up, for Bobtail became the origin of the so-called "shaggy-dog stories."

The source of these dry tidbits of irony, which may or may not be termed stories, goes back to ancient Greece, where comedians enjoyed setting up a hero for a short fall. Indeed, the basis of all shaggy-dog stories is that they lead you to believe one thing, and then give you another.

During Prohibition in America, the same style of storytelling popped up again. This time around it featured "shags, shag-nasties, and ragshags." These were rough-shod characters—bums, alcoholics, and other down-at-heels folk. The stories generally dealt with the ironies of life under the influence; they always carried a punch line, and they too were called "shaggy dogs."

In the 1940s the stories turned into nonsense jokes, which played upon the mundane and offered a tongue-in-cheek reprisal, the punch at the end. Then, in the 1950s, the stories became tagged to a primarily tailless, but not entirely humorless, working dog of the English countryside.

It had gone this far, so now it went all the way. Into the comedy club, by way of the back door, came the good-natured, fun-loving, hard-working Old English sheepdog. The dog, growing quickly in popularity, inspired a lot of laughter. Being an amorphous-looking fellow helped and so did his bundly, bag-of-surprises personality. Of course, with both the dog and the stories, what you see is not what you get.

Shaggy-dog stories were an antidote to the Atomic Age, a world undergoing drastic psychic and physical change. It was a time where anything might happen and stories of outrageous dogs with mounds of rumpled fur were in keeping with the unpredictable tempo of the time. If humans were acting like dogs and dogs were acting like humans, what was the difference? No one knew which end was up anyway.

Here, then, are a couple of vintage shaggy-dog samplers:

> Once there was an American businessman, who read in the lost-and-found section of the newspaper that a British gentleman had lost a shaggy dog and wanted it back. Touched by the Englishman's caring so much for a dog, and knowing that he was travelling to London, the American found a dog that fit the shaggy's description. Then, when he went to England, he sought out the address printed in the lost-and-found ad. That very day, he brought over the dog and presented him at the door. A butler met them with a cold, uncurious stare. However, seeing the shaggy for the first time, the butler looked horrified. "Sir," he said, "not *that* shaggy!" and he slammed the door.

> Once a businessman was traveling by train and he chanced to enter a car where an Englishman was playing chess with a shaggy dog. The businessman watched with great fascination as the dog quickly won the match. Surprised, the businessman remarked that he was amazed at the dog's prowess.
>
> "Do you enter him in tournaments?" he asked.
>
> The Englishman replied that the dog wasn't that good.
>
> "You see," he said snidely, "he lost the previous two matches."

As the fifties came to a close, shaggy-dog stories got shaggier and shaggier until there was no dog there at all. The stories turned tail and became bizarre twists of wit that featured animals of all kinds. Though they were still called shaggy dogs, the tales starred parrots, horses, cats, and almost any member of the animal kingdom.

In the 1960s Disney's *The Shaggy Dog* proved that a good joke was worth a movie. Starring Fred MacMurray and Mouseketeers Tim Consodine, Tommy Kirk, and Annette Funicello, the film is about a teenager who turns himself into a sheepdog.

Actually, the story was loosely based on a novel written by Felix Salten, who wrote *Bambi*. The lovable shaggy cast for the film was an Old English sheepdog of champion parentage, who, as it turned out, had only a few obedience lessons before tackling the role. This caused his trainer to call him "a real method actor." But whether this was true or not, Disney Studios knew what the public wanted—a shaggy, behind the wheel of a souped-up jalopy.

The film turned out to be more than a string of incidental laughs. It proved to a generation of parents that funny dogs and crazy teens were just the same—largely misunderstood and, for lack of a better way to put it, pretty shaggy.

The Lore of the Dog

Part floor mop, part rug, part bundle—all of these combine into what we've come to know as the lovable, laughable shaggy dog. Complete with bob tail, this drover's dog of the nineteenth century has a great bark and a gait that rolls and rollicks like a bear. He has a somewhat traceable lineage, but an untraceable expression on his curtained face. However, the seemingly introverted dog behind the furry veil is overtly friendly.

Square proportionately, the Old English sheepdog is full-boned, deep in the chest, and despite the hanging forelock, impressively watchful. His tail is bobbed, sometimes at birth, but mostly when the puppy is four days old. His affectionate name, Bobtail, comes from this characteristic. Coat coloration is any shade of grey, grizzled, blue, and with or without white markings.

Frequent brushing is needed to keep the coat from getting matted. Also, it should be noted, the fur makes a first-class wool for knitters. He stands 23 inches in height and weighs 50 to 60 pounds.

Bobtail is known as a "dog of character." One might, then, fill in the blank. . . . What kind of character do you imagine him to be?

Well, he can be just about anything; he'll do well in almost any climate and he's handy as a pocket. Indoors or outdoors, he adapts nicely. As a dog who knows his affection is secure among the human family, he exhibits confidence, charm, and warmth. Sled dog, watchdog, drover's dog, film star—Bobtail's lived many lives.

As a popular joke, his persona thrived, and he became as a result a popular breed in America.

Bobtail is not boisterous, demanding, or overwhelming. He seems to fit in with whatever crowd he's thrust into—whatever, wherever, whomever. Ultimately, though, his character is so large it's rather hard to define. He's just a big bundle, and if this is true then it's equally true that the bundle's beloved.

In fact, belovable.

PEKINGESE

The Little Lion Dog

MARIAH FOX

THE LION DOG of Tibet resembles the Pekingese, but in Asian legend, the Lion Dog is a combination of the eagle and the lion, an heraldic creature of Chinese myth. These so-called Hand Dogs were recorded in old Chinese chronicles. Once the hand of a human was laid upon a newly hatched eaglet, so the legend went, it would turn into a Chinese Lion Dog. Eagle's nests were, therefore, often sought out, not only for eagles but dogs.

In the migration of Buddhism from India to China, the myth of the king of beasts became fused with the faith of Gotama Buddha. The result was that the good lion at the Buddha's heels turned Canidae—and all the better to serve the master.

The myth exalts the small dog because he was able to change back and forth from a dog to a lion, and was, in this sense, a shapeshifter. His guardian nature (dog) could also become a man-bearing beast (lion) or even a kind of heraldic steed.

In Japan, the myths of the Buddha were further refined. Thus, the Lion of Buddha became the Dog of Fo. In native art, this dog was represented as a Pekingese. An eleventh-century Japanese painting shows the entry of Buddha into Nirvana. Beside his praying disciples, there is a sacred Lion Dog. He is shown lying on his back, feet in air—the familiar pose of the Pekingese.

———

THE SYMBOLISM OF the Lion Dog was not lost on the great Kubla Khan, grandson of the greatest warrior monarch of all time, Genghis Kahn. His thirteenth-century court, heavily influenced by Lamaist Buddhism, contained both lions and dogs. The lions, supposedly, lay in attitudes of courtly feline circumspection, while their tiny counterparts, the little Lion Dog Pekingese, played fearlessly about their curved claws.

IN 1861 DURING the European invasion of Peking, British and French officers came upon a shocking sight. In a shuttered and sequestered chamber, the body of the Imperial princess lay dead in her royal robes. Before she'd taken her life, she gathered about her five sacred Lion Dogs. These ancestral guardians, whose distant relatives had once watched over the dead woman's forefathers, were so small and yet so grand as they kept their loyal, circular watch around their mistress.

GENERAL DUNNE PRESENTED one of these "sleeve dogs" to Queen Victoria, and thus a living myth was unveiled to the wonderment of the Western World.

Independent of the Chinese, however, there is some evidence that a Lion Dog, or something like it, may have existed in Europe prior to the recorded historical importation. For example, a painting by Albrecht Dürer, the Flemish master, shows such a dog. Its image is of tufted tail and lionesque head, and lest anyone think the work was a fantasy, it ought to be noted that a contemporary of Dürer's drew a dog that looked exactly like it.

The British naturalist Thomas Bewick, in his *History of Quadrupeds* (1790), depicts a Lion Dog, by name, saying only that it is a "small and rare variety." Dog authority M. O. Howey asks: "Was this abortive attempt to produce a lion dog in Europe a reflection of Eastern mysticism—perhaps a symbol of 'the Lion of Judah,' or the Dog of Fo, or was it merely a freak idea of an imaginative mind?" Of course, we shall never know.

The Lore of the Dog

The Pekingese is the quintessential cuddly miniature. Distinguished from English toys and from the toy spaniels by his long low body and short legs, he has deep, soft, straight hair, and wooly rather than a silky coat.

The muzzle is short and the eyes full, but not pushed out and the dome is prominent. The tail is the pompom variety of other toy spaniels, but the ruff of chest and the feathers on thighs, sides, and forelegs surpasses these dogs.

The colors vary widely in the breed; almost any color can be found on a Pekingese. Generally, this breed weighs from 8 to 10 pounds and the average height is 6 to 9 inches.

Suspicious of strangers, yet affectionate with his master or mistress, the Pekingese is so brave as to be considered foolhardy. The dog looks the part of his antique background—quaint and finely drawn as the dynasty art of ancient China. Long ago, the theft of such a dog in China was punishable by death, and perhaps some of the dog's insouciance comes from his sacred and inviolate past. To look at a Peke, one might imagine they're just cute little oddities—pretty, dainty, delicate, but not too durable. Nothing is further from the truth, for the true-bred Pekingese is courageous, combative, and bold. Possessing much self-esteem, he's a fine watchdog, having been specially bred for that purpose in Chinese antiquity.

POMERANIAN

The Little Lapp Fox Dog

JOHN BREDIN

THE POMERANIAN RESEMBLES nothing so much as a small fox, but this dog's bloodline is lupine, stemming from the spitz dogs of Lapland and Finland. There are, of course, claims, hither and yon, that say the ancestor of the little spitz fox is Chinese, Egyptian, or Greek. And there are Greek vases, Chinese poems, and Egyptian murals that attest to such a possibility. Naturally, there are those who scoff at this, saying that the Pom undoubtedly came from Pomerania, where a group of Finns settled in Samogitia. So what, you have a right to ask, is the bottom line? And is there one?

There are a number of dogs, developed in central Europe during the nineteenth century, that have similar markings and also the physical appearance of the Pom, which is commonly considered to be a spitz type, whose closest relative might be the handsome snow-coated Samoyed. Other dogs that have this look are the keeshond, the Norwegian elkhound, and the schipperke. This group of spitz family members is probably traceable to Iceland and Lapland, having migrated from such places as Finland and Siberia, where their fur and tough physique proved them useful in many ways.

If this is so, one wonders why the dog was dwarfed to the degree that he is today. Beauty may be the only reasonable answer, for there is something quite extraordinary in the Pomeranian's coat of angora fluff. The head is that of a darting fox, but the tail is carried up and along the back in a way that no self-respecting fox would emulate. Yet all attention is drawn to that amazing abundance of pillowy fur. Edward C. Ash has written: "Man is not entirely responsible for the coat. The cold wind made it, and Man merely improved on what the cold wind had created."

Spitz dogs were utilized in almost the same way as the buffalo by the North American Indians—as food, shelter, fuel, and religion. Spitz flesh was edible, an Asian delicacy, in fact. But in the cold north, the entire dog was divided into a perfect economy of utility. Both dead and alive, the dog was valuable as a commodity; his coat was a comfort against the wind; his flesh was favored for roasts and stews; his skin made an excellent window, and his sinew was the source of thread. The women of some northern climes wore little else than dog-skin dresses. Mostly, though, the hardy spitz pulled and hauled sledges. Native women treated pups in much the same manner as their own babes, holding them to their breast. This practice was not peculiar to northern people, for in Italy it was not uncommon in the eighteenth century to find women suckling fox kits.

The early explorers of Canada were greeted by spitz dogs who also had a large amount of wolf blood. Such pack animals were described as "pointed-faced dogs" and were considered fox dogs as well, though it was quite clear that they were really domesticated wolves. The proof, so called, was that they howled like wolves and were unable to bark like dogs. Although the Indians ate such dogs, the animals were treated as family members and were often seen walking into the tents at night and eating out of the peoples' porridge bowls, as if accustomed to eating like men. Wedding oaths were consummated by fox-dog libations: a draft of fox blood shared by the happy couple at a wedding. Fox-dog fleece made fine mattresses and it was also believed that when a man died, his soul would be joined by that of his favorite dog, who would be killed at the time of the man's death.

In the Siberian steppes the fox dogs were really Samoyeds, and the grinny little Pom certainly has the same expectant face as the smiling Sammy. However, in China the breed that most resembles this family of spitzs is probably the Chow. In any case, the dog was commonly eaten in Siberia and there were butchers whose main job was to prepare dog hams, dog legs, and such meats of varying canine perfection. On special feast days in China, it was customary to eat dog, and when a certain official was asked once why he looked so well, he answered that his diet contributed to his health, adding that every morning he consumed thirty eggs, a pint and a half of good wine, and one dog leg.

Fox-dog myths are as rampant and profuse as the customs that accompany them. The Lapps believed that they were descendants of the dog clan; each individual of the clan had his own dog spirit. North of Norway, Sweden and Finland, and well into Russia is the country known as Lapland; all of it is north of the Arctic Circle. The native Laplanders are the Reindeer People. Europeans considered them—and still do to some extent—to be wizards and sages, whose shamanic power came from the spirit of the dog. A household spirit always watched over the hearth of the Russian Lapp families; they offered him food at every meal, but they were relieved when that dog spirit left the house and went elsewhere. The Swedish Lapps have musical signals, melodies, and tunes to drive their dogs. This spiritual form of encouragement was shown in the contemporary film *Iron Will.* The American protagonist inherits his father's wolf dog who has been Indian-trained to the sweet notes of the bone flute; the dog won't budge without the commencement of his secret, personal song.

Lapp dogs were also used to guard house, family, and most importantly, the reindeer herd. In the ancient Lapp and Finnish culture, as shown in the national Finnish epic, the *Kalevala,* the poetry of dog guardians is sung:

> *Still the castle dog was barking*
> *And the yard dog still was barking*
> *And the furious whelp was baying*
> *The island watchdog howling.*

The Lore of the Dog

The Pomeranian, smallest member of the spitz type dog, is a toy with a foxlike head and bright, dark eyes. The ears are pointed and triangular. The tail is turned over the back and covered with long fur. The coat is soft and fluffy underneath, but the outer coat is harsh and sticks straight out. The Pom has a real mane, fluffing out like lion's ruff, and he must be groomed on a daily basis or the coat will become matted. The Pom comes in all solid colors, and is sometimes particolored. Maximum height is 12 inches and the average weight is 11 pounds. It is not uncommon, however, to see dogs much smaller and lighter weight. As in the other toy breeds, when dogs are bred in miniature, health problems can occur. Bulging eyes, missing teeth, hip dysplasia, and bad temperament are just a few of the unfortunate things that can happen to the miniaturized Pomeranian.

The natural temperament of the Pom is spirited, spunky, and bristling with curiosity. He likes the outdoors, yet does well in an apartment as long as there is plenty for him to do. Poms have a rather quick temper—they guard their food and toys, for example—so young children and other domestic pets need to give them consideration in this regard. The Pomeranian's bark is larger than the dog, and consequently, they make good watchdogs, who are always a bit wary of strangers.

The Pom is not a lazy dog with a preference for pillows rather than sidewalks. Instead, the dog is active, a hearty little fellow, who loves a good romp.

POODLE

The Dogge of Changes

MARIAH FOX

GERMANY, DENMARK, AND Italy believe the handsome, water-tight poodle is theirs, but it seems only fair to place the dog's lineage in France, where his probable ancestor was the North African barbet, a water dog and retriever of distinction. Today's French poodle was originally named *caniche*, stemming from *chien canne,* or "duck dog." Germany can lay claim to the word, if not the dog itself: Poodle is derived from the German *pudeln,* which means "to splash about in the water."

We know that the poodle is an old breed because we have visual record of some of them in paintings as early as the thirteenth century. Poodles also served as artist's models for Botticelli in the sixteenth century and Rembrandt in the seventeenth century. The smallest of poodles, the toy, was introduced in England in the eighteenth century when the white Cuba toy poodle became quite popular.

Reportedly, this dog came to England from the West Indies. Queen Anne admired a troupe of these dancing sleeve dogs when they first whirled upright to music in England. Ever since poodles of all sizes have danced to music of all kinds. Their performance charm as seen in circuses and floor shows is no less than their fancy footwork, but these dogs love to make people laugh and people love to laugh at them.

A<small>NOTHER FAMOUS ATTRIBUTE</small> of the poodle is his prowess as a swimmer. Bred to retrieve ducks in cold water, the dog's heavy, curly coat is left long around the joints, so that it works like a diver's wetsuit keeping the vulnerable body parts warm. Hunting also brought the smaller toy poodles into prominence, as they proved delicate diggers of truffles in the damp, fragrant forests of France.

I<small>N THE SIXTIES</small>, shortly before he won the Nobel prize for literature, John Steinbeck parlayed the poodle into such prominence that it is questionable whether he wrote *Travels with Charley* as a dog book in the guise of a travelogue, or a travelogue in the guise of a dog book. Whichever it was, Charley, the French poodle, is as piquant a person as you'll meet in literature—modern or ancient.

Charley's got charm without pomp, grace without grandness, beauty without boastfulness: "Charley's combed columns of legs were noble things, his cap of silver blue fur was rakish, and he carried the pompom of his tail like the baton of a bandmaster. . . . If manners maketh man, then manner and grooming maketh poodle."

However, it's Charley's sixth sense that Steinbeck comes to appreciate as a man whose mortal defense is trussed (trust) in his dog. Charley's infallible sense of the prevailing wind, whether good or bad, is a matter of clairvoyance. Moreover, Charley's moods are human, his attitudes a combination of provincial and high-born, his ways sometimes perverse, sometimes pathetic— but always amusing—and so like us, his admirers.

Overall, this dog's comical presence endeared readers to a book that surpassed the typical travelogue by a seasoned master. If Steinbeck did—as he claimed—model his book after Stevenson's *Travels with a Donkey in the Ardennes,* then he more than matched it; he bettered it. For what is a donkey next to a dog? And as he might have said himself, What is a dog next to a French Poodle?

S<small>TEINBECK'S POODLE-WRITING</small> (<small>POODLING?</small>) goes back to a Parliamentary Broadsheet, dated 1643, in which figures an inestimable white poodle, owned by Prince Rupert. This dog was the gift of Lord Arundel at the time that Prince Rupert was imprisoned in Linz by the emperor.

And what a perfect poodle he was, a Poodle par excellence; not only could he tell the difference between a Cavalier and a Roundhead, but Boy, as he was known, could bark most effectively at Parliament. His unfortunate death on the battlefield on Marston Moor could only have been caused by a soldier "who had skill in necromancy."

The latter comment reflects the fact that people in Boy's day believed that a "familiar" or Devil's accomplice, and Boy was definitely regarded as one, could be a dog as well as a cat; History, then, assigns this, the first poodle known to us by name, a very special place.

Boy's origin and accomplishments are many. As the myth goes, Boy was once a white woman who was changed into a handsome white dog, who was made to watch over the prince and keep him from mischief. His talents included prophecy: dates, times, and occurrences. He could, moreover, find anything that was concealed from view and liberate it for the betterment of the king and Parliament.

Boy was also endowed with the gift of language, not merely one but quite a few. He was able to tell gold from dross in the character of a man just by what he preached or professed to believe. Boy's own language was said to be a mixture of "Hebrew and High-dutch." Spies had no opportunity to hide their vain secrecies from Boy, who, after translating what they said, passed it on to the king. In physique, Boy was entirely "weapon-proofe." Word had it that daggers glanced off him and his armored skin was "anointed overwith Quick-silver." Of Boy, it was jokingly said that "he usually lets his mouth as a trap, and catcheth bullets as they fly." Under his tail, the myth went, he wore a brace, in which he voided bits of leaden ball, thus to have them ready for his master's reuse.

Boy was also called "a Metamorphosis Dog," a "Dogge of Changes," a shape-shifter of sorts. One day he'd be Philip the Shoemaker; the next, Tom the Barber. Nor were these two appearances his limit, for mingling himself with "the good apprentices," he came to resemble M. Bostock, the book-binder's boy. But his greatest trick was to pass a black cloud over the prince himself so that he might appear to be "the Appleman at Dunsmoreheath, the Netfeller in Coventry, and the Old Woman in Warwick."

Clearly it was no accident that John Steinbeck's Charley won so many American hearts, and then went on to win the world's. For, just as Boy was no common boy; Charley was no mere Charley. Whether necromancy, literary fantasy, familiar spirit, or Canidae incarnate, Poodle is Dogge as Dogge is Man.

The Lore of the Dog

The handsomely composed poodle comes in three sizes: standard, miniature, and toy. A long, fine head, slightly peaked with an elegant, unpointed muzzle, sits upon the poodle's well-proportioned shoulders. The body is neither long nor short, but so finely balanced that the dog is considered one of the most comely of all breeds. Sitting upright in a chair, or in the front seat of a car, he resembles a person.

The dog's brow is thoughtful and even a trifle intellectual, though some might say—and be wrong—that the poodle is an airhead.

The eyes are almond and very bright, the ears long, wide, flat, and fringed. With a deep chest and a tail highly set and usually docked, the poodle's coat is frizzy and the hair is dense and fine with a wooly texture. If one leaves the coat hanging, or corded, the dog is known as a corded poodle. If not corded, then it may be cut into an amazing array of styles.

The poodle comes in solid colors. Height for the standard poodle is over 15 inches; the miniature is 15 inches or less; and the toy is 10 inches or less. Weight for the standard poodle is 44 pounds; the miniature and the toy are not specified.

The poodle's personality is most attractive, which accounts for his large popularity. This is a dog that doesn't enjoy being alone, who likes constant company and the favors of good conversation and witty exchange. More than most breeds, Poodles seem to have mastered a deep understanding of our language, and they take commands and directives exceptionally well.

Poodles perform as fine hunting dogs and watchdogs, and in both activities they are versatile and responsible. They despise being ignored or relegated to the menial status of "other dogs." Although often considered high-strung, most experts agree that poodles are more super-sensitive than other breeds. It's been said that "a first-rate dog has no wish to be a second-rate human," and no dog is better suited to this phrase than the poodle.

PUG

The Pug of Puggery Way

JOHN BREDIN

SOME SAY RUSSIA, some say Holland; most swear the pretty little pug's an old Chinese secret. The truth is, we don't know exactly the origin of the pug but we do know what he looks like. This small, flat-faced, punchy bodied, tail-curled dog, looks like nothing other than a miniature mastiff. However, this Dutch connection may be in more than looks alone. The myth goes that the prince of Holland was once attacked at night, his army completely taken by surprise. As the night-guard ran to warn the prince, the enemy came at his heels, but a pug woke the prince by jumping on his face, giving him just enough time to slip out of his tent and flee the advancing army. Thus was the pug known in Holland as "the hero dog of the Netherlands."

GENERALLY ACCEPTED IS the view that the pug, like his great shadow, the mastiff, is a product of the East. Elasticity of the skin is an attribute, a conformational virtue of this dog, and it was believed that the wrinkles on the pug's forehead actually represented something other than loose skin. The "Prince Mark" was a vertical bar in the pug's wrinkles forming the Chinese character for prince; and thus the dog became princely, by virtue of this identifying feature. Other Chinese intimations are these: The dog was said to resemble a monkey; yet with bulging eyes and rolling gait, it was also said to be leonine. Take your pick, both are animals revered in Chinese mythology.

THE NAME "PUG" probably comes from the Latin *pugnus,* which means "fist," because the profile of the pug may be regarded as a clenched fist. There are those who claim that the word also means "monkey" because the dog was bred to look monkeylike, a perfect companion in the royal court. The latter was also a term of endearment in the English language, as in "you cute little pug;" or, "you dear little monkey." Whatever we think of the animal's origins and names, it's clear that the dog's place in history is well established. Stories and tales show that he was primarily a ladies' dog of the lap variety for more than two hundred years in Europe. In this connection, his name, converted into a kind of cute slang, meant "best friend," "pretty face," and even "lover boy." By 1780 the English dictionary stated that a pug was "something tenderly loved." This meant, or could mean, a friend or a lover.

As WITH THE name, so went the fashion of ownership—once again, reminiscent of the poodle and other breeds, we have a "dog of changes." Up and down goes the carousel of fortune; the pug's up one minute, down the next. By the end of the eighteenth century the pug was almost extinct in England ("Every dog has its day."). In the early part of the nineteenth century, owing to the popularity of the Italian greyhound and the toy spaniel, our poor little pug fell farther out of fashion in England, though in Holland and France he was de rigueur.

What brought him back, beside the tides of chance, was his undeniable cuteness. Pugs were touted as dogs that would race upon the carpet as horses upon the turf. They were spotlessly clean and so well aligned that fanciers looked for the famous distinguishing facial features that defined the purest of pugs: three hairs to each mole on the face. Yet ultimately the pug was revived because of an unexplained need; women wanted the dog so badly that by the end of the nineteenth century he was a finely produced black-market item, comparable to today's most elusive, highly priced Havana cigar. The curio aspect, the collectability of the pug was written all over the dog's crisply groomed features. Not only was the mole hair quotient discussed and sought, but the precise angle of tail curve was also bantered about. For instance, the male dog's tail curled right, the female's went left; perhaps in correspondence with certain martial arts maneuvers of the Chinese.

While well-bred young ladies might faint at the sight of something ill-bred, the pug, too, might imitate such admonishing virtue by appearing to keel over at the sight of an "uncouth individual." Pugs could flutter eyelids, turn up their already turned-up noses at all things disdainful. However, pugs were also most useful in the healing arts, skilled at pulling out fevers, relieving headaches and drawing off serious maladies, attracting the sickness unto themselves. (Today, experts agree that the medicinal aspect of these dogs has something to do with the common comfort and empathy they offer, but it's also been disclosed that they can reduce the symptoms of high blood pressure "just by being around.") Nor was the pug's charm felt only by the wealthy, for in the eighteenth century in Italy, a countess's pug was known to have been suckled by "a common woman," who was endeared to the little animal as if it had been her very own child. This was not an unusual circumstance, as finely bred pugs were the equal of finely bred children, and mothered as such.

Two myths of the historical sort come from the classic dog book, *This Doggie Business*, by Edward C. Ash:

> It became a fetish to exhibit Pugs at shows bedecked in necklaces, sometimes necklaces of considerable value in which the dogs got their feet entangled, much to their misery! Then came the famous Pug-dog Show at the Aquarium in London. The promoters had put on a show-man outside the hall to advertise the show, and he walked up and down shouting with tremendous force: "Na! Then!—Na! Then! This WAY to the Puggery!"
>
> Passersby—hearing this cry, and seeing that the charge to enter was very small, without any idea of what such a thing as a Puggery might be, but judging by the shouts of the man that it was likely to be exciting went in increasing numbers and came out flattened!
>
> A few years later a law case was fought over the ownership of a Pug-dog at Marlborough Street, and Mr. Hannay, the magistrate, bewildered by the claims of both sides, told each lady in turn to call the dog, hoping by this means to find out who indeed was the owner. The first lady cried out: "Moppy! Moppy! Come along Moppy!" And the Pug was overwrought with joy at finding its mistress again. Then the Pug-dog was taken back and the other claimant was given her chance. She cried out: "Jem! Jem! Come to your mistress Jem!" And the Pug-dog jumped up and ran to her in a state of Pug-like devotion. Mr. Hannay on this found the problem more than he could understand, and refused to make any order!

It's clear, at least to us that the mystifying little gamboler, the tiny horse, miniature lion, diminutive mastiff is just a cute little pug. He's really no mystery at all. Since the earliest time, this dog has always tried to please—whomever, whatever, wherever. And what's wrong with that? It's the very medicine we seem to need: If nothing else pleases, at least we, as frustrated humans, can be pleased by a dog. Onward, then, to the Puggery!

The Lore of the Dog

The pug has long been the favorite of monarchs ever since his earliest history in Asia and Europe. Such figures as Empress Josephine of France, Madame de Pompadour, Marie Antoinette, and William of Orange had pugs. Recently, the Duke and Duchess of Windsor had a number of pugs, who traveled with them wherever they went. This is a most comical canine, whose devotion to master/mistress is both legend and fact. Perhaps one reason why the rich and famous have always adored pugs is because these dogs make them laugh. Pugs are admirable tykes who love a good laugh, and at their own expense, too.

Physically, the pug is a square, compact creature with well-developed muscles. The head is large for the dog's size. The muzzle is short and flat, the skin on the head deeply wrinkled. The eyes are big and round, and protrude just a bit. The ears are small, triangular, and velvety soft. Pug tails are famous for being carried high and over the hip, a double curl being the best conformation. Their fine, silky short fur comes in apricot, yellow, fawn, silver, and black. They always have a dark mask over the face and ears, giving them a monkeyish cuteness. Pugs stand 10 to 11 inches and weigh 14 to 18 pounds.

The classic pug personality is amusingly friendly. Yet there are those who say that pugs are sulky and standoffish with anyone they don't know well. These dogs were not really designed with children in mind. Historically, they have been raised and fondled by loving adults. Sensitive to heat and cold, they do best in an environment that is not extreme in either direction. However, while they seem to have had capacious luxury in their past, these dogs do not mind small quarters or the good and simple plebeian life.

Pugs were bred for companionability, not hunting prowess. They guard, yet they're not guardians by trade. Their "medicinal uses" were many and varied, as hinted at above, and one of the cures they offered involved eating or drinking that which a person feared might be poisoned. This may or may not have led to the old custom of feeding a dog a bit of one's own malady (dogs were sometimes given a strand of human hair between two pieces of bread, and if the dog coughed, the sick person was cured). The extra heat given off by a small dog was believed to draw away the feverish heat of a human being; thus pugs were often used to relieve a burning brow. Historically useful as friends and relations and, psychologically, as mirrors for human moods, this little dog made himself invaluable to many a monarch by lifting a frown into a smile. And many a humble and suffering soul.

RHODESIAN RIDGEBACK

The African Lion Hound

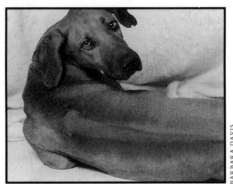

BARBARA DAVIS

W HEN THE FIRST Europeans came to South Africa in the sixteenth and seventeenth centuries, they brought greyhounds, bloodhounds, Great Danes, mastiffs, and terriers. The dogs of the Hottentots, or Khoikhoi, sprang from ancient Canidae stock, and these tame hunting dogs, when mixed with European hounds, made a superior lion dog, an animal with the wild blood of the African continent. This is the Ridgeback, a breed related to dingoes and other wild dogs of Africa and Australia.

The ridge of fur, however, which gives the dog his name, is permanent in him, while in the wild dogs it's visible only when aroused. The Ridgeback's bristle of opposing fur is an indelible remnant of the dog's past and it gives him a regal crest as well as a formidable posture. Curiously, the only other brown dog that has a ridge, which is formed by the hair growing forward, is found on the island of Phu Quoc in the Gulf of Siam. According to the Kennel Club of Great Britain and the Kennel Union of Southern Africa, "It is unclear whether ridged dogs appeared spontaneously in two parts of the world, or if they first appeared in Africa and then through commerce, moved with humans to Asia."

In 1877 a missionary, the Reverend Charles Helm, introduced the breed into Rhodesia, where big game hunters gladly adopted it. Once trained to hunt lions in teams—one dog for the hunt, two for the flank—Ridgebacks immediately found their calling. Three dogs could attack and subdue a pride of lions. They are still said to be the only breed of dog that can keep a lion at bay and alive.

As sight hounds, Ridgebacks hold their quarry on line, but their sharp sense of smell is invaluable on the veldt. The Ridgeback can travel for twenty-four hours without any water and he shrugs off harsh insects and rough terrain as calmly as he does inhospitable weather. Here is a lion-hearted hunter of the tall grass, who is also a soft-mouthed, silent-footed bird dog. The coarse, short hair is tick-proof and the Ridgeback, in addition to his hunting talents, is an excellent watchdog, especially on the prowl after dark. (This is because they were used on African farms to protect the farmer's sleeping stock.)

THE ANCESTOR OF today's Ridgeback appears in a number of Aboriginal myths, among them the prophecy given to them by the moon: "Dog shall tear Hare to pieces because Hare is responsible for forfeiting humankind's bid for immortality." Another Bushman myth explains why hunters always place the shoulder-blade bones of the Springbok out of reach of the hunters' dogs. The reason being that if ever a dog should happen to gnaw them, the hunter's aim would no longer be true.

THE LAMBA PEOPLE (central Bantu of northwestern Rhodesia and the Belgian Congo) also speak of the Ridgeback's ancestor, a primal dog who appears in a number of folktales which explain the nature of the hunt; the permanence of fire; the unprovoked bark; the compliment not given to a dog deserving of it. Some dog sayings among the Lamba are cautionary asides for human conduct; the dog being interchangeable with a man in terms of virtue. One proverb says: "Come back, my little dog, hunting is for every day," which seems to be the same as saying, "Tomorrow will be better" or "No one knows what the morrow may bring."

LOVE OF DOG stands above parental care among the Zulus of South Africa. As in European myths, where the dog is a prophet of death, the Zulus tell how the dog belonging to a king's son once sang out during a time of war, "Sing with me, my father, about your only son."

When the people heard this, they knew it was a mourning song, and that the king's young son was already dead in battle.

The story is also told of the practice of grinding the bone of the oldest dog in the village and making a medicine of it. Medicine men performed this rite when an epidemic ravaged their village because it was thought that by ingesting the sacred dog medicine, people thus afflicted would live to be as old as the venerable dog whose bone they had been given.

The Lore of the Dog

Physically, the Ridgeback is a handsome, upstanding, athletic dog. He is symmetrical and, like the quarry he was originally trained to hunt, leonine. His ears are hound's ears, square at the end and pendulous.

The serious-faced Ridgeback may be considered a rather circumspect and dignified dog. The attentiveness in his manner is reflected in the way he walks and stands—with great pride.

Colors range from light wheaten to red wheaten, with short and sleek fur. The legs are long and strong, excellent for endurance, and the pads feature a protective tuft of fur wedged into them, enabling the Ridgeback to walk on hot sand and other abrasive surfaces.

The Ridgeback is a sight hound whose hunting skills permit him to track, chase, and confront a lion. And yet this is a dog of docility in the home. His quiet, confident composure is observable in his obvious enjoyment of children. He is watchful, and gentle.

Ridgebacks are clean, almost odorless dogs, who are seldom quarrelsome, adapting easily to town or country living. However, due to their size—25 to 27 inches at the shoulder, weighing 65 to 70 pounds—they need plenty of exercise.

ROTTWEILER

The Butcher's Dog

BARBARA DAVIS

THE ROTTWEILER, LIKE the Great Dane and other large dogs, is descended from the Molossian mastiff of Tibet. The Romans, so far as we know, had Rottweilers as herd dogs and household guardians, as evidenced by two Rottweilers carved in stone upon the portal of a Roman home.

These proud, robust dogs remained in Great Britain after the Roman conquest, but, in time, they finally found their way to the German town of Rottweil, where they were bred primarily for cattle herding. Their owners were the butchers of Rottweil and the name itself refers to the red tiles of the town's rooftops.

Legend holds that men and dogs drove their herds to market as equals in the task. However, highwaymen were a real threat in those days and the butchers placed their full purses upon the necks of the dogs. Thus did the Rottweiler's reputation as the best of all guardians come into being. As purse wardens they were so good at their job, no thief would risk life or limb to challenge them. And when they walked about during the day, a bag of coins jingled at their necks and rang with each well-placed step.

Toward the close of the 1800s, cattle drives by dog were replaced by the railroad, and so the Rottweiler found himself out of a job. In 1900 only one Rottweiler could be found in the town of Rottweil, but within a few years, the qualities that made the dog the prince of guardians allowed him a new occupation: police work.

———

Today, the rottweiler combines the traits of a multifaceted background. He is notably a companion whose passion is to protect the property of his owner.

The Rottweiler came to America in the early 1930s and in the past ten years has become the most popular guard dog in the country. An outstanding recent example of the Rottweiler's dedication as a guardian appeared in the Associated Press news story of the dog known as Samantha. This legendary Rottweiler saved the life of three-year-old Blake Weaver by staying at the boy's side for twenty hours.

Barefoot and wearing only shorts and a T-shirt, Blake had strayed off into the deep woods of the Ocala National Forest of Central Florida. During the chill January night, Samantha, the family Rottweiler, stayed close and kept the boy warm. Through the night, as wind chill factors brought 30-degree temperatures, Samantha stayed on guard and blanketed the boy. The following day, Samantha led Blake to the dirt road where four hundred searchers were plying the woods, looking for him. He was found uninjured, owing, the physicians' claimed, to the dog's care. Today, Samantha the Rottweiler is an honorary Marion County Deputy.

In teutonic mythology dogs like Samantha were not deputized, but they were depicted in stone and sculpted on bronze. Warriors bearing the body of Siegfried are shown flanked by huge Rottweilers, and the hammer of the Teuton god, Thor, is symbolically carried in the mouth of a dog that is the very image of a Rottweiler.

The tale of Thor's hammer has a strange doglike twist to it. The myth tells how the sacred hammer was stolen by a giant named Thrym. He vowed to return it only when he had first married the goddess, Freyja. She flatly refused him, so to get back his thunderbolt, Thor pretended to be Freyja. Dressing in the goddess's clothes and wearing a veil over his face, he passed unnoticed until he reached Thrym's castle. Then his first meal with Thrym nearly gave him away, for he ate an entire ox and eight large salmon, after which he quaffed three barrels of mead.

Thrym's unruly eyebrows raised on seeing this; well he knew that no woman could possess such a hearty appetite. But Thor had a ready explanation at hand. So great was his desire to be with Thrym, that he'd eaten nothing on his travels, and was therefore ravenous with hunger.

Thrym, still suspicious, reached across the table and ripped off Thor's veil. What he saw was the ruddy face of a god and the lightning eyes that danced therein.

Yet before Thrym could say anything, Thor explained that his face merely betrayed the love that lay within him. And he begged Thrym to get on with the wedding vows.

These words calmed Thrym as no others could, and so he ordered the great hammer to be brought in. Then, according to custom, he placed it on his bride's knees. Thor quickly grasped the weapon and slew Thrym on the spot. Thus ends the tale.

And where does the dog come in?

This old myth is not only preserved in balladry, but there is an Icelandic chair made in the Middle Ages that reveals a carved hammer closed in the mouth of a dog: a huge square mouth clamped upon a massive, mythical hammer.

Is this Thor's dog? Or is it a comment on the nature of the guard dog; that the mouth of the dog is lightning and can strike the unwary just like Thor's hammer. "Beware," the chair says, "who comes in this house is watched over by eyes as keen as Thor's and a mouth as strong as his hammer." And the dog chair sits before the fire, four-pawed and eager, ready to greet friend or foe.

The Lore of the Dog

Tough and rugged describes him best, but he is an historic worker, an outdoor dog of distinction. The Rottweiler is medium large with a compact build. The head is wide between the ears and squarely sculpted. The ears are small, triangular, and pendent. With a broad chest and front feet slightly shorter than the back ones, the Rottweiler is a dog with great hind-end traction.

The coat is invariably black (some are pure black) with brown markings; the fur is short and thick. The tail, customarily docked, may also be short and horizontally carried. Height is 24 to 27 inches and weight averages at around 110 pounds.

Rottweilers have become the dog of choice for people who value a conscientious guardian. They are exceedingly self-assured and aloof around strangers. Inherently, their desire is to guard. As fighters, they are also exceptional, having once been used to bait bears and bulls.

Young Rottweilers, if not socialized and given instruction on their future work as guardians, will become over-protective. It is not uncommon to find a trained dog following his master/mistress from room to room. They like to keep eye contact on the family.

According to the American Rottweiler Club, "the dog may not be able to distinguish between a bear-hug greeting of family or friend; they may regard such actions as hostile advances, and this also includes shouts, laughter or screams." Therefore, the Club advises some caution and suggests that a definite responsibility must come with this dog's ownership.

An interesting fact about Rottweilers is that, whether properly trained or not, they still sometimes try to bluff or even bully not only strangers but their owners. In spite of the Rottweiler's tendency to be the ultimate watchdog, he is quite tranquil and a good companion.

Rottweilers are fine with children, but this depends, of course, on the particular dog and the individual children.

SAINT BERNARD

The Alpine Mastiff of Great St. Bernard Pass

JOHN BREDIN

THE ANCESTOR OF the Tibetan mastiff was probably brought to Switzerland by the Romans some two thousand years ago. Most likely the breed was then mixed with the Great Dane and the Great Pyrenees to give us the big-boned St. Bernard that we know today. Officially, the dog first appeared on a Swiss coat of arms in 1350.

The name Bernard comes from Archdeacon Bernard de Menthon, who founded an alpine hospice in a treacherous pass between Switzerland and Italy. There, the first European St. Bernard was bred as a guardian, companion, and search-and-rescue dog.

The relationship between the monks and the St. Bernard happened quite by accident; or perhaps by providence, they might say. For, right from the start, the big heavy-coated dog naturally took to the snows and demonstrated a native desire to seek out avalanche victims.

Case histories from the earliest times show that this remarkable animal, with little or no training, went about his work with professional ease and rugged determination. The result, in retrospect, is three centuries of rescue service in the Alpine mountains, and that translates into the saving of thousands of human lives.

Barry was the most celebrated dog in human history. He lived at the Hospice of St. Bernard (from 1800–1814) and, in his brief and legendary life, saved forty human lives, though myths have swelled the number to well over one hundred. He also ensured the immortality of his breed as the rescue dog of the century. The dog's personal name, Barry, became so well known that it was subsequently associated with the breed, as in "a Barry dog."

THERE ARE MANY myths based upon not only the life of the dog, but his imagined death. None of these are supposed to be true, but all form a fabulous hoar-frost of mythology around the dog and the breed. One myth, for instance, relates that Barry went out on the last night of his life to search the mountainsides, deep in snow, for any lost travelers. A man buried in snow saw the dog and called for his aid, and Barry ran toward him. Now the half-frozen traveler believed that what he really saw coming to him was a wolf, and struggling with his gun, shot Barry dead.

As if this story weren't fantastic enough, other fables were laid on top of it; in one of them, the noble dog not only rescues the half-conscious traveler, but licks him all over with his warm tongue to revive him, and it's in the midst of this life-saving activity that the crazed man shoots and kills the great dog. The fixation for Barry and the desire to make known his larger-than-life characteristics seemed to have inspired his preservation in physical as well as spiritual form. He can be seen today in the Museum of Natural History in Berne, Switzerland.

THE HISTORY OF the St. Bernard would seem to be a success story; however, it's surprising to learn that the breed almost disappeared at one time due to a breeding experiment. The monks of the St. Bernard Hospice had made the St. Bernard indomitable by mixing his blood with that of the larger and heavier-furred Newfoundland. But the resultant dog was so heavy-coated that he was actually unsuitable for rescue work—the great weight of his coat just slowed him down. The monks then abandoned this plan and gave the dogs away, but as fate would have it, the give-aways became popular with other Europeans, particularly the English. It was Heinrich Schumacher, a dog lover and breeder, who dedicated his life to the preservation of the original short-haired "Barry breed" St. Bernard. Through the latter part of the eighteenth century, he not only supplied purebred dogs to Switzerland, but he also spread them around the world. In the United States the long-haired St. Bernard was, at first, readily adopted, but over time, and continuing to the present day, the short-haired dog has returned to ensure the original Swiss standard of excellence.

———

The MOST FAMOUS St. Bernard myth was wrought out of experience and hearsay by the American novelist Jack London. In his great dog hero, Buck, a hybrid St. Bernard, London creates an animal archetype: the dog that risks his own life to save others. No book about dogs has ever bettered Jack London's masterpiece, *The Call of the Wild* as it explores what E. L. Doctorow calls "the complex spiritual life of a dog." In the novel the man and the dog are cast as archetypes in prehistory, secret sharers of the primordial fire. This is one of those rareties: an adult animal tale that is psychologically binding and accurate. The main virtue of the story is that we share in the atavism of Buck's mythic, or superdog, qualities. In the end, when Buck leaves civilization to run and howl with the pack of wolves, we go right along with him. Today's urban mythology of the St. Bernard calls into question not only the dog's prowess as a life saver but his reason for existence.

IN THE POPULAR film *Beethoven* and in the earlier myth of *Peter Pan* by Sir James M. Barrie, the conundrum of the too-big dog is humorously resolved. In Barrie's tale the oafish St. Bernard, Nana, is the family nursemaid. This remarkable dog fetches pillows for the children, pours medicine for them, and can even arrange alphabet blocks in their proper order. However, she's too large for the Victorian home in which her master reminds her: "Nana, the children aren't puppies."

On the night of Peter Pan's most auspicious visit, Nana, having gotten under Mr. Darling's feet once too often, is tied up outside. Who can forget that Nana finds Peter Pan's shadow? Dogs are the ones in Celtic mythology who see beyond mortal eyes and venture into the netherworld. Nana, the good St. Bernard, is seer, nurse, and savior rolled into one, but, because she's too big, she is tied to her dog house and can't go to Neverland.

The moral is clear—it's just not a dog's world, it's a people's world, one in which dogs are given responsibility only to have it wrested away because they take it too seriously.

Beethoven, an updated Nana of a contemporary California ranchhouse, likes to snatch bacon off the kitchen table. He's too big for picket-fence parameters, but he is ever watchful of the children. Like Nana, Beethoven is also locked out of the house "for his own good." Although his child-concerns are ignored, or unseen, by all but the children, Beethoven acts as a safeguard against human error, rescuing a drowning tot in spite of his confinement.

Underneath the gags this film asks some serious questions, a few of which were also raised in *Peter Pan*. One of them is fundamental: Do we really need such a big dog in a confined urban environment? The answer comes in unison from the children whose instincts, in the film anyway, have not been dulled by the trials of adulthood. Big dogs, most children believe, have big hearts.

According to Jack London, "Buck was content to adore at a distance. He would lie by the hour, eager, alert, at Thornton's feet, looking up into his face, dwelling upon it, studying it, following with keenest interest each fleeting expression, every movement or change of feature."

The St. Bernard's capacity for adoration is even larger than the dog itself, and when we grow so weary of life that we no longer need such reminders of love, we'll no longer require dogs at all, let alone large ones.

The Lore of the Dog

This gentle giant is easily recognizable for his greatness of size, particularly the enormity of his squarish head and the broad, heavy tail—upcurved in motion, down when still. The forehead is furrowed, giving him a worried, working dog's mien. The muzzle, deep and four-sided, adds to the seriousness of his face. The ears are medium size and, like a logger's cap, thrust out a little before dropping.

Coloration is usually red and white with the fur being either short or long. The short-haired coat is dense but smooth-lying. The long-haired coat is slightly wavy, not too shaggy, and of medium length. The long-haired breed is less adapted to rescue work, since the coat collects ice and snow until it is almost too heavy to be borne.

St. Bernards are strong-legged and big-footed with powerful toes. Height is from 25 to 27 inches; weight can be as light as 110 pounds and as heavy as 175 pounds.

Known in literature and in film as a wonderful friend of humankind, the St. Bernard is loyal, tranquil, meditative, hard-working, fully focused, and agreeably gentle. These dogs are not noted for guarding skills, though they will do adequately at the task.

St. Bernards are not dogs of leisure, but nor are they demanding of constant activity. Their inclination is to be useful, to sense danger, to be present when the time comes for them to act.

They are not usually fond of small dogs, but they love people without reservation.

SALUKI

The Desert Dog of Saluk

JOHN BREDIN

SUMERIAN MURALS AND carvings dating back to 7000 B.C. depict this oldest of breeds as the purebred of kings and sheiks. The saluki also figures in ancient songs and chants, and his presence in the Bible is the very definition of the word dog.

The name "saluki" has the ring of antiquity; it is, in fact the Arabian desert town of Saluk, which is no more. The Moslem people, who have declared the saluki a gift of Allah, believe the dog to be not a dog at all—for dogs, by definition, are unclean. The swift saluki, *el hor*, the "noble one," is allowed to sleep on the sheik's sacred carpet. As the gift of Allah, he is also a bringer of acceptable hunted meat, which otherwise (if hunted by another dog) would be considered unclean. The prized dog is also allowed to eat from the same dish as his master. Moreover, Arab women have been known to nurse saluki pups at their breast along with their own babies. There's also a story of the Arab customs official, who, seeing a saluki's bill of lading marked "dog," refused to stamp it until the paper was dignified to read "saluki."

The historic desert hunt was initiated with a hawk as harrier and the saluki as follower, driver, and killer of game—hares, foxes, antelope, and gazelle. One Arab said of his dog, "When he perceives a gazelle cropping a blade of grass, he overtakes her before she has time to swallow it." In truth, the hindquarter drive and thrust of the saluki can put him at measurable speeds of forty or more miles per hour.

THE CRUSADERS WERE said to bring salukis back to Europe with them, but the dog wasn't known there until the mid-nineteenth century. The first salukis in England were Persian rather than Arabian, and larger in size. Later, toward the end of the nineteenth century, Arabian salukis came to England from Prince Abdulla in Arabia. During World War I, more were brought in, and England's Kennel Club recognized the breed in 1922; the American Kennel Club recognized the breed in 1927.

In Mohammedanism it is believed that a mysterious power inhabits certain beings and certain things; this gentle force that flows from the natural world envelopes the sleek saluki, and is known as *baraka*. *Baraka* is present in such worldly disparities as brides-to-be, camels, mountains, and, of course, the swift el hor, saluki. The dog's telescopic sight is the gift of Allah; so is his fleetness of foot. And both are likewise said to be possessed of *baraka*. When a dog can outrun an Arabian gazelle, one of the fastest creatures on earth, how can the dog not be driven by the force of *baraka*?

Where men fail, the saluki does not. Arabs, in the hunt of old, carried their salukis in the saddle; today they are carried on the seat of a four-wheel-drive Jeep. This is so they're rested when the time comes for them to run. For it is then that the power of *baraka* is unfurled and set forth to run its course with fate.

The Arab hyperbole is thrown out, but not in jest, as a man laughingly says, "My saluki will catch a gazelle and bring him down even if that gazelle would spring up to the stars and vault over the moon."

MOHAMMEDANS HAVE A saying that describes a greedy person as "One who would not throw a bone to the dog of the seven sleepers." This dog, a saluki, was known to have guarded seven youths who were fleeing for their lives during the realm of Emperor Decius around A.D. 250.

The Koran tells of the youths' long uninterrupted sleep—three hundred and nine years—during which time they were watched over by a great saluki guard dog, whose forelegs were stretched in the mouth of the cave.

It is said that the dog spoke to the youths in a prophetic voice (the voice of Allah), saying that he loved those who also loved God, and that he would watch over them. Such myths earned the saluki the right to enter paradise. One interpretation of the story of the seven sleepers is that the saluki in the myth, like Anubis, is the emissary between the worlds of life and death.

Another Arab folktale is about the Beni-Kelb, the Sons of the Dog. The women of this tribe are fair and human in presence, but they say the males have no speech because they are "white hounds." The folktale further says that when an old person's beard is white with frost, these dogs beckon him to their tents, where, after regaling him with meat and drink, they devour him.

The "devouring dog" theme is akin to the Seven Sleepers' saluki guardian. Metaphorically, to be eaten by one so holy as a blessed dog is to be reborn, to enter the force of *baraka*, to be one with Allah.

The Lore of the Dog

The far-seeing eyes of the saluki are set in a comely, narrow, tapered face. The long ears, tail, and legs are feathered with silky fur and the body, deep-chested, long-legged, and elegant, is made for chasing antelope. With a sleek coat of varying color—white, cream, fawn, red, grey, black, and tan—the saluki is the picture of symmetry, a desert-bred animal of antiquity. Tufted, hardened pads allow the saluki to run over hot, rough surfaces without injury.

In addition to their running skill, they can also turn abruptly with their quarry and continue to move gracefully at a gallop. Height is 23 to 28 inches; weight is 50 to 55 pounds.

The saluki is a self-assured master of the limelight, but does not do as well in situations of shared glamour. His love of sighting things, his enjoyment of the hunt, the chase, the run, make him fun to watch. Though the saluki is reserved among strangers, he is a good companion with the family, gentle with children, affectionate but not demonstrative.

As watchdog, the saluki is unaggressive yet protective. It is not recommended to keep one with other, smaller animals, because of the saluki's hunting instinct.

SAMOYED

Dog of Sun, Dog of Moon

BARBARA DAVIS

THE SAMOYED PEOPLE come from between the White Sea and the Yenisei River of Siberia. Nomads and reindeer herders, the Samoyeds owned dogs that were originally used for driving dog sleds across the Siberian steppes. Later the dogs came to be used for shepherding reindeer. European and Asiatic Samoyed dogs have also been used for this purpose, and for guarding the herds against the predation of wild animals. These were also the sled animals chosen by Nansen, Scott, and Shackleton for their Arctic and Antarctic expeditions. In a region where the frozen air drops low enough to fell the tundra crows on the wing, a dog that can endure the winter is a miraculous creature indeed. The Samoyed can, and does, handle his environment with great tenacity of spirit and physical adaptation. How does he adapt so well? Partly due to the way the dog is so well padded and layered with fur.

Samoyeds have sun–white, straight-haired outer coats of fur, while their inner coat is a softer duckdown shield against the cold. As *National Geographic* states: "countless Arctic suns and snows have bleached his coat to a striking white. . . ." Such a coat is reflective and the tufts between the toes act as snowshoe padding in the deep drifts. Moreover, the soft white undercoat, when brushed out, has yet another purpose—though not for the dog. This fur has been used for centuries by the Samoyed people, who spin it into yarn and weave it into fine woolen clothing.

————

More than a century ago the Samoyed dog was brought to England where owners discovered what the natives of the Siberian steppes had always known: Their dog is very loving and considerate of humans. They learned as well that the word "Samoyed" (pronounced *Sammy-yed*) means literally, "living off themselves," which is a reference to both the people and the dogs they raised. There is an incredible self-sufficiency bred in these loyal, hard-working animals whom their original trainers called "Bjelkiers," which means "white dogs that breed white." Historically, the Samoyed is relatively new to America. The standard was first approved by the American Kennel Club in 1963. As stated earlier, the importation to England took place around 1889. Roald Amundsen's expedition (December 14, 1911) brought a Samoyed lead dog to the South Pole, the first time any non-native creature set foot or paw upon these snows.

Myths of the American Indian that deal with white dogs are plentiful. Deities of the Jicarilla Apache, who reside in northern New Mexico, are said to have a variety of dogs, among them a glittery white dog, representative of the sun and moon. The old Iroquois white-dog sacrifice was a rite that induced the dog spirit to travel to the world above and bring messages to the Great Spirit. White dogs were sometimes sacrificed in the old Chinese custom in which their blood, spilled upon the city gates, helped to ensure the safety of the inhabitants. A pint of hot blood taken from a white dog was also a cure for ghost encounters, fevers, and insanity. European dog myths include the white dog of death. The sight of such a dog invariably presaged the death of a family member. In some parts of Wales the color of the dog ghost is of great importance. The vision of a white dog means that a dying person, or someone soon to die unexpectedly, will be saved from Hell and will go on to Heaven.

The Lore of the Dog

The Samoyed has the sturdy "spitz-look" of a medium-size sled dog: deep chest, strong legs capable of great endurance. The head is wedge-shaped with a tapered nose, the lips are black and slightly curved, which gives the dog the famous "Samoyed smile." The eyes are dark and almond shaped and the ears are thick and erect. The tail is long, covered with beautiful fur, and curved over the back. The coat is "double," with an undercoat of soft wool and an outercoat of longer fur that stands straight out from the body. There is a ruff around the neck and shoulders. Samoyeds are most often pure white, but they can also be white-and-biscuit, or all biscuit.

The height is 19 to 23 inches and the weight 35 to 60 pounds.

The coat of the Sammy can be used for yarn, if mixed with other fiber. The fur is odor-free, and somehow resistant to most stains and dirt. Moreover, the Sammy is meticulous at self-grooming, much like a cat. In hot climates, the fur is best left uncut because the outer coat is a protection against sunburn.

Most northern breeds are unsuited for guarding, and while the Samoyed falls into that category, the dog's use as a reindeer shepherd makes him a better watchdog than most of the other sled dogs. The Sammy is sometimes thought to be difficult to train. This is not true, but the breed does show impatience with regard to obedience training and the performance of repetitive tasks.

Sammies talk with an *"aroo,"* or soft *"woo-woo,"* like the Malamute, but they also bark.

SCHNAUZER (MINIATURE, STANDARD, GIANT)

The Schmoozy Schnauzer, Large, Medium, and Small

MARIAH FOX

ROGER CARAS HAS this to say about the breed that sometimes is accused of sporting diamonds and pearls: "Schnauzers, and particularly the miniature schnauzer, are like poodles: a breed that people get silly about. You are far more likely to find the poodle or the miniature schnauzer wearing a diamond-studded collar than any other breed. People often comment on that adversely, usually in relationship or at least with reference to starving children. . . . Buying your schnauzer or any other dog, thirty-seven custom hand-knit sweaters from an extremely expensive store, as one New Yorker has been reported to do, is again playing games with being rich. It has nothing to do with dogs. Nothing of that kind does. Ah, but how often dogs take the rap."

The schnauzer's rap, if such it is, comes about because he is such a fine companion dog, and has been for at least five hundred years. Albrecht Dürer portrayed a standard schnauzer as far back as the 1490s, but all three breeds were founded in Württemberg and Bavaria in the nineteenth century, where it was primarily known as the wire-haired pinscher, or what we call today the standard schnauzer. This is the oldest of the three breeds, the miniature being the newest at around the turn of the century.

The giant schnauzer, which was crossed with various herding dogs, as well as the Great Dane and perhaps the Bouvier des Flandres, was an excellent cattle-driving dog, and, today, is a household guardian, a police dog, and a companion dog in Europe and America.

Roger Caras clarifies the three breeds, pointing out that the terms miniature, standard, and giant "would seem to imply one dog in three sizes, instead of three different dogs. The latter is the case." He goes on to say in his classic *A Celebration of Dogs* that all three schnauzers make excellent watchdogs, but that the giant is "most impressive," and so large that fanciers use them to pull carts.

The miniature, though small in stature as his name implies, has a noisy terrier's bark that can be alarming to an intruder. "It doesn't have the basso profundo of the larger dogs, but it can put up enough thunder to advise intruders that they are no longer unnoticed. Being unnoticed is what skulkers in the night want, and any good noisy dog can rob them of that. All schnauzers are good at that task."

The standard will revert to type when left entirely alone, or out of doors. This means the dog's ratter instincts are strong and though these dogs do not go to earth the way terriers do, they will get very excited about chasing a rat.

A TALE ABOUT a schnauzer came to us from a friend, Karel Werner, a teacher who, during the Second World War, lived in Prague. He was a young man in the spring of 1939 when the Germans occupied Prague. The Nazis were all over the city, and it was no longer safe for a Jewish boy to be out on the streets at night. Jews were also forbidden to attend high school, and all males between the ages of nineteen and forty had to register for duty in German labor camps.

And so it was that one evening, while saying his last farewell to some old friends, Karel was seen walking home from Wenceslas Square in the dark, where he was captured by a group of German soldiers. These men, not really knowing what to do with the boy, made him sit in the back of a truck that was carrying soldiers to another part of the city.

Karel knew that he might be shot for jumping off the truck, but he did so anyway, vaulting off the side as rifles were raised and rounds fired at close range. He ran fast and crazy, zigging like a rabbit as the bullets cranged against the cobbles of the street. Then, finding himself in an alley, he ran the length of it and entered a five-story apartment building from the rear door. He took the stairs six at a time and arrived breathless on the top floor. The apartment doors were all closed, none ajar. He banged on them with his fists, begging to be taken in. No door opened. At last, knowing that he was being followed (he could hear the soldiers downstairs), he sank to his haunches in the recess of a doorway.

Almost immediately, he heard loud German-speaking voices in the corridor. The soldiers had come and Karel could hear a large dog on a tight chain, dancing in place, whining to be set free. All at once the big dog was released. The soldiers stayed where they were at the opposite end of the hall, but Karel heard the bolt of a rifle slide into place. Methodically, the dog, heavy-footed and well-muscled from the sound of his feet, came down the hallway, sniffing at the front of each door. The silence was deafening; Karel breathed as quietly as he could, but his hands were trembling on his knees, which he'd drawn up to his face.

Door after door received the intent inspection of the dog. Karel heard the click of claws as he set forth, then the nosing of the floor in front of each door, as he came closer and closer. Then, all at once, the dog was there, in front of him. Karel's eyes were wide open and so were the dog's. They were face to face now, the dog standing, Karel hunched into the recess of the deep doorway. Their noses almost touched. Karel saw that the expression on the animal's face was one of great doubt and wonder. He'd found something, but was it the thing his owners wanted him to find?

They stared, the boy and the dog, neither one moving a muscle. Then the dog broke the trance and moved back. Karel expected him to go for his throat, but the dog turned and went to the next door, head down, sniffing; then the next door and the one after that. Then he swiveled on his feet and came clicking back the way he had come, but he never glanced at the doorway occupied by Karel. He went back to the soldiers, who joked among themselves, lit some cigarettes, and went back downstairs. To Karel, each loud footfall was a reprieve.

Years later he would remember that the dog's face looked like a man's; it was big and bushy-bearded with eyes that had a deep Bavarian seriousness in them. To this day whenever Karel sees a schnauzer, large, medium, or small, he gives him a warm welcome: "Hello, old savior," he says.

The Lore of the Dog

Roger Caras describes the schnauzer's face as "Whiskers 'en bush' " and in his opinion, such facial appendages do something elegant for the dog, along with his bushy eyebrows. In fact, the dog's strong, blunt muzzle is decorated with mustache and chin whiskers on all three of the breeds. Of course, the face of the giant is nothing less than imposing, while the standard comes complete with terrieresque dignity, and the miniature is a bit more compact, but also more comical, yet fully convincing as a guardian when he wants to be. These dogs, all three, are exuberant about life and they show it with animated face and athletic body.

The miniature is the smallest version of the family, and has a long head and dark, oval-shaped eyes. The ears are usually docked to a point and the coat is coarse with a dense undercoat. The color is salt and pepper or black. Height is 12 to 14 inches and weight is 13 to 15 pounds.

The miniature breed is a family-oriented dog, so devoted that he truly resents strangers. His whole being resounds in the effort of pleasing the family, especially one particular member. Few breeds show more willingness to learn and more elasticity in accepting training techniques. Miniatures do not tire of playing games, for their focus is probably more acute in this than the average person's. It's not a good idea to start a game with this dog that is over too quickly.

The standard schnauzer, like his cousins, is a good watchdog, companion, and friend. He was originally a carriage-and-watchdog in the stables, as well as a ratter in the barn. In all of these roles, he was admirably suited and self-styled to please. His terrier attitude was, and is, curious, dependable, and acceptably menacing when needed. The standard schnauzer is medium in size and ruggedly built. The head is long, the eyes oval and dark, and the ears docked to a point. The coat is coarse and wiry, never wavy or straight; colored salt-and-pepper or black; and the dog's beard, mustache, and eyebrows are the most noticeable features of the face. The height is 18 to 20 inches and weight around 33 pounds.

The giant schnauzer was a cattle driver in the mountains of Bavaria where he was most likely bred from a cross between a standard schnauzer and a black Great Dane. This dog, due to his great size, needs an enormous amount of exercise, primarily running. In terms of features, the giant looks like his cousins, but he is much, much larger. His head is long, the eyes are oval, the ears point-cropped (or not). The wiry and dense coat, as with the other schnauzers, needs regular grooming. Usually the giant is pure black, but occasionally you'll see a silver or salt-and-pepper schnauzer. The height is between 25 and 28 inches with a weight of 70 to 75 pounds.

The giant schnauzer is an independent dog and if not trained early can become aggressive. Harsh training won't work at all with this breed; the dog will become instantly rebellious. In general, schnauzers have a sense of their own worth and a feeling that they know what to do in a given situation; they need, moreover, to be able to trust this worthwhile intuition.

SCHIPPERKE

The Little Captain of Belgium

JOHN BREDIN

THE SCHIPPERKE HAS always been a worker, a little tough of the dockyard nights. Small he may be, but soft he is not. The Skip is one of the most dangerous ratters in the business. Owners testify that you just don't know the dog until you've seen him shaking his head with a ball or toy. The neck muscles of the Skip are very strong, as are the jaws, and this diminutive dog can swiftly dispatch a rat. The sharp, foxy schipperke is surprisingly athletic and lives to a great old age, but these are just a couple of his well-known virtues.

THE NAME MEANS "little captain" in Flemish, and as the workman's pet, watchdog, and professional ratter, the Skip, as he's known today, became an indispensable companion dog long before his fame brought him into "the doggie business." The Belgian Schipperke Club, though, was started in 1888, shortly after the breed was introduced. In 1890 one of the first tracts written on the schipperke appeared in England and in it mention was made that the dog was known as the "spits" in Belgium, but because the Pomeranian was already known as a spitz dog, this name eventually lost out to the present one.

Around the turn of the century in Belgium there were quite a few breeds answering to the name of schipperke. These were city dogs bred to keep down the rodent population on the barges in the canals. Naturally, they were also boat dogs, skippy little agile fellows on the narrow decks, whose thickness of fur enabled them to swim in frigid water without fear of drowning or contracting hypothermia.

One dog authority during the 1930s attested to the fact that there were three kinds of Skip in Belgium at the turn of the century. Supposedly, each vied for the title of "correct breed." There was, for instance, the Brussels Skip, wide in front and short-headed; there was the Louvain variety, short-coated with long narrow ears. However, it was the Antwerp dog, so called, who received the most appreciation for attractiveness, and became, for a time, the correct breed of the day. The latter may very well be the prototype for today's standard.

EARLY FIFTEENTH-CENTURY MYTHS in Europe speak of a tail-less black dog whose presence is an incarnation of the devil. Was this possibly the schipperke? Some say the mystery dog was originally a shepherd that was bred down in size, so the myth may have some basis in fact. Of course, any black animal during the time of the medieval witch hunts was a candidate for deviltry, but the Skip's lack of tail figures here as well, since taillessness is a quality of goats and pigs, both of whom have had a lineage with the old hellish myths.

WHERE DID THE myth of the devilish black dog come into being?
Probably it goes back to, times of mourning, dark times, ancient associations with moonlessness and darkness, and with humankind's feeling of helplessness at night. Lethal black dogs of mythology come in all shapes and sizes and spring from all countries on earth. In fact, only Argentina, it would appear, has a black dog myth of virtue rather than perilous and incontrovertible fate.

In China, tailless black dogs, *p'eng hen,* are thought to be demons. Large black coastal dogs, demons of Welsh folktale, appear with blazing eyes and baleful breath. Scotland's fairy dogs are not large, but like a small calf, their tails are curled over their back. They are noted as green and white in color, yet their presence is only felt at night when such distinctions are almost indeterminable. The footprints of the *cu sith,* or fairy Canidae, are always in a straight line like a fox, the animal the Skip most resembles, some say.

In DEVONSHIRE, ENGLAND, dog phantoms attack church and school at midnight, dropping a furious hail of stones from the sky. The same myth is also found in Jamaica along the north coast, where people speak of both the Scottish *cu sith* and the Devonshire phantom dogs. The Afro-Jamaican folklore also involves a burning calf that rolls down a hill with rattling chain, symbolic, some storytellers avow, of slavery. But could this also be the calflike *cu sith*?

O NE OLD SCHIPPERKE story has nothing to do with devil dogs but dogs that fight rats with devilish glee. It seems that when the Caribbean island of St. Thomas was under Dutch rule, a man on the boat docks at night saw a most amazing thing. It was a schipperke chasing ground rats that took to the trees. The dog, introduced from Europe, sent the rats off the docks where they had no choice, if they were to remain alive, but to adapt to an alternative environment. As these little dock dogs had no interest in tree-climbing, the rats—timidly at first, then boldly—adapted to their new life by learning to leap, squirrel-like, from branch to branch.

The Lore of the Dog

The schipperke, short and compact, is lively and mischievous. The head and face are decidedly foxlike in appearance. The ears are triangular and sharply pointed. The absence of a tail (for most members of the breed), the presence of a ruff, and the jet-black soft fur of the schipperke set the dog apart from any other. The double coat—a fluffy or downy undercoat—keeps the dog warm in cold wind, water, and wet weather. Schipperkes stand 12 to 13 inches and weigh up to 18 pounds.

According to schipperke owner Amy VanDenberg, this breed is, in a sense, ownerless:

> We are allowed to become their people. Life with schipperkes is a continual challenge. They are so inquisitive and quick that their people must constantly try to outwit them. For example, if a schipperke is sternly disciplined, you may bring out his vengeful nature. Sweet and entertaining as the dog is, he can't seem to resist setting up surprises, if he thinks you deserve them. When one of ours was disciplined—a spank with a hat—the dog later sought out this article and defecated in it to show his disdain for the punishment that had been meted out at his expense.
>
> Schipperkes teach their people to be neat: to put shoes away in the closet, to place clothes all the way in the hamper, and to

keep pens and pencils well away from the edge of tables. Our first love, Saba, appears to wish she had thumbs. She has stolen many pens and pencils, becoming frustrated when she can't use them as we do.

Stemming from the shepherd blood, which they are known to have, schipperkes have an obvious herding instinct. If my husband and I are in different rooms, the dogs pace back and forth between the rooms until we are in the same place. Only then will they settle down. People who raise these mischievous bundles of energy and crafty intelligence consider them a big dog in a small package.

THE SCHIPPERKE IS first a companion and a watchdog. On the barges of Belgium where he earned the nickname of "Little Captain," this dog was the protector of his barge and the guardian of all people aboard. Although schipperkes have also been nicknamed "Little Black Devils," they've earned a special place in the hearts of their owners.

SCOTTISH TERRIER

The Hardy Highlander

JOHN BREDIN

THERE ARE THOSE who claim the Scottie is the oldest indigenous breed in Great Britain. Knickknacks, for one thing, bear this out: Originally named the Aberdeen terrier, the dog was cast as a magnet, a playing card, a stuffed toy, and in novels he was the tagalong of detectives and outdoorsmen. For more than twenty years in America alone, the Scottie reigned as one of the top ten most popular breeds. Today he's a little off the roster of public favor, but ever on the verge of coming back.

These brave little earth dogs, as they've been dubbed, are irrepressible warriors and devoted until death do them part. They spark up at anything, bark up any tree that looks squirrelly, run about and bob about, and dance to an imaginary bagpipe. Maybe that's why they've been so popular—there's an intensity in the face, a curiosity that defies comparison. They like people, the doings of people, and they're participants, not onlookers, so they get into a lot of mischief, but not the irremediable, mastiff variety. Mostly they make us laugh.

HISTORICALLY, THE SCOTTIE was bred in the Highlands of Scotland to go after the fox and the badger. Digging into cairns was his specialty, though holes of any kind draw his attention right away. The claws and furious paws work in simultaneity, a whirring of intent that closes them in on their quarry. King James I of England delighted in the dog's insistent personality and persistent hunting prowess, and sent off six of them to the nobility of France. Toward the close of the nineteenth century, there were a number of dogs resembling the Scottie, who enjoyed basking in this kiltie dog's fame. Experts say the true breed comes from the Skye, West Highland, and the Aberdeen terrier. Bred to keep his character—the feistier the better—and the well-known comical face and figure, the Scottie was nonetheless a hardy Highlander, a working terrier, who would rather fight than quit.

America adopted the little guy with no holds barred. In the thirties, forties, and fifties the country was Scottie crazy. And all because, according to *National Geographic,* commercial artists saw in the dog a persona well-suited to fame and fortune—notably theirs. The ubiquitous Scottie appeared in ads, as miniature figurines, as knickknacks, as pieces of sentimental cuteness, the sight of which, even today, among Baby Boomers will bring an immediate smile.

Not only did artists celebrate the Scottie, but writers got into the act as well. They lavished praise on the bewhiskered face, the intelligent almond eyes with their Scottish wisdom all a-sparkle. Rudyard Kipling's *Thy Servant a Dog* probably sold more Scotties than any other famous literary figure, but then Holling Clancy Holling's *The Book of Cowboys* didn't do such a bad job either. In France, a cartoonist in the 1920s launched a fad for both Scotties and wirehaired Scottish Terriers. The cartoon was called "Ric et Rac" and the Scottie in it looks more like a paperweight or a bookend than a dog, which may have accounted for another fad, for all we know. In *The Book of Cowboys,* Holling ornamented the pages of the book and the tales he told of real life "out West" with two children and their favorite Scottie, Biff, who jumps over the sagebrush just like a jackrabbit.

One of the most famous Scottish Terriers of the 1940s was Fala, the inseparable companion of Franklin Delano Roosevelt. His full name was Murray the Outlaw of Fala Hill. In April 1945, when news of the President's sudden and unexpected death shook the nation, Fala was there in the corner of the room. However, at the moment that Roosevelt was pronounced dead, the little Scottie leaped up, crashed through a screen door, and ran wildly to the top a hill while barking at something only he could see. There on the hilltop, the little dog kept a long vigil. Naturally, this was not the first time in history that a dog saw something which everyone else seemed to have missed.

The Lore of the Dog

The Scottish terrier stands square on his feet; he's a little longer than he is high, but this is a square deal of a dog, even-tempered most of the time, hot-tempered some of the time, and, occasionally, a combustible spitfire. Scotties have a long head, but with the abundance of whiskers, they appear as square as their body type. The bushy eyebrows, mustache, and beard present not a dog but a dark-faced Scotsman. The eyes are small, glittery, and almond-shaped; the ears are small and pointed. The tail goes straight up and adds to the little dog's jaunty personality. The Scottie's coat is long, thick, and wiry with a soft undercoat. Although black's the most common color, the coat can be grey, sandy, wheaten, or brindle.

When running, the dog carries himself with a rolling gait due to his powerful hindquarters and his broad chest. Reaching out, the Scottie's fore-legs turn in, and he rocks and rolls as he runs, not unlike a bear cub. While his most notable persona is one of twinkling humor, this dog can also be dour and sometimes even disagreeable if he is not in preferred company. Human visitors, unannounced, can expect a torrent of noisy barks, and animal guests are simply unwelcome.

Scotties have a reputation for independence, but care should be taken for early training so that the terrier trait of aggressiveness doesn't overtake the dog's normally good nature. They are diggers and will go to ground for any reason whatever. Generally, they are not recommended for families with very small children—Scotties do not like to be "manhandled." These are high-spirited, lovable little dogs with a witty sense of what life's all about. They like cities as well as towns, but, naturally, the country's their own special province.

SHAR-PEI

The Dragon Dog of Kwun Tung

MARIAH FOX

THE NAME SHAR-PEI in English means "sand dog," which describes the texture of the skin when stroked against the grain. This uniquely cast coat is what gives the dog a furrowed face and form, a curiously wrinkly charm. Once known as the rarest breed in the world, artifacts featuring these "tomb dogs," as they have been called by archaeologists, date back to the Han Dynasty (A.D. 220) in China. These were herding, guarding, and hunting dogs, which people say resemble, not only a pig, but a hippopotamus; this is due to the high-set tail, small ears, large round muzzle, and wrinkly skin of the dog. In truth, the ancient breed is believed to have Chow, Great Pyrenees, and Tibetan mastiff in his bloodline.

The dog's ancestry resonates with mythology and history, the two being almost inseparable in this breed. Shar-pei owner Heidi Merkli writes:

> The appearance of the shar-pei is unique in many ways. The blue-black mouth and tongue is a trait shared with the Chow Chow. It was believed that in ancient times, the dark mouth of the Chow Chow, which was exposed when the dog barked, would ward off evil spirits. The first shar-pei may have appeared as a mutation of the Chow Chow. Known as a fighting breed, the shar-pei was shaped according to dog fanciers of long ago. The toes of the shar-pei were slightly turned out, which was thought to help the dog

with balance, as well as a sign of strength. This is a characteristic which resembled that of the Chinese Crawling Dragon with feet pointing east and west. A shar-pei's tail should denote bravery and a dog who carries his tail between his legs, and not up and over the back in a tight or loose curl, is considered cowardly.

The origin of the shar-pei can be traced to the province of Kwan-Tung in China where he was regarded as a great and noble dog of war. With the establishment of the Communist regime, the dog population in China was decimated. The shar-pei and other court dogs were viewed as ill-fated reminders of an elite class that was no longer in existence. To own a dog, by Communist decree, was to invite severe penalties, both economic and physical. The dogs themselves were destroyed whenever they were found. Thus a fine, aristocratic Canidae bloodline of two thousand years might have come to a close.

However, owing to the efforts of Mr. Matgo Law of Hong Kong, the shar-pei was brought back in sufficient numbers to permit the breed to flourish and also to allow exportation. Matgo Law, by himself, called for dog fanciers around the world to help save the noble shar-pei from extinction. His plea was heard, the dog was saved, and the world is ever grateful. The Hong Kong Kennel Club registered the shar-pei in 1968 and since then the breed has grown in popularity in America.

ONE OF THE great myths featuring a mastiff ancestor of the Chinese shar-pei occurred some four thousand years ago. The story tells of Emperor Kao-hsin who, seeking to vanquish a tribal foe named Wu, offered his daughter's hand in marriage, plus large tracts of land and one thousand pieces of gold, to anyone who could bring him his enemy's head.

No one saw Pan-Hu, the emperor's five-colored dog, raise his head and listen intently to the offer. Nor did anyone see him get up afterward and leave the palace. But he did these things as a man might have, and sometime later he returned, carrying the rival chief's head by the hair. On seeing this extraordinary sight, Emperor Kao-hsin declined his offer; however, his own daughter demanded that the promise be kept.

Pan-Hu, so the myth goes, carried his bride home on his back. They lived together in a cave in the Southern Range. Their children, six daughters and six sons, grew up and married each other. They lived freely, answering to no man and to no rule other than their own. They wore clothing of bark, dyed five colors in honor of their father, and they had tails made of the same material.

Today there are Chinese provinces that still celebrate this old myth. In some, Pan-Hu is worshipped as an ancestral being and sacrifices are made to him at the turning of the New Year and at other sacred seasons.

The Lore of the Dog

The shar-pei is a medium-size, square-bodied but well-proportioned dog, with an alert face and a lordly, scowling, snobbish, intelligent, and dignified manner. The head is large and proudly carried and covered with wrinkles. The mouth is solid bluish black; the ears are small and close to the head, and not pricked. The tail is carried over the back in a tight or loose curl. The coat is sand-grained, harsh to the touch, and comes in solid colors: black, cream, fawn, chocolate, or red. The height is between 18 and 20 inches and the weight is between 40 and 55 pounds.

Shar-pei owner Heidi Merkli states that the dog's skin has "a prickly texture when stroked against the grain. In ancient times, it was said that the shar-pei's ears were no larger than a human thumbnail, just large enough to cover the opening of the ear."

The personality of the breed is described by the American Kennel Club as "essentially independent and somewhat standoffish with strangers, but extreme in his devotion to his family." According to Heidi Merkli,

> The shar-pei is an alert, reliable, loyal, incredibly intelligent breed, with a sensitive, calm, and independent nature. One night my husband and I went to bed as usual with Bubba, our fifteen-month-old shar-pei, soundly sleeping in his crate by the side of the bed. Bubba was a good sleeper, in fact it was his second favorite thing to do. However, around 3:05 A.M., I awoke to Bubba sitting by the side of the bed staring at me. He then started to pace in and out of his crate. I wasn't sure what was wrong since he always slept straight through the night. Ten minutes later the fire alarm went off in our sixteen-story apartment building. We rushed out of our apartment and climbed down eight flights of stairs with my husband carrying Bubba. . . . Our lives had been saved by our shar-pei, whose devotion to family set off his own inner alarm before anyone knew there was a fire.

The shar-pei, once bred to ward off evil spirits with a plaintive bark, seems to have remembered his ancient training very well. For smoke, in many Chinese myths, was not only the intimate of fire, but the familiar of dangerous ghosts. In this respect Bubba was right on cue.

SHETLAND SHEEPDOG

The Little Sheepdog of the Shetland Islands

BARBARA DAVIS

T

HE SHETLAND SHEEPDOG, as the name implies, comes from the Shetland Islands of Scotland. Although there are no physical records of the dog's lineage, one can assume it's as old as the islands themselves, for these gentle working dogs have a quiet intensity and only the fittest of the fittest could have survived the cold climate on an island that yielded their owners so scant a livelihood.

If man and dog thrived on these lonely isles, it was only due to a striving and obstinate nature, much like the bare-boned rocks that stubbornly poked out of the soil and refused to be dislodged. So the Shelty has a hardiness as ungiving as granite but as soft as moss.

The breed was recognized by England's Kennel Club in 1909 and was acknowledged in 1911 by the American Kennel Club. Shelties found homes on sheep farms and ranches throughout the United States where they were, and are, a vital part of family and work life.

A

N OLD SHEPHERD'S tale of the Spanish Southwest tells of a small black-and-white sheepdog that haunted the hills of the Devil's River and Conchos country of East Texas. She wasn't exactly a ghost dog but the Pastores, who inhabited that land, thought of her as one because she was abandoned by her mother when her eyes were still closed. She was raised, so they say, by an old Ewe, so the little dog never knew she was a dog at all, and some say she wasn't one. More than likely, they say mysteriously, she was the spirit of dog and sheep combined.

When, as a pup, she was too little to know better, she stayed among the sheep, keeping close to the mother ewe, whose milk nurtured and sustained her. But, in time, the pup grew into a dog, and the dog had the sense that all herders have, and soon she was herding the sheep with which she was raised; and cutting out whatever ones she wanted for her own.

Now the Pastores noticed their sheep were vanishing, but they had no idea where they'd gone. A suspicion grew in them that the little dog was leading the sheep into some ghostly canyon somewhere. But how could they prove it? Their own sheep herding dogs wouldn't attack the thief, if thief it was, and so the stealing went on, unpunished, and unseen.

Talking among themselves in the flickering light of their campfires, the Pastores reasoned upon the situation, trying to draw some sense out of it.

One old man said, "This dog was suckled upon the milk of the sheep. The sheep is in her, therefore, as well as the blood of her kind." The pastores nodded in agreement because what he said was reasonable.

Then another man spoke: "I believe this little dog is turning our sheep into ghosts, for where do they hide? We know nothing of them, except that they disappear." The talk went back and forth, but in the end, it was decided to make a trap for the ewe-dog, as they called her, to see if through some trickery, she might be caught and brought under their control.

So a male sheepherding dog was let go one night and the Pastores hoped that he would mate with the ewe-dog and force her to settle down. After a few months, he did just as they'd hoped—he led them right to her.

Sure enough, she had a litter of pups hidden away in a cave. Time passed and the Pastores realized that their sheep were no longer being taken from the flock.

Now the pups grew up, black and white, and low to the ground, and were the most remarkable sheepdogs the Pastores ever saw. Some said they resembled a rodent, the gopher; others said they saw only the ewe in them.

In any event, there was a time in that dry mesquite country, when, if a man were selling a dog, he would say: "This is the grandchild of the great ewe-dog of the Devil's Creek and the Conchos." For she, as everyone knew, was part sheep and part dog—the best and most useful portions of each, it was said. And so saying, raised the value of their dog by much more than mere money. But where were the stolen sheep the Pastores had lost? No one ever knew.

The Lore of the Dog

In appearance, the Shelty is a small, rough-coated collie. The body is long but perfectly proportioned. The head is refined, tapered. The small ears, high on the head, are three-quarters erect. Alert and watchful, the dog has a goodness of face, a quality typified in collies, in general; a face finely tuned to whatever is going on around it. This dog is one of the most responsive dogs in the Canidae family.

The coat is double: the outercoat long and straight, the undercoat short and dense. The colors are black, blue merle, sable, black and white, black and tan, and tricolored. The long tail is fringed and the mane is thick. The forelegs are feathered. Height is 13 to 16 inches at the shoulder; the weight is not specified.

The Shelty is devoted and docile, an excellent watchdog, a fine family dog, a good outdoors companion. As a worker, this breed barely needs to be trained because of the years of herding, guarding, and working that are imbued in its blood. These dogs are deeply loyal and affectionate with family members, but they are reserved when in the presence of strangers. Their work ethic is such that they will substitute other activities for "watching or herding sheep." This can be helpful, if you have children playing in the yard, but the dog may not permit or understand the entrance of "new players" or drop-in guests.

SIBERIAN HUSKY

The Sled Dog of the Siberian Steppes

JOHN BREDIN

THE SIBERIAN HUSKY gets his name from the people of the cold North, the Eskimos. The name, however, was first used in Alaska where it described the rugged Esky, or Eskimo, work dog commonly known today as the husky.

For roughly three thousand years, the Inuit people of Siberia bred huskies to herd reindeer and to pull sleds across the snowy wastes. Selectively, Eskimos bred a dog that was perfect for his chosen profession, herding and sledding. He was commended for strength, pulling-power, confidence, sharp attention, and seemingly unlimited endurance.

Today varying opinions are offered for the dog's traits and personality. For instance, some say that his gentle nature comes from centuries of affection and care given by his tribal masters, the Arctic and sub-Arctic cultures known as the Chukchees, the Koryaks, the Kamchadals, the Samoyeds, and others.

There are those who contend, though, that this superlative work dog was isolated within a pack and pretty much left to his own devices, which were sometimes said to be brutish and cruel. In Greenland, for instance, the dogs lived freely eight months out of the year, during which time they behaved as members of the pack, fighting for food, females, territory, and status.

The sled dog that had to contend with the forces of nature, and whose pack leader was invariably a man first and a dog second, did not know of such things. His life was based upon toughness, loyalty, and dependence upon—not one—but two leaders.

However, there is conflicting opinion on this, as well. Indian dogs are said to be more dependent upon their driver, a man, than their leader, a dog. Whatever the case, the Siberian husky is a dog that serves, at best and at worst, a hierarchy of leadership.

The relationship of man and dog and sled, as a triumvirate against the environmental mirror of wind, ice, and snow, has been beautifully expressed by the poet James Williams in his unpublished short story "Lessons of the Ice."

William's intimate experience with Alaskan Eskimos and their dogs sheds vital light on a little known subject. At first, upon arriving in the glaring world of the North, he is lulled into what he terms the "Arctic aesthetic":

> The dogs ran powerfully, excited with anticipation of a hunt, pulling the sled with a steady pulsing tireless rhythm. They had been nearly starved all winter and were anxious for fresh meat. They settled into a steady pace, the sleds gliding, almost floating, side by side on the soft snow.

But the transcendental beauty of the immense snowscape soon turns into a noose in which Williams finds himself snared. His friend O'gungucq has warned him to tie his dogs and anchor his sled well while the two men are seal hunting. "Did anyone tell you those dogs are crazy, especially the lead dog?" O'gungucq asks.

On returning after the hunt, Williams realizes that his anchoring efforts have run amuck; his dogs are loose.

> My lead dog had escaped after all. Several of the other dogs were loose too, or tangled in their harnesses. Three of my seven dogs were running around. Two others had tangled themselves together and were struggling to free themselves while limping backwards and forwards.

Surrounded by northern ice and glittery empty mountains, Williams feels himself drifting into helpless anger as his friend tells him, "I told you to tie them up good." After which he drives his own well-behaved team of tail-curled Huskies off into the failing light.

> I stood there alone in the snow watching until he disappeared over the white hills. He had left me alone and when I realized he was

not coming back the cold seemed even colder, the faint light dimmer, and all hope extinguished like a spent match.

Thinking that nothing worse could happen to him, Williams discovers one last surprise—the lead dog has eaten its harness. "It even ate the rope that I had used to tie it with." In addition, "Once free, it chewed on the other dogs' harnesses and helped them to get loose."

Hope is not lost, however, as he convinces himself that his future lies with the capture of the lead animal. As night comes on, he steels himself for the taking of the crazy lead husky. This he accomplishes with amazing resolve. He stares the dog in the eye and says in an unwavering tone: "I am going to catch you and you are going to let yourself be caught."

It happens just that way, with the dog conceding to his wish, and the other dogs soon following suit. Miraculously, running in the darkness behind his dogs, Williams wends his way back to the small Eskimo village where he is greeted with surprise—it seems that no one thought he would make it back alive.

That evening after a dinner of fresh seal meat, I walked into the starry night to where the dogs were tied. The village kept over eight hundred dogs. I listened to the muffled movements and their quiet aspirated barks and yipping, thankful that I was home, thankful that my dogs had stayed with me, even if they were a little crazy.

Wolf blood is, of course, a factor in the husky's temperament and the Indians who crossed huskies with timber wolves got a lead dog who was loyal to his driver and easily disciplined by him as well. As natural leaders, or kings, as they were called in the North country, these huskies were in great demand. Yet, it's also been said that once placed in a group of their own kind, they're pretty much incapable of working in harmony. Perhaps James Williams's experience stems from this mixture of blood, or perhaps it's just the way some dogs, like some people, behave when they know their leadership is in question.

THE HUSKY'S ENTRANCE into America came about during the early 1900s when fur traders brought them in from Siberia. The first team of Siberian huskies ran in the All-Alaska Sweepstakes Race in 1909 and their small stature was, at first, misunderstood. Spectators called them "Siberian rats."

In 1910, the Siberians won the race, and, for the next ten years, they dominated this and many other such races. The most famous race was the so-called Serum Run, which was not a matter for idle spectators or bettors. The huskies carried life-saving serum through minus 50-degree gales to Nome where there was a dyptheria epidemic. These same dogs later went on tour in the United States to promote the breed, but it wasn't until 1930 that American Kennel Club membership was granted.

THE SIBERIAN ESKIMOS of Unisak, in the Bering Straight, believe that Dog was created by Raven and his wife. Dog was fashioned out of Raven's tough fingernails. Another myth comes from the Reindeer Chukchees of Siberia. The Creator made Dog out of wood, they explain. One day later, this dog with the heart-spirit of an indomitable tree was pulling a sled driven by a man.

THE MOST COMMON myth of the North is that of the Dog Ancestor. The Siberian Mongols believe that their ancestor was a dog, or was nourished by one, and this corresponds, conversely, to the fact that some Eskimo women suckle puppies as if they were their own.

The Buriats, another Siberian people, claim that long ago all men were born as dogs, while all females were born as women. But just as life came from dogs, it also is said that "life went to the dogs," meaning that these magnificent creatures were credited with the gift of life and death.

The Yenisei Ostiaks of Siberia tell how they found their first "Dead" and when the Creator heard the people's wail, he sent Dog to comfort them and show them how to turn death into life. In many such tales, however, Dog is proven to be quite forgetful, and in this case he disremembered his real purpose. Instead of teaching resurrection, he taught the art of earth-burial, giving death a ceremonial existence and rationale.

A SIBERIAN SHAMAN'S song celebrates Dog's funny memory. Here is a great animal who cannot forget what he once did; or what he is; or what life and death really mean. The shaman, seeing Dog look upon the grave of a man, sings out: "Oh, look at this dog / He stands crosswise and looks back."

As do we, the people.

The Lore of the Dog

The Siberian husky is medium-sized with a well-furred, compact, and powerful body, ideally designed for hauling, pulling, and carrying. The face is foxlike and the eyes, usually brown or blue, are offset with a white mask, which gives the dog an optimistic look.

Smaller and lighter-boned than the other sled dogs of Alaska, the Siberian has far surpassed his competitors in speed and endurance. The husky features erect ears and feet with fur between the toes and pads, enabling him to move freely on ice and to be unhindered by wet snow.

The tail curves over the back when the dog is in motion, but it falls straight or low when he is standing still. Siberians have a double coat: The inner is downy and the outer is composed of straight, soft fur. While lovely to look at and to touch, Siberian fur has an annoying habit of attaching to everything. All colors and markings are the norm. Height is 20 to 23 inches; weight is 30 to 60 pounds.

The Siberian husky's a hard worker whose personable nature comes from his work environment. In order to be a good sled dog, he must be nonaggressive, protective, and focused on his work. His athleticism, his rather recent wolf ancestry, his tolerance for extreme temperatures make him a great outdoor dog.

In small indoor quarters, the Siberian husky may become restless. If you leave this dog in your fenced backyard with nothing to do, he may create something to do; perhaps he will dig large holes, or tunnels, or even caves.

A watchdog he isn't; his attention seems elsewhere. Siberians need and enjoy exercise, as they are tireless runners. There are conflicting reports on the dog's receptivity to other breeds, children, and even people outside the family. Although they're sociable, they're also territorial.

WEIMARANER

The Good Gray Ghost

MARIAH FOX

THE ORIGIN OF the silver-grey weimaraner is wrapped in the grey woolen mist of *Wenzels Krone*, the old term for Bohemia. There in the early nineteenth century Prince Esterhazy introduced Carl August of Weimar to some unusual hunting dogs. Another tradition tells us that "the hunter among kings and the king among hunters," the Grand Duke Carl August (1757–1828), and his noblemen, bred the dogs on his own estate in central Germany. Still older traditions favor the idea that this dog has "the mark of the hound" and that his portrait, or something like it, may be found on medieval tapestries—only then his hair was thicker and furrier and his ears longer and floppier, and his head altogether more square.

In fact, the only thing that seems to hold the dog to a well-bred conclusion is his misty color—grey as the dawn, old as the remarks that are made about him. That, and the literature of his amazing tracking ability, are considered as fairly reliable evidence of the dog's descent from the ancient scent-tracking hounds of old Europe. How far back might the dog's lineage extend?

As with all of the oldest breeds, the hoary trail always leads to Egypt. There, according to historians, Louis IX of France, better known as Saint Louis, learned of the dog on his first crusade. After returning to France, he obtained a pack of them, and these became known as *"les chien gris de Saint Louis."*

By the end of the fourteenth century, most French noblemen owned some of the royal grey hounds. Not surprisingly, they made excellent gifts; thus were the greys passed on from court to court. And thus did their legend grow, for medieval knights—when not in combat—were upon the hunt; and when not on the hunt were bragging of same, so the lauded dogs grew larger in stature, if not in fame.

Time passed, and the silver-grey phantom of the forest became a storied part of table boasts; a statuesque sculpture to celebrate the life of the hunt; a character of tapestries, tableaus, and illuminated manuscripts.

THE FINEST OF the medieval running hounds were those used as "lymers." These were the elite corps of dogs, trained and handled by lymerers, or on-lead handlers. The German term for the dog, however, is *"leithund,"* a hound that tracks on a lead. However, the effect of the weimaraner's ancestor being given this special status is that the lymers, lead dogs, usually lived in the handlers' homes. The close bond that developed between the handler and the grey followed the dog well into the twentieth century.

Some experts explain the weimaraner's fondness for special treatment by recalling the old dependency of lymerer and lymer. The introduction of firearms and the end of the big-game hunting era in central Europe gave breeders a new incentive for specializing. The hunting dog of choice thus became the pointer, and the weimaraner's bloodline was thus mixed. The cross with pointers (he became known as the Weimar Pointer) added a tincture of vivacity to an already tenacious hunter. The grey kept his true color(s) and his prowess in tracking, yet he now honed the art of showing where the prey or quarry lay.

It was at this point that Grand Duke Carl August entered the weimaraner's story, and, supposedly, perfected the breed. By the close of the nineteenth century, the good grey ghost had earned the honorary title of "Forester's Dog" and was generally considered the king of the hunting dogs.

THE MYTHOLOGY OF the weimaraner begins not in "the old days" as with most major breeds, but in America in the early 1950s. Postwar Americans were looking, it seems, for anything that might be labeled "super."

In 1950 *Look* magazine featured an unknown dog from Germany, the weimaraner. He appeared on the cover and was called the new "wonder dog." Suddenly weimaraners were everywhere. One was the darling of President Eisenhower; another belonged to actress Grace Kelly.

The wonder dog was unleashed, as it were, to a very naive public. These were the days, remember, when people believed everything they read. Wei-maraner myths amassed in all the magazines. One story said that this superdog had been a well-kept secret for 137 years. Writers of the time told of Germanic secret weapons, megabombs and megaplanes, of which the postwar period was still brimming. The mystery dog, well-kept under century-old wraps, was just another Germanic secret suddenly come to light. A dog that could out-track the American bloodhound was just what people expected from the archaic, ducal castles of Bohemia. Legend had it that the weimaraner would leap fifty feet off a bridge into swift water just to retrieve a duck. Housewives buzzed about the grey dog that rescued children, and which, they'd heard, would even answer the telephone—or at least pick up the receiver.

The fifties public not only believed in hype, it worshipped at its altar. People knelt at the fount of the fabulous, the mount of the mysterious. They loved the wonderful, the magnificent, and the spurious. It didn't matter that hype validated hype, becoming in the process pure myth.

So, the weimaraner that answered the telephone—listened to the voice at the other end. Would the cunning creature really speak into the receiver? Researchers claimed that the dog loved intimacy, and was curious beyond belief. Yes, came the verdict, the weimaraner would dislodge the phone and, hearing a voice on the other end, respond. One author said the dog's eerie presence on the phone was not talkative, but merely "heavy breathing."

Writer Jack Denton Scott reported in *Field and Stream* magazine,

> One rainy day not too many months ago, the aforementioned Jack Baird was walking on his land in Wappingers Falls, New York, when he fell, twisting his left arm under him. His other arm was in a sling, and he had fallen in a deep brook which snakes through his property. He couldn't get up, was weak from an illness, and rapidly drowning. His weimaraner bitch, Diana, stood watching him for a moment. Then, quickly sensing the danger, moved over to Jack, worked herself under his left arm until he could hoist himself out of the water on her strong back, and slowly dragged him from the stream.

Other tales, and there were many, unfolded. The "Gray Ghost," as Scott affirmed, "has arrived." But along with the true tales were the untrue ones, also reported, but not vouched for, by Scott.

For instance, there was the following odd endorsement: "This dog, this weimaraner, can run effortlessly beside an automobile traveling at the rate of 38 miles an hour, and pull ahead of the car and not even appear winded."

Scott himself claimed that his own weimaraner pup practically trained itself: "I yard-broke this pup in five days, taught him to retrieve in two weeks."

A hunter bought a weimaraner pup, and kept it from the smell of a game bird for a year and a half. Then he took him for a ride in his car. "I came to a likely looking alder run, stopped and got out. Fifty yards from the road this weimaraner came to a beauty of a point. I thought it an accident or something, walked up, and wham! out goes a woodcock."

Finally, even the former president of the Weimaraner Club stated: "Everything anyone says about these dogs is true." America signed up, too— at least for one bottled-up, buttoned-down moment in the 1950s.

By 1990 the superdog had dropped in popularity to number fifty. The price of success had come down hard on the dog. Overpopularity had caused the price of ownership to soar to four figures in the fifties, while the quality of the breed plummeted—a clear case of supply and demand on a crash course with popular mythology.

However, while putting the past into perspective, we should remember that history often follows mythology, and not the other way around. The silver-grey ghost was so-named because of his catlike stealth in hunting and his sterling talent for problem solving. Take one look at this thinking dog's sparkling, speaking eyes, and you'll see that this isn't hype at all. He looks, he thinks, he acts, and in that order. All in the blink of an amber eye. Yes, the dog is something of a myth. But one that is decidedly manmade.

The Lore of the Dog

The silver-grey weimaraner pointer is a dog fashioned of adjectives, sculpted out of superlatives with his noble robe: a coat of velvet grey, silver-tinged. The body and build of this dog is that of a rangy, muscular uplander, broad of chest, long-limbed, and with the hindquarters of a crouching cat.

The head is fine and aristocratic. Ears with rounded points hang down in perfect symmetry. The eyes are amber, blue-grey, or grey, and have a fascinating look of fixation, of undiverted interest in all that is going on. The tail is docked, the feet are webbed.

The height is 23 to 27 inches and the weight is 55 to 90 pounds.

The breed was developed to meet the needs of the nineteenth-century German forester. He became, therefore, a tracker, pointer, and retriever who worked at a steady, tireless pace, which was characterized by thoroughness rather than speed. He loves water and will swim with indefatigable determination.

The weimaraner's temperament is forged of tough aggressiveness and incredible softness. The dog's sensitivity is well known. Other pointers work for the love of the hunt, but the weimaraner works for love of the huntsman. This is true of their training and background, and the dog won't function properly when kept in an isolated kennel.

Weimaraners demand human companionship; kennel life wounds their dignity. Easily trainable, therefore, by a gentle trainer. Some say the dog can be trained by merely watching another dog. As for intelligence, the grey ghost has a great problem-solving aptitude, and much of the legendary status accorded to the breed is not altogether inaccurate.

They're curious and learn from their experiences. The dog's predatory and roaming instincts make it necessary for him to have a fenced yard. He can be aggressive toward other breeds and may be too boisterous around younger children; older ones, however, are fine and he will be watchful of them.

The weimaraner's temperament is strong and the trainer must exert an equal or greater measure of strength in training him; however, this should never be harsh or the dog will become very rebellious and/or difficult.

WELSH CORGI (CARDIGAN AND PEMBROKE)

The Fairy Heeler of Wales

MARIAH FOX

MOST AUTHORITIES CLAIM separate histories for the Cardigan Welsh corgi and the Pembroke Welsh corgi. Although they were interbred (and not officially separated as two distinct breeds until the 1930s), they came from two distinctly different places. Their root-ancestry, therefore, is quite apart.

The Cardigan is the older of the two breeds, having been brought to Wales by the warrior Celts of Central Europe in 1200 B.C. The ancestry is traceable to the dachshund. The Pembroke was brought to Britain by Flemish weavers, courtesy of Henry I, in A.D 1107. The ancestry is spitz, keeshond, and schipperke.

As a working dog the Cardigan corgi accepted the unique position of heeler for the tenant farmer of Cardiganshire, Wales. Since the Crown owned most of the land that surrounded the farmer's home, he was only permitted to use that grazing area which he occupied.

There was, therefore, much competition for land usage among the local farmers and they had a vested interest in ever increasing their "occupied territories." Heelers, rather than herders, were trained to disperse cattle by nipping at their heels, a most dangerous occupation. Their job was to push the herds out into larger and larger quarters; this gave the individual farmer more legal space with which to graze his stock.

After the division of the Crown lands into private ownership, it was then fenced off by each of the crofters. As a result driven stock was no longer needed, and the corgi was out of a job, until he was crossed with a herding dog, the collie. Then his job changed and he was given to herding, as well as his old preoccupation of heeling.

T̲HE PEMBROKE CORGI had little or nothing of the dachshund characteristics. However, later crossings with the Cardigan made him a stockier version of this dog. The Pembroke, having a gentler personality than the Cardigan, became a more successful house pet.

The Pembroke of Buckingham Palace, first introduced by the Duke of York, subsequently made the breed famous. For the Duke became a king and the gift dog, Roseval Golden Eagle, was offered to Princess Elizabeth, who later became a queen. In many of Queen Elizabeth's portraits, her beloved corgi appears beside her.

Anne G. Biddlecombe, of the Welsh Corgi League of Great Britain, suggests that those interested in the corgi should listen to the legend told by an ancient bard. For the corgi is, indeed, a poet's, a storyteller's dog, a fairy heeler, a magical little beast sent to us from mystic realms.

Corgis came from the green and golden valleys of the grandfathers, men who toiled with their cattle and their ploughing. And as the men ploughed, the wives made cheese. One day a farmer's children found two pups playing in a hollow like fox kits. Their coats were burnished gold, shining like pieces of satin. Their forelegs were short, straight, and thick, their heads like a fox's, and their eyes kind and gentle. Long of body were these dwarf dogs and without a tail behind them.

The children stayed all day and learned to love the dwarf dogs, sharing their bread and water with them, taking them home and putting them in a basket by the hearth. Now, when the farmer himself came home, he asked his children, "What are these?" And they answered, "We found them on the mountain, playing in a hollow."

Then the farmer said, "Surely, these are the gifts of the fairy folk, who keep such things. Corgis, fairy heelers, they are, and the little people—" and here he broke into song:

Made them work the fairy cattle
Made them pull the fairy coaches
Made them steeds for fairy riders
Made them fairy children's playmates
Kept them hidden in the mountains
Kept them shadowed in the lee
Lest the eye of mortal man see.

Now, the corgis, taken in by the farmer, prospered in the care of his children, for the fairy spirit was in the dogs. It was in the lightness of their step, the quickness of their turning, their badness and their goodness, their love of mortal masters.

So, in the valleys and the mountains, from the little town of Tenby, by the Port of Milford haven, to St. David's Head and Fishguard, in the valley of the Cleddau, on the mountains of Preselly, lives the Pembrokeshire corgi.

For those of doubting nature, who scoff at tales of old, look to the backs of these wondrous dogs, and see if they've got the ancient saddle marks, where the fairy warriors rode them, as they ride them still at midnight in the middle of summer, riding, riding when mortals are sleeping.

The Lore of the Dog

Presently the royal Dog of England, the corgi is neither English nor royal, being the fairy steed of Welsh myth. In Welsh *cor* means "dwarf" and *gi* means "dog," so the corgi is, literally, a dwarf dog.

Both the Pembroke and the Cardigan Welsh corgi are low-set, extremely sturdy, heavy-boned dogs, longer than they are high.

The Cardigan has a bushy fox tail and the Pembroke has hardly any tail at all. The eyes are medium size; dark for the Cardigan, hazel for the Pembroke. The ears are big and foxlike, carried erect by both breeds; however, in the Cardigan the ears are larger and more rounded. The Cardigan's feet are, once again, larger and more round.

The coat for the Cardigan is short and stiff with a good undercoat. The Pembroke coat is thicker and softer and of medium length. Both coats come in reddish brown, fawn, sand, black, and tan. White patches occur in both breeds on feet, chest, and neck. Height is between 10 and 12 inches and weight is less than 30 pounds.

The corgi is a tough, funny, friendly dog. Like most herding dogs he adores children and watches over them carefully. As a work animal—heeler, ratter, and guard dog—the corgi is serious and businesslike. But as a family companion, he enjoys being included in all affairs of the house. He has a great sense of humor and, when not at work, a playful view of life. Work, however, is important to him. In Welsh law, he is recognized as a cattle dog as far back as A.D. 920. Small though he is, this dog has pluck and stamina, quickness and agility. His tactics on the farm may be seen today on a city walk, when, somewhat without warning, he'll see something out of line—a garbage bag, for example—and start to nip at its heels, and he'll duck and jump about, as if to evade the bag's flying hooves.

Exercise is important in his daily regimen. In addition to walking, he seems to require a certain amount of free running. Like many low-slung dogs, who often live in urban environments, the corgi can develop a weight problem, particularly if not given enough exercise.

YORKSHIRE TERRIER

The Yorkie of County Yorkshire

JOHN BREDIN

Bred in the nineteenth century from Skye and other terriers, the Yorkie is a special breed with characteristics all his own. To begin with, he may be one of the only breeds that must withstand hair in curlers, and though he likes to run like a rabbit in the clover, he's rarely given the opportunity because of the precious mantle of silk fur that he wears. Owners, in fact, have been known to insure their Yorkies' fur for fabulous sums. Yet the dog's history reveals a rough-and-tumble tyke, whose passion for ratting was well-known in Yorkshire, England, where the dog was first bred.

He was a miner's companion, accompanying them down damp, dark, unlit tunnels; and he was also a ratter in the cottonmills of the same region. In both cases, however, the Yorkie was also put "into the pit," his own private gladiatorial chamber to fight rats caught by millhands and miners. This was a sporting terrier, then, not just a companion, who helped kill rats.

The Yorkshire terrier ascended from the mines and mills of the nineteenth century to become, around 1880, a Victorian lady's pet. His appearance in the United States occurred at about this time, and the dog's popularity with film stars and the well-to-do has been assured ever since his arrival.

Mel Young, who raises Yorkshire terriers, explains that their ferocity with regard to rats is an awesome sight to behold:

> Here is a dog who weighs, in some cases, less than the rat, and is just no bigger than a minute. I am speaking here of the large variety of Florida palmetto rat. It may seem a bit macabre, but our twenty-pound cat likes to go outside and hunt the rats, for the express purpose of delivering them to our Yorkies. He brings them on order, so to speak. If we have Yorkie puppies, he brings in mice or smaller rats. If we have the full grown dogs in the house, then he delivers the big rats. He comes in the cat door and drops them on the floor.
>
> The next thing you hear is the whirring feet of the Yorkies— only the females; the males do not go after the rats—as two or three females take off in a blinding flash. The rat doesn't have time to face off at all before a dog hits him like a torpedo and, with one flick of the head, kills him. There is nothing faster, in my opinion, than the quickness of a Yorkie when going after a rat, except the little throw of the head that breaks the rat's neck. You'd have to see it to believe it. (These females, by the way, are also the more aggressive watchdogs and barkers, if anyone unannounced is at the door.) But the odd thing about this cat-rat-Yorky business, is the way the cat participates. He seems to have an exclusive arrangement with our dogs, and after he's delivered the specified goods, he sits back and watches with great curiosity and interest. He's never, to my knowledge, even wetted the fur on one of those rats he brings in.
>
> We have one little lady Yorky who has always done this funny thing. She was raised in a plastic swimming pool (dry, not wet), but ever since birth she's seemed to like water a lot. In the summer, when it's very hot, she likes to get into our big five-quart water dish, which is left out for all the dogs, including our Doberman pinscher, and paddle around. If I drop in an ice cube, which she likes to chase after and bite, she'll just hop into that dish and paddle around, playing with the ice cube.

The Lore of the Dog

The Yorky is a well-proportioned, compact terrier with a small flat head and black, dancing eyes. The ears are V-shaped and usually erect, but sometimes they stand halfway up. The tail is customarily docked and carried slightly higher than the level of the back.

The coat is impressively long, sometimes as much as 24 inches—which means it hangs all the way to the floor. It is soft, shiny, and perfectly straight. Overall, the dog is steel-blue with golden areas on the head, chest, and legs. The hair on the head is so long that it needs to be tied up in a top-knot to keep it out of the little dog's face. The height is around 8 inches at the shoulder and the weight is about 7 pounds.

When the puppies are born, they are naked, but they soon turn black and start to look like young Doberman pinschers, or Rottweilers. Their next growth phase is that of little monkeylike creatures, too cute for words. The last phase is the silky-haired, attractive adult dog.

They are good with children, but only if they are raised with them, and they are very affectionate with their families. As watchdogs, the females are said to be best, fearless and territorial. Males, if they have been raised among female siblings, will tend to let the females do the work.

About the Authors

GERALD AND LORETTA Hausman, in addition to owning more than thirty different dogs (not all at one time), are the authors of two cookbooks and the editors of several anthologies. They presently live in Bokeelia, Florida, with a Great Dane, a dachshund, an Akita, a Siamese cat and a Blue-fronted Amazon parrot. As devotees of dogdom, they have not only owned many dogs, but have also made a lifetime hobby of studying their characteristics and habits. Gerald Hausman's popular Native American bestiary, *Meditations with Animals,* has been translated into foreign languages and has gone into many editions and printings. Both he and his wife, Loretta, have been students of animal behavior since the early sixties. The research that went into the present volume was extensive and goes back to the first written volumes on dogs that were originally published in the seventeenth century. The Hausmans spent much of their time interviewing dog owners and breed club representatives to complete *The Mythology of Dogs.* Furthermore, the oral tales that they have included come from virtually every part of the planet where dogs are known and loved.

Bibliography

Allen, Glover M. "Dogs of the American Aborigines." *Bulletin of the Museum of Comparative Zoology at Harvard College,* Vol. LXIII #9: Cambridge, Mass., 1920.

American Kennel Club. *The Complete Dog Book.* New York: Howell Book House, 1992.

Ash, Edward C. *Dogs: Their History and Development* Vol. II. New York: Benjamin Blom, Inc., 1972.

Ash, Edward C. *This Doggie Business.* London: Hutchinson & Co., 1934.

Aymar, Brandt and Sagarin, Edward. *The Personality of the Dog.* New York: Bonanza Books, 1964.

Baring-Gould, M.A. *Curious Myths of the Middle Ages.* New York: John B. Alden, n.d.

Barrie, J. M. *Peter Pan.* New York: Henry Holt, 1987.

Beethoven. MCA Universal Home Video, 1992.

Boone, J. Allen. *Kinship with All Life.* New York: Harper and Row, 1976.

Bordeaux, Edmond, S. *Messengers from Ancient Civilizations.* San Diego, CA: Academy Books, 1924.

Borland, Hal. *Penny.* Philadelphia & New York: J. B. Lippincott & Co., 1972.

Botkin, B. A. *A Treasury of American Folklore.* New York: Crown Publishers, 1929.

Botkin, B. A. *A Treasury of Western Folklore.* New York: Crown Publishers, 1929.

Brewer, J. Mason. *Dog Ghosts and Other Texas Negro Folktales.* Austin, Texas: University of Texas Press, 1958.

Bruette, William and Donnelly, Kerry. *Complete Dog Buyer's Guide.* Neptune City, Va.: T.F.H. Publications, 1979.

Carmer, Carl. *Pets at the White House.* New York: E. P. Dutton, 1959.

Cavendish, Richard, Editor. *Man, Myth and Magic: The Illustrated Encyclopedia of Mythology, Religion and the Unknown.* Freeport, Long Island, New York: Marshall Cavendish Ltd., 1995.

Brunvald, Jan Harold. *The Choking Doberman and Other "New" Urban Legends.* New York: W. W. Norton, 1984.

Caras, Roger. *A Celebration of Dogs.* New York: Quadrangle, The New York Times Book Co., 1982.

Coblentz, Catherine, C. *Animal Pioneers.* Boston: Little Brown & Co., 1936.

Coren, Stanley. *The Intelligence of Dogs.* New York: Bantam, 1995.

Courlander, Harold. *A Treasury of Afro-American Folklore.* New York: Crown Publishers, 1976.

Dale-Green, Patricia. *Lore of the Dog.* Boston: Houghton-Mifflin Co., 1967.

Davidson, H. R. Ellis. *Myths and Symbols in Pagan Europe: Early Scandinavian and Celtic Religions.* Syracuse, New York: Syracuse University Press, 1988.

Debo, Ellen Weathers. *The Chinese Shar-pei.* New Jersey: T.F.H. Publications, 1986.

Dinesen, Isak. *Out of Africa*. New York: Vintage Books, 1965.

Dobie, J. Frank. *Man, Bird and Beast*. Vol. III. Austin Texas: Texas Folklore Society, 1930.

Doctorow, E. L. *Selected Essays 1977–1992: Jack London, Hemingway, and The Constitution*. New York: Random House, 1993.

Dorson, Richard, M. *Folklore and Folklife*. Chicago, Ill.: University of Chicago Press, 1973.

Dracott, Alice Elizabeth. *Simla Village Tales or Folktales from the Himalayas*. London: John Morray, 1906.

Fairfax, Thomas. *The Complete Sportsman*. London, 1689.

Farrar, Janet and Farrar, Stewart. *The Witches' Goddess*. Custer, Washington: Phoenix Publishing, 1987.

Fletcher, Walter, R.. *My Times with Dogs*. New York: Howell Book House, 1980.

Fox, Michael W. *Understanding Your Dog*. New York: St. Martin's Press, 1972.

Gonzales, Andrew. *With Aesop Along the Black Border*. New York: Negro Universities Press, 1924.

Graves, Robert. *The White Goddess*. New York: Ferrar, Strauss & Cudahy, 1948.

Gray, Charles Wright. *Dawgs*. Garden City, New York: Garden City Publishing Co., 1925.

Howey, M. O. *The Cults of the Dog*. Essex, England: C. W. Daniel Ltd., 1968.

Iron Will. Walt Disney Pictures, 1994.

Jones, Tim. *Dog Heroes*. Kenmore, Washington: Epicenter Press, 1995.

Kipling, Rudyard. *Collected Dog Stories*. Garden City, New York: Doubleday & Co., 1934.

Kipling, Rudyard. *Thy Servant, A Dog*. Garden City, New York: Doubleday, Doran & Co., 1931.

Kirk, Ralph. *Six Breeds*. Freeport, New York: Books for Libraries Press, 1923, 1970.

Kjelgaard, Jim. *Big Red*. New York: Holiday House, 1945.

Knight, Eric. *Lassie Come Home*. New York: Dell Publishing, 1940.

Larousse Encyclopedia of Mythology. New York: Prometheus Press, 1959.

Leach, Maria. *God Had a Dog: Folklore of the Dog*. New Brunswick, N.J.: Rutgers University Press, 1961.

Lee, F. H. *Folktales of All Nations*. New York: Tudor Publishing Co., 1930.

London, Jack. *The Call of the Wild*. New York: Vintage Books, 1990.

Lorenz, Konrad. *King Solomon's Ring*. New York: Thomas Crowell Co., 1952.

Lorenz, Konrad. *Man Meets Dog*. Boston: Houghton Mifflin Co., 1955.

Lovett, Sandee. *The Newfoundland Dog—A Living Legend*. Cedar, Michigan, 1994.

Lowell, Michelle. *Your Purebred Puppy*. New York: Henry Holt, 1990.

Man, Myth and Magic. Vol. III. Freeport, Long Island, New York: Marshall, Cavandish Ltd., 1995.

Mery, Ferdinand. *The Life, History and Magic of the Dog*. New York: Grosset and Dunlap, 1968.

National Geographic Society. *The Book of Dogs*. Washington, D.C.: 1927.

National Geographic Society. *The Book of Dogs*. Washington, D.C.: 1958.

McLauren, Tim. *Keeper of the Moon, A Southern Boyhood*. New York: Anchor/Doubleday, 1991.

Miller, O. Victor. "Hot Grits and Blue Yonder." *Albany Magazine*. Feb. 1996, unpaginated galley.

Miller, O. Victor. "Warning: Objects Are Closer Than They Appear" *Albany Magazine*, Sept/Oct. 1991. pgs. 37–39.

Nicholas, Anna Katherine. *Shar-pei*. New Jersey: T.F.H. Publications, 1990.

Patrick, Ted. *The Thinking Dog's Man*. New York: Random House, 1964.

Patridge, Eric. *The Shaggy Dog Story: Its Origin, Development and Nature*. New York: Philosophical Library, 1954.

Peter Pan. Walt Disney Home Video. 1953

Pferd, William. *Dogs of the American Indians*. Fairfax, Va.: Denlinger's Publishers, Ltd., 1987.

Readers Digest Association. *Reader's Digest Illustrated Book of Dogs*, 2nd rev. Ed. Pleasantville, NY: 1993.

Scott, Jack Denton. "The Gray Ghost Arrives." *Field & Stream* magazine. October, 1947.

Scott, Walter. *Guy Mannering or The Astrologer*. Boston & New York: Houghton Mifflin, 1912.

Schuler, Elizabeth Meriweather. *Simon and Schuster's Guide to Dogs*. New York: Simon and Schuster, 1980.

Steinbeck, John. *Travels with Charley*. New York: Bantam Books, 1966.

Suares, J. C. *Hollywood Dogs*. San Francisco: Collins Publishers, 1993.

Thobey-Marcellin, Marcellin, Phillipe and Pierre. *The Singing Turtle and Other Tales from Haiti*. New York: Farrar, Straus & Giroux, 1971.

Thomas, Elizabeth Marshall. *The Hidden Life of Dogs*. New York: Pocket Star Books, 1993.

The Ugly Dachshund. Walt Disney Home Video, 1965.

Those Wonderful Dogs. National Geographic Video, 1994.

Titcomb, Margaret with Pukin, Mary Kawena. *Dog and Man in the Ancient Pacific with Special Attention to Hawaii*. Honolulu, Hawaii: Bernice P. Bishop Museum Special Publication 59, 1969.

Trew, Cecil G. *The Story of the Dog and His Uses to Mankind*. New York: E. P. Dutton & Co., 1939.

Turner and Hooch. Touchstone Home Video. 1989.

Walker, Barbara G. *The Women's Encyclopedia of Myths and Secrets*. San Francisco: Harper and Row, 1983.

Walker, Barbara G. *The Women's Dictionary of Symbols and Sacred Objects*. San Francisco: Harper and Row, 1988.

Watson, James. *The Dog Book, Vol. I & II*. New York: Doubleday & Co., 1916.

Weinrich, Beatrice Silverman. Translated by Wolf, Leonard. *Yiddish Folktales*. New York: Pantheon Books, 1988.

White, E. B. *One Man's Meat*. New York: Harper & Brothers, 1942.

Williams, James. "Lessons of the Ice." Unpublished story, 1996.

Woley, Eleanora. *The Symbol of the Dog in the Human Psyche*. Wilamette, Illinois: Chiron Publishers, 1990.

Wylder, Joseph. *Psychic Pets: The Secret World of Animals*. New York: Stonehill Publishing Co., 1978.

Index